SOUND THE ALARM
The Maui Disaster That Sparked A Global Awakening

By Shane Buell, Traci Derwin, & Stephanie Pierucci

SOUND
THE
ALARM

THE MAUI DISASTER
THAT SPARKED A GLOBAL AWAKENING

SHANE BUELL
TRACI DERWIN
STEPHANIE PIERUCCI

PIERUCCI
PUBLISHING
ELEVATING WORLD CONSCIOUSNESS
THROUGH STORIES.

Copyright © Justice Now, LLC 2024
Sound The Alarm
Untold Stories From The Disaster That Sparked An Awakening

Published by Pierucci Publishing, P.O. Box 2074, Carbondale, Colorado 81623, USA
www.pieruccipublishing.com

Cover design by Stephanie Pierucci

ISBN
Ebook: 978-1-962578-34-9
Hardcover: 978-1-962578-48-6
Paperback: 978-1-962578-50-9

Library of Congress Control Number: 2024941712

Pierucci Publishing books may be purchased in bulk at special discounts for sales promotion, corporate gifts, fund-raising, or educational purposes. Special editions can be created to specifications. For details, contact the Special Sales Department, Pierucci Publishing, PO Box 2074, Carbondale, CO 81623, or Publishing@pieruccipublishing.com, or toll-free telephone at 1-855-720-1111.

If you have tips, videos, images, or interest in contributing to the upcoming documentary "Sound The Alarm," please personally email Stephanie at Stephanie@pieruccipublishing.com.

CONTENTS

PART ONE:
SMOKING GUNS

PART TWO:
GOVERNMENT FUNNY BUSINESS

PART THREE:
ACTION NOW

DEDICATION

To The Reader:

    We dedicate this book to our readers who are at various stages of supporting this global awakening. For your courage to question a highly propagandized narrative and to see beyond psyops. For your willingness to get involved locally either through Facebook evangelism or by representing your family values as a member of your local school board or youth group. For your caution in voting out the swamp and voting in the resistance to the WEF, UN, and totalitarian, self-interested entities. For the business owners who refuse to kowtow to fake "green" programs that are doing more harm than good to our beautiful earth. And most of all, for the people of Maui and especially Lahaina: we will not rest until you have justice.

To Our Team:

    For their support and input in writing this book, a special thanks goes to: Bennett DeBeer, Steve Bock, Paul Deslauriers, Clyde Holokai, Anne Williams, Jim Derwin, Spice Prince, Bruce Douglas, Forensic Arborist Robert Brame, Steve Slepcevic, Mike McKeenan, Norman Sollie, Sam Eaton, Matt "Matty" Schweitzer, Melissa Black-Law, Matt Weinglass, Bodie Pacheco, and Eric West. A very special thanks goes to Jon Kinimaka who named this book and didn't want recognition. Please enjoy his sweet Hawai'ian inspired lullabies here: https://www.youtube.com/@jonkinimaka9391

SECRET

FOREST FIRE AS A MILITARY WEAPON

The battle was fought
in the forest of E'phraim;
and the forest devoured
more people that day
than the sword.

II Samuel 18: 6, 8

From the "Secret" 1970 report
"Forest Fire as a Military Weapon"
commissioned by the U.S.
Department of Defense.

BOWL OF LIGHT

By Elijah Kalā
Instagram @SonOfOahu
Shared on May 9, 2024

As we rise as a people, a community, and a collective, one of the most vital components of this journey is ensuring your light lives on in love.

As much of the challenges we face in society at large, we all face similar challenges in our personal lives.

These challenges can, as cliche as it sounds, "make or break you". These challenges also reveal our true nature to ourselves and the ones around us.

I have learned that the most challenging part of facing hardship is MAINTAINING YOUR LIGHT.

Our light, representing our Godly nature is that of love, compassion, understanding, acceptance, balance, harmony, peace, and that which contributes to the betterment of ALL, is of the highest sanctity.

Our light is sacred, our mana is divine, our love is the power existing at the highest vibration of the universe.

Therefore, it must be honored, acknowledged, and shared with those who can see its power. Through hardship, we are often put in a crossroads as children where we learn to either stand by the integrity of doing what is pono, or choosing another solution that ultimately is not of the light.

We take this behavior and carry it through to adulthood, not knowing that every time we choose something other than the light, we inadvertently diminish our own illumination.

Over time, as we use this internal compass, we devolve to becoming less and less of our true selves, and more of what disrupts the universal order within & without.

No Laila...
Care for your light...
Honor your light...
Protect your light...
Cultivate your light...
And let it shine.

Me ke aloha a me ka mana kapu o Ke Akua,
Kalā

A HAWAI'IAN POEM
by Prince William Charles Lunalilo, 1860

King William Charles Lunalilo Courtesy of Lunalilo.org[1]

"E Ola Ke Ali'i Ke Akua"
(Composed by Prince William C. Lunalilo in 1860)[2]

God Save the King
(English version by the Reverend Lorenzo Lyons)

Ke Akua Mana Mau,
Ho'omaika'i, pōmaika'i
I ka Mō'ī!
Kou lima mana mau,
Mālama, kia'i mai
Ko mākou nei Mō'ī
E ola ē!

Eternal, mighty God,
Bless from Thy bright abode
Our Sov'reign King
May Thy all powerful arm
Ward from our sire all harm
Let no vile foe alarm;
Long may he reign!

Ka inoa kamaha'o
Lei nani o mākou
E ola ē!
Kou 'eheu uhi mai
Pale nā 'ino ē
Ko mākou pule nō
E ola ē!

Royal, distinguished name
Our beauteous diadem,
Long life be thine
Thy wing spread o'er our land
From every foe defend,
For thee our prayers ascend,
Long live our king!

I mua ou mākou
Ke 'li'i o nā Ali'i
E aloha mai
E mau ke ea ē
'O ke aupuni nei,
E ola mau mākou
Me ka Mō'ī.

Before Thee,
King of Kings,
Of Whom all nature sings,
Our prayer we bring.
Oh let our kingdom live;
Life, peace and union give,
Let all Thy care receive,
Bless Thou our King!

---

2   https://puke.ulukau.org/ulukau-books/?a=d&d=EBOOK-KS12.2.9.8&e=-------en-20--1--txt-txPT----------

PUBLISHER'S NOTE

This book is designed as a tool to ignite your critical thinking skills and the truth evangelist within you. Whether your platform is X.com, Friday night bingo tables, or a church pulpit, your voice is an especially wonderful part of this awakening.

We ask that you review, discuss, and question everything you read in this book.

This book is merely a book of questions, not accusations. It is full of public information that we have been honored to compile in one succinct, organized way.

We have made special efforts to verify and fact check information, leaving over 80,000 words on the cutting room floor from our initial manuscript due to our unwillingness to accept "anonymous" testimony, claims without video or picture evidence, or rabbit trail conspiracy theories that take away from the most important mission: to restore Lahaina to her rightful landowners and guardians.

Neither Pierucci Publishing nor the authors: Traci Derwin, Shane Buell, Stephanie Pierucci, or any of our friends or affiliates intend to promote fear, further misinformation, nor fuel negativity. We believe that it is our sacred duty to ask questions that further world consciousness, even when those questions are seemingly unanswerable and altogether difficult.

The authors are not and have no plan to be involved in any legal motions or proceedings on Hawaii at the time of publishing this book. We are merely citizen journalists reporting information that has been provided by experts much smarter than we are. No information in this book, on podcasts, in social media, or websites is deemed to be medical or legal advice, and we are not medical or legal professionals.

Some names might have been changed or altered in order to protect the identities of first-hand witnesses. We have done our best to cite all sources to the best of our ability and to reject any information that we deemed unreliable, including using the full legal names of our sources and eyewitnesses.

Please consider sharing this book with someone you care about, as the intention of this book is to honor the victims of the Lahaina tragedy through our quest for answers and, ultimately, for the truth.

INTRODUCTION

During the final moments of editing this book, Traci Derwin and Shane Buell presented evidence of curious fire behavior in Ruidoso, New Mexico where a fire started on June 17, 2024 and is, at the time of this writing on June 23, 2024, 0% contained.

There were many similarities between the Ruidoso fires, the Paradise, California fires, the Chile fires, the Texas fires, and other fires in Europe and beyond, some of which will be discussed in this book. For instance, items melting that require a temperature far hotter than a normal wildfire. Discussions in the local government of short term housing reorganization and other legislation in "Community Development" have been recently proposed in Ruidoso, similar to the "Working Group" and "Emergency Proclamations" on Maui. But what struck us, the authors, most, was the fact that in Ruidoso, like in Paradise and other places, no alarms sounded.

One eyewitness stated that a fireman showed up at his home ordering him to evacuate before a warning or alarm was ever sounded.

This is among many of the red flags we're becoming accustomed to seeing in fires that don't appear to be natural in places that, consistently, have been earmarked for development by local legislative bodies.

Speaking at Amherst College in 1962, President John F. Kennedy once said, "what good is a private college or university unless it is serving a great national purpose?" He then said, "privilege is here, and with privilege goes responsibility."

The authors of this book are not victims of losing our homes or loved ones in the Lahaina fires, but inspired by words such as President Kennedy's, and we feel privileged to have been spared in our respective homes, but responsible to serve a great national purpose. That great national purpose is awareness of what happened on Maui and justice for Lahaina. We dream of seeing the people of Lahaina return to their homes. We understand that it's highly unlikely that it will ever happen. And that's why we're writing to you today.

Throughout the pages of this book we'll illustrate to you various ways the elites and globalists have torched everything from homes to family values, and we'll pay special attention to celebrating the fact that we're coming out ahead, even though it looks dark. Of course, it always looks darkest before dawn! We are in an awakening, which is why the subtitle of this book was chosen, "The Maui Disaster That Sparked An Awakening."

More of our readers have visited Maui than any other place that appears to be the victim of a directed energy or other nefarious attack. Because Maui has been referred to as the "heart chakra of the planet" by many, including in Stephanie's first book about the Maui fires, *Burn Back Better*, we believe that people are particularly incensed about Maui. And with that comes action. We are delighted to see that Maui has sparked an awakening in people all over the world. In fact, two of the authors of this book were unbelievers; Traci and Stephanie didn't believe that it would be possible for globalists or nefarious actors to get away with an intentional incineration of a town before Lahaina. Lahaina was their wake-up call. And over the past ten months, it's haunted them every moment.

You, too, might be haunted by what happened in Lahaina and/ or what is now happening in Ruidoso (although thankfully far less fatalities that we can see,) or what happened in Paradise or even Chile. You, too, might be dually inspired with a sense of deep purpose and renewed vigor to make your life count and your voice heard. Throughout this book we'll provide you with many inspirational stories and even actionable steps to make your voice heard and to turn your anger into productive action.

For instance, Stephanie has invested time literally walking the streets in Lahaina and talking to boaters returning to the docks at Lahaina Harbor about detoxification post-fires. (See "An Urgent Message" in the beginning of the book.) Other men and women from Honolulu to Houston invest time sharing Traci and Shane's videos from the YouTube channel "Brush Junkie" with Hawai'ian lobbyists and legislators with the hopes that they'll have an impact on an endlessly corrupt Hawai'ian government. Those of you reading who have large platforms online have hosted Stephanie Pierucci after *Burn Back*

Better launched or other voices such as Representative Elle Cochran on your shows.

We can't give a strategy to each reader, but we trust that we've been through enough in this book to give you inspiration to find your calling and your lane with regard to seeking justice for Lahaina.

We will not be forced into the Great Reset.

Lahaina is among the last-ditch efforts by globalists to see what they can get away with.

And by purchasing and sharing this book, you join us in saying "no."

Each Hawai'ian Island Has Ominous Writings On The Walls...

We the authors feel tremendous concern for any community in which "TOD Corridor," "Sustainable Development," "15-minute city," "SMART City," "Eco-barrio," or other plans are being proposed or, God forbid, approved. These are the areas that we believe are most vulnerable to "mysterious fires" such as the one on August 8th in Lahaina.

In previous YouTube videos on Traci's channel, "Brush Junkie", Traci and Shane have shown that the State of Hawai'i has a "Strategic Plan"[3] to redevelop each island according to "Smart" growth principles, just like they're doing with the "West Maui Community Corridor"[4], which was planned years before the Lahaina fire but was a virtual match to the burn zone.[5] We'll go into much more on the Maui plans later in this book. These so-called "Smart" cities are now often rebranded to various other names, such as "Community Corridors", "Commercial Corridors", "15-minute cities," or even "10-minute cities," in the case of Līhu'e on Kaua'i.

---

3   https://planning.hawaii.gov/wp-content/uploads/State-TOD-Strategic-Plan_Dec-2017-Rev-Aug-2018.pdf

4   https://www.westmauicommunitycorridor.org/_files/ugd/b59736_9d548b7fc8c94629a a7724647a7ead82.pdf

5   https://www.youtube.com/watch?v=MTb88U_ui8U

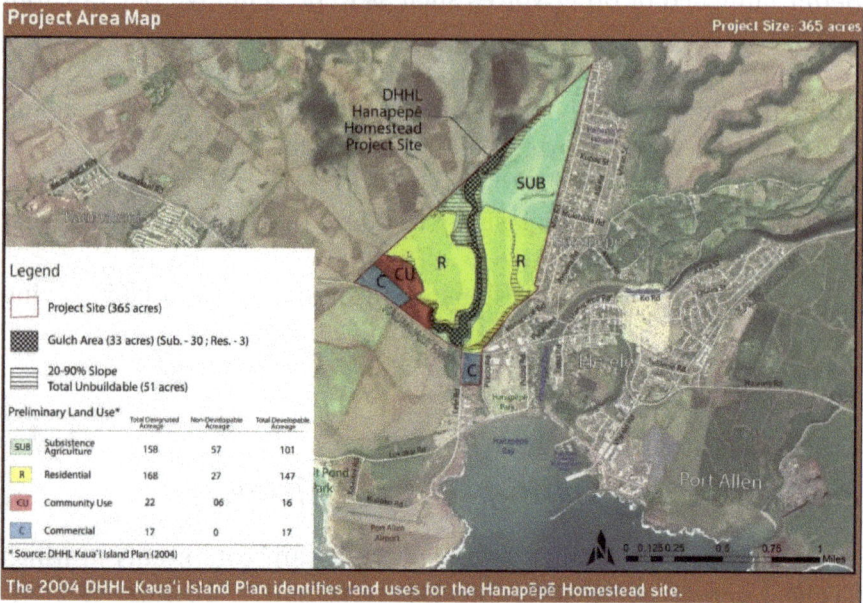

The 2004 DHHL Kaua'i Island Plan identifies land uses for the Hanapēpē Homestead site.

In their video titled "Kauai's 10-Minute City Plans!," Shane mentioned another project on the island of Kaua'i called "The Hanapēpē Infill Redevelopment" plan, as seen above.[6] This is a 3-phase housing development on the Hanapēpē Homestead site just west of Moi Road that has recently finished Phase One of its construction and is ready to begin clearing the remaining land for Phases 2 and 3, as seen in the following image.[7]

---

6   https://youtu.be/r09L_E-iWVM?si=KufoURv6_upazTrT&t=1337
7   https://dhhl.hawaii.gov/wp-content/uploads/2012/05/Island_Plan_Kauai_2004.pdf

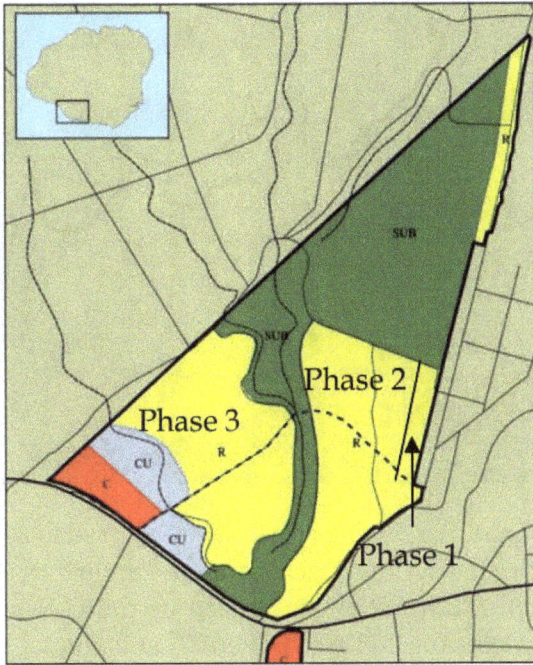

Figure 10.3

Hanapēpē Residential Phasing

At the time of writing this book, a brush fire had broken out around noon on July 15, 2024, starting just west of Moi Road (as seen in the next image), on the very same Hanapēpē Homestead site where the Hanapēpē Infill Redevleopment plan was ready to begin phase 2. Residents in Kaumakani were ordered to evacuate, while the County of Kaua'i activated its Emergency Operations Center and power lines were deactivated to limit liability until the fire was contained.[8]

Kaua'i resident David Parsons III told KHON2 News that he saw "little tornadoes" that were seen "across the horizon".[9]

---

8   https://www.youtube.com/watch?v=5ui3gzhCgCM
9   https://youtu.be/x0xgvhVey84?si=i0lH5tjzkeY177jL&t=66

This is just one of many fires that have occurred in zones that were scheduled for redevelopment according to "Smart" or "Sustainable" growth principles that were introduced by the U.N.'s "Sustainable Development Goals for 2030" (SDG 2030) and adopted by cities and counties world-wide, especially across the State of Hawai'i. Shane had seen this happen so often before that he wasn't shocked by it at this point, but Traci and Stephanie thought it was noteworthy to include here because it's another example of the same thing happening again in Hawaii.

The fact is that every Hawai'ian island has been included in the "State of Hawai'i Strategic Plan for Transit-Oriented Development," which aims to redevelop each of the islands and their cities into Smart islands and Smart cities, just like they are trying to do with Lahaina on Maui. These plans also exist for virtually every other city and county in the U.S. as well as every N.A.T.O. country in the United Nations.

Book Beginnings

"The World Will Be Saved By the Western Woman"
The Dalai Lama

As Traci and Stephanie first began writing this book, it was hard not to remember that statement and imagine what the Dalai Lama had in mind when he praised the resourcefulness and passion of the Western woman with the phrase, "the world will be saved by the Western woman." We had many "girl power" moments. But our party was incomplete without Shane. What started as a spark became a roaring fire, so to speak, when Shane agreed to co-author with us. He was the perfect intellectual and spiritual complement to our mission.

Nevertheless, during our time researching over the past ten months, we the authors have found that although there are many remarkable and brave men behind-the-scenes analyzing scientific, meteorological, and forensic evidence and sharing it online, the women involved in the movement to see justice for Lahaina are particularly assertive. We've been impressed with the civic and community engagement among the women. They're signing and sharing petitions, showing up to provide public testimony, and spearheading community action. Throwing caution to the wind, many brave women such as Representative Elle Cochran have had no hesitation about plainly stating that there were at least 1,000 souls who perished in this tragedy.

We hope that by reading this book you will, too, find that the spark in you turns into a passionate fire, and that you will get involved. First, please set this book down and sign the petition for a transparent, public investigation and hearing that you can find at www. mauicommunityinvestigation.com.

Next, if you live in Hawaii, please pay attention to Traci's "Brush Junkie" channel on YouTube where you'll learn about upcoming opportunities to get involved by submitting your testimony or appearing at local legislative and community meetings or hearings. You will find Traci on YouTube at https://www.youtube.com/@brushjunkie6384.

Please also follow Eric West on YouTube for more information about getting involved locally. You will find Eric on YouTube at https://www.youtube.com/@hawaiirealestateorg.

Goto www.SwitchForLahaina.com and learn about a simple way to support individuals and families affected by the Lahaina fire.

Consider Supporting Citizen Reporting of the Truth on Maui. Visit http://www.TruthMaui.com

*

Your authors are continually inspired and fueled to see that this movement isn't restricted to men in suits and boardrooms. The community is activated, incensed, and impactful, as you'll learn about in this book. The remarkable network of justice seekers for Lahaina has tentacles across all socioeconomic levels, classes, and even many countries; both men and women. We receive emails daily from watermen, doctors, marine biologists, special forces veterans, and so many wonderful mothers and members of the community.

We, the authors, aren't so sure we're going to save the world, but this book is our prayer to save Maui. And yes, we are *that* afraid for Maui's future.

PART ONE:
Smoking Guns

CHAPTER ONE:
There Will Be No Rebuild?

In January of 2024, Stephanie began the New Year on the island of Maui meeting with people involved in the cleanup of Lahaina, people in local Maui government, people from Lahaina, some who'd lost their home, many who'd lost family or friends, and engineers, environmentalists, and people in disaster recovery.

After nine days of interviews, the most shocking story Stephanie took away with her was the insistence by some experts that the people of Lahaina would never be rebuilt. This incensed Stephanie and almost made her wonder, "What the heck am I doing all this work for, if there's never going to be a rebuild?"

The most ominous report Stephanie heard was from a team of disaster recovery and private security specialists who are based out of California, Florida, and Hawaii. They worked in Lahaina as well as scores of other fires around the world. One of these experts, Samuel Eaton, plainly stated, "People will *ask* the government to take their land; they're going to make it that hard."

Eaton believes that it will be *at least* four to five years before people could get into their homes in Lahaina, and that there were a handful of obstacles that would be put into place before they could return. Among them include:

1. Every home will require a permit for rebuild;
2. Every permit will need about 12 months to get approved;
3. You will need 3–4 permits;
4. Only one may be approved annually (Hawaii is notoriously slow in granting permits);

5. All houses must be built on stilts 17 foot above the water/land (Jersey Shore did this);
6. Due to required easements between neighbors and from a person's driveway, most likely a 1,000 square foot home would be reduced to as little as perhaps 300 square feet—so these big Hawai'ian families surely couldn't fit in there comfortably;
7. Most of the homes in Lahaina were owned outright, meaning they were NOT insured because they were family homes. Insurance was denied to family homes because the insurance companies required a bank loan, which makes the families from Lahaina vulnerable to red tape and back office foolery;
8. The homes must be zoned henceforth for underground utilities;
9. Property taxes will be reinstituted.

Hence, our fear at this time is that people will have so many hoops to jump through that they won't ever return to Lahaina. As you'll read in Part Two, there is yet another reason people may never return to their homes in Lahaina. The government has been assertively looking to declare eminent domain over the entire inhabitable West side of Maui. This essentially means that the government will do what they wish with these properties; regardless of who "owned" them and whether or not they were commercial or residential.

Our fear is also that Lahaina will not be restored to the people, but turned into a "Smart City" that boasts a "sustainable, carbon-neutral, low-emissions, no gas vehicle permitted" type of concentration camp.

Many of the locations we'll explore in this book have plans for "sustainable developments" in their county records. This is no accident. The 1984 "doublespeak" is evident in the political propaganda in Lahaina and, ultimately, throughout the "climate alarmism" movement. Up is down, left is right, sustainable developments are really unsustainable prison camps fueled by false climate change claims.

From his book description "Climate and Energy Lies: Expensive, Dangerous and Destructive,"[10] former Wisconsin State Senator Frank Lasse writes:

---

10   www.truthinclimateandenergy.com

Across the modern world, we are being told that the climate is heating up, creating a climate crisis. This well-funded propaganda, commonly called "Climate Alarmism," is founded on lies. These "Climate and Energy Lies" will impoverish communities, states, and entire nations, robbing citizens of their freedoms. What's more, the psychological fear triggered by Climate Alarmism is used to control populations. To herd them into making decisions that favor corporations and politicians, at the average citizen's expense. At its core, Climate Alarmism is a tool in a dark globalist political and corporate agenda.

Energy inflation and bureaucratic meddling for the sake of reducing greenhouse gasses are the first steps toward global control through Climate Alarmism. The "Green" movement is financed with borrowed tax money, oppressive regulations, and ever more expensive electricity and energy. This adds to the $34 trillion U.S. national debt. The West scrambles to purchase wind towers, solar panels, batteries, and electric car components from the world's greatest polluter and Alarmism beneficiary, totalitarian Communist China. "Green" Chinese products are made with dirty coal power, near slave labor, and almost no environmental protections. They are often more detrimental to earth (and our national debt) than fossil fuel energy.

However imaginary the climate crisis is, the threat of prosperity and freedom disintegrating is real. We shouldn't fear climate change, we should fear climate change policy![11]

In Lahaina, many homes were built one-hundred years ago. Affording setbacks, roadways, sprinklers, underground utilities, and easements are expenses that will be out of reach for most people who lost their homes or businesses. Eaton's fear is that people will give up and **ask for the settlement check.**
After Hurricane Katrina, lots of properties were not rebuilt for these reasons. In Lahaina, approximately 2,700 structures were incinerated. Prior to the fire, Maui County invested in green energy projects instead

---

11 www.truthinclimateandenergy.com

of fire mitigation. At two of the three points of potential arson on the island, it's clear that dry brush had not been mitigated, which fueled the fire toward Lahainatown with the (engineered?) strong winds.

In a later chapter we'll also point out that the local government was highly inept. In fact, Maui Emergency Management Agency director Herman Andaya had no experience in Emergency Management.

Maui Emergency Management Agency Administrator Herman Andaya speaks during a news conference in Wailuku, Hawaii, on Wednesday.
To his left Maui's Mayor Bissen and Hawaii Governor Josh Green to his right.
Mike Householder/AP

On August 8th, hundreds of 911 calls were made reporting destruction; some of them included parents calling terrified that they were "stuck" in the fire with children. Some of these calls included reports that there was no water to fight the fires. In fact, it took five hours to release the water which Deputy Director for Water Resource Management Kaleo Manuel is on record stating was due to "equity."

As these calls were pouring in, Andaya exchanged a disturbing series of text messages with MEMA administrative assistant Gaye Gabuat on August 8th. Mind you, many had perished, up to 1,000 souls by our estimation, while Andaya and Gabuat were still "LOL'ing." Those text messages include the following statements, showing a nonchalant attitude that still sends chills up our spines.

3:53 p.m.
Gaye Gabuat to Herman Andaya: "Lol. Poor chief looks so overwhelm. Chief is wanting help from the military. Not sure of what."

4:01 p.m.
Andaya to Gabuat: "This is crazy. How is everyone holding up?"

4:03 p.m.
Andaya to Gabuat: "Should I come home?
Gabuat to Andaya: "PIOs are funny. There are 3 of them and they look scared and overwhelmed....I think they need a hug lol to calm down."

9:37 p.m.
Andaya to Gabuat: "How's the other fires?"

Gabuat to Andaya: "Still burning"

Andaya to Gabuat: "Wow ... Lol"

Gabuat to Andaya: "Now we have Kihei fire near Pulehu Road."

Andaya to Gabuat: "You just keep making my day."

10:58 p.m.
Hawaii Emergency Management Agency administrator James Barros to Andaya: "LtG just called...Very concerned."

Andaya to Barros: "Yes....this is really bad. I'm flying back tomorrow."[12]

---

12 https://www.hawaiinewsnow.com/2024/04/19/ag-report-maui-wildfires-shows-lack-urgency-former-mema-head/

One reason your authors continue to work on unveiling the truth on Maui is not only our respective personal connections to the islands, but because what we saw in terms of gross incompetence at a minimum was plainly murder. Those who survived were required to ignore the police and road blocks. Alarms were not sounded on an island with the most robust alarm system in the world. No text notifications nor sirens alerted people, which may have saved countless lives.

Since the fire, the island has seen an uptick in suicides and crime. Stephanie's experience on the island illustrated that many of the survivors are suffering "Survivor's Guilt." Others are terrified of losing their temporary housing. Many are camping on beaches, having already given up on FEMA finding them a short term or long term rental. What's more, some report that working with FEMA is plagued with so much red tape that it isn't even worth arguing with the FEMA representatives. Still others did report that by filing early claims with FEMA, they were lucky enough to find housing on the island. Among locals, those who were put up in private homes versus small hotel rooms where many hotel proprietors don't even allow them to use facilities in the hotel feel like they've won the lottery; one reported that he was afraid to tell his friends lest they get angry that he won the "FEMA" lottery.

More likely if FEMA is working with families, our understanding is that FEMA is offering families $1,600 to move off Maui; breaking up the fabric that makes this community and the network Maui needs to make sure the needs of families are met as the government legislates through the cleanup.

On an island where the average cost of a home was already $1,200,000 and the average condo going for $800,000, Lahaina was one of the few working class areas. It is said that $5.5B would be required to rebuild Lahaina. However, our concern is that it will be much more profitable for the government to turn this former working class town into a veritable Disneyland instead of preserving what once was. Those who are responsible for the fire are likely to benefit from it.

With housing having disappeared overnight and the town losing $17,000,000 daily in tourist income as of January 2024, our fear is that if people do not read this book and take any action within their capacity, there will be no rebuild.

CHAPTER TWO:
Our Kuleana

Kuleana is a uniquely Hawai'ian word and practice loosely defined as "responsibility." When we the authors think of the word *Kuleana* in relation to the true Hawai'ian meaning, we don't think of the "responsibility" to make our kids dinner, although that's important. But rather, we see it more as a deeper purpose, such as protecting those childrens' lives. *Kuleana* also has significance as a purpose that creates harmony; as we practice our *kuleana*, the beneficiary gives back to us in some way.

The authors have chosen to work continually on the project of *Sound The Alarm* and *Burn Back Better* as part of a deep purpose or responsibility, a calling that has a reciprocal relationship, such as the original Hawai'ian word suggests. For instance, care for the environment is a reciprocal relationship; if you take care of the environment, the environment gives back to you and your family.

As far as our *Kuleana* with regards to continually uncovering, researching, evaluating and sharing information about the Lahaina fires, we have found that the relationship between reporting and receiving, the "reciprocal" part of our work for Lahaina includes sounding the alarm for the whole world to understand that it isn't just a tragedy on Maui, but a looming threat for all communities, particularly where sustainable development plans have taken root. The work we do to help Hawaii gives back to us in our assurance that it makes the world a safer place. That is why we continue in this work; it doesn't deplete us; it invigorates us because the work gives back in creating a safer world for our families. That is, provided you, the reader, pay very close attention to the third part of this book and work alongside us in continually spreading truth and sounding the alarm in your communities.

A few months before embarking on this second book about Maui following *Burn Back Better*, published in October of 2023, Stephanie listened to a radio spot somebody sent her called "Something Wicked This Way Comes" by Scott Kesterson. The voice in this interview clip is unknown but the original broadcast was on BardsFM Episode 2724. The host states, "The U.S. government is f*cking the people who lost their homes in the Maui fire... 2,207 homes burned down... since the Maui wildfire, not a single building permit has been approved. Not one..."

Our author, Stephanie Pierucci, was homeless in 2021 after a legal battle to protect her son from an experimental gene-based therapy cost her life savings and nearly two years of hefty earnings. It is the memory of that desperate time that fuels Stephanie to continue fighting for Lahaina because being homeless, as a single mother no less, can have indescribably difficult moments for both the parent and the child. Her heart has remained soft toward anybody who doesn't have this basic need; shelter and security.

The radio broadcast continues and has been transcribed by the authors of this book:

> *The insurance companies haven't been able to pay anything because the United States government won't even allow the insurance adjusters into the area. Where all they wanna do is go in there and verify that these buildings have burned down. They wanna verify how extensive the damage is for each of the homes that they insured. And for a lot of these homes it would be as easy as driving up, taking pictures of a burned down property, verifying that the home no longer exists, and then they could cut a check. But the U.S. government won't let them do that. And the U.S. government won't let anybody rebuild. And here's the wildest part. Because the insurance adjusters can't verify that these homes burned down and because the United States government won't approve a single fucking billing permit, all of these people are still paying their mortgages. These people no longer have homes. But because they're not approving building permits and they're not allowing the insurance adjusters in, the banks are still charging these people a mortgage. These people are paying a fucking mortgage on houses that don't even exist and many of them are getting foreclosed on. Like, imagine how ridiculous that is. Your house burned to the f*cking ground.*

Your insurance company wants to go out there. They want to go see the burned down house, take a picture, and cut you a check. But the government in the interest of "helping people," I guess, won't let them do that. So the banks get to keep collecting the mortgage payments and if you can't make the mortgage payments on the house that isn't even f*cking there anymore, they get to foreclose on the property and now the bank owns the land where your house used to be. And all of this is happening because the government will not approve any building permits and won't even let the insurance adjusters in. But yeah, you guys keep celebrating that Biden visited there for four hours. I'm sure that's some comfort to these people."

Many of our readers from every continent have experienced this same level of incensed, indignant rage at what is happening to the people of Maui post August 8th. We encourage you to never stop feeling that rage as you fight alongside us for the people.

What Brought Us Here?

Throughout this book, you'll hear stories and perspectives from these three authors who were all in quite different locations at the time of the August 8th fire in Lahaina.

Traci Derwin

Traci Derwin was with her family during the time of the Lahaina fire. At the time, she ran a sizable YouTube channel called "Brush Junkie," in addition to being a busy mom and wife. As she'll admit, she wasn't cozying up to any Alex Jones types nor the conspiracy theorist next door in 2020. She didn't take a stand against the Covid-19 shots and had no problem with taking the first round, including a booster. By any measure, Traci was not the woman you'd have pegged to suddenly devote her life to uncovering a nefarious crime or call out corrupt global elites.

Traci grew up in an area called Kaneohe on Oahu, about thirty minutes from Honolulu, where her father and his family are from. On the paternal side, she is a fourth generation Japanese living in Hawaii, which is fairly typical on the islands. Her paternal-grandmother was born and raised in Kona, having had a father who immigrated as a train conductor and a mother who passed away from a brain aneurysm when Traci's grandmother was an infant. Traci's grandmother would say, "I was still drinking from my mother's breasts when she passed." Unlike other Japanese immigrants, none of her ancestors worked on plantations. Rather, her grandmother left the Big Island of Hawaii and worked at the Ilikai Hotel on Oahu most of her life. Traci's grandmother took care of her sister and her while their parents were at work. So her childhood is infused with her grandmother's lessons about being loving, dynamic, and a hard worker.

Traci remembers being required to learn the Hawai'ian language as a child growing up on the "windward side" of the Koolau mountain range, where wind would hit and release rain regularly. Needless to say, it was unlikely that fires would start or be sustained in such conditions. She remembers that she was enamored with fire as a little girl and would start them regularly, even though it was difficult on account of the moisture in the brush and air surrounding it.

When Traci learned that Lahaina was burned by a fire, she found it to be odd; growing up, she'd heard the sirens many times in Hawaii, and they were praised as the world's most robust alarm system. The State of Hawaii tests the sirens regularly; she recalls that growing up, they were sounded many times during hurricanes or tsunami watches.

The Lahaina fire struck Traci as especially odd when former Maui County EMA Director Herman Andaya said that he decided not to sound the alarms because he thought people would run toward the fire. The notion was unbelievable to Traci, and even downright offensive.

Alongside her suspicions about the alarms, Traci found more strange details surrounding the fires, including equally strange parties involved, especially at the level of the local government. Before she knew it, Traci found herself as the leader in a movement of people who were formerly the "anti-vaxxers" and "tin foil hatters."

But without judgment, Traci forged ahead, driven by curiosity and her love for the people of Hawaii, having a come-to-Jesus about the community that investigates most of what they hear as "crimes" before coming to conclusions. Traci's integrity and flexibility enable her to work with people from the other side of the political aisle in order to get to the truth.

Her journey of reporting on the Maui fires lit within on August 20th, which was the same day that "hurricane" Hilary hit the Los Angeles area, while she was living in Southern California. There were also two small earthquakes at the same time. She got alerts on her phone for all three! Traci had already been hearing about the devastating fires in Maui and remembered hearing that the people of Maui did not receive a single alarm, siren, or alert on their cell phones. At that moment, an alarm went off in Traci's heart and mind. She already had her suspicions about the state's handling of the Lahaina emergency, but when the alerts began blowing up her cell phone for this August 20th "rainy day" (which was all the hurricane amounted to), along with two small scale earthquakes, her suspicions began to burn.

Over the coming days, Traci had several conversations that confirmed she wasn't being melodramatic. That's when she made her first video to share about what she thought was going on and to express her concerns about criminal negligence on Maui. To date, that video has been seen by over a quarter million viewers. Viewers can easily identify moments where Traci's voice wavers; the fire had just occurred two weeks prior and, having been born and raised on Oahu, viewers see that she is tremendously affected.

Up until that day, Traci had devoted her YouTube channel to discussions about makeup and makeup brushes. Her following amounted to 1,220 subscribers and a very modest income that barely covered her makeup and brush addiction. Throughout her time providing these makeup tutorials, she knew deep down that she had more to offer the world. Little did she know, the world would soon respond to her courageous inquiries about Maui. At the time of writing this book, her YouTube channel following has increased more than 2,600%, making her among the most respected citizen journalists devoted to the Maui fires.

Traci was pleased when that original video that has received over 260,000 views reached 1,000 views, so she seized the opportunity to post another video celebrating the cultural and historical significance of Lahaina. After putting her children to sleep the following evening, she was surprised to see that she had over 20,000 subscribers, and that number was increasing rapidly. Previously, she would gain one or two subscribers per day, but suddenly, she was getting a new subscriber every couple of seconds. The video was going viral; the world wanted to hear more of Traci's thoughts on Maui, the fire, and the beautiful people of Hawaii.

Traci called her husband, who was on his way home from a meeting, to tell him about the strange activity in her YouTube analytics. He didn't believe what she was telling him. He stated, "If you're at 150,000 views by tomorrow, that's certifiably viral." Traci's husband works in online marketing and wagered that the activity was a coincidence. Sure enough, the next morning, she had far more than 150,000 views. Her email inbox was flooded with messages, including one from Alexander & Baldwin, Hawaii's premier commercial real estate company owned by Blackrock, who are among the largest landowners on Maui. Alexander & Baldwin wanted to make it clear that Kaleo Manuel, who was the director of the Department of Land and Natural Resources (DLNR) at the time, was a beloved member of the community and they suspected he was being used as a scapegoat for the lack of water. They emphasized that he was certainly not at fault for the lack of water in the hydrants. Manuel was "reassigned" after the fire, then reinstated to his position, only to resign shortly thereafter.

The reality of the world's response to her video filled her with both heat and euphoria; in that moment, Traci felt aligned with her purpose in a way she'd never felt. In 2008, Traci lost her father, who was a man of integrity with strong opinions about politics. The realization that she was doing a service to the world and honoring her late father's legacy was the lighted match thrown onto a heap of dry brush that propelled her forward to keep investigating.

Traci's deep understanding of the beauty and power of the Hawai'ian land and culture made the Lahaina tragedy even more potent and personal for her. Since her first viral video, Traci hasn't looked back; she has only gained momentum as an intrepid citizen journalist.

Stephanie Pierucci

Stephanie wrote the original book on the Lahaina fire called *Burn Back Better: A Perfect Storm or A Perfect Crime*, which is the most thorough investigation of the August 8th fires, until now. Unlike Traci Derwin,

Stephanie has been on the front lines of the fight against unlawful mandates, well aware of the corruption at play.

In 2021, Stephanie found herself at a "political dissident" rally at a local church in Aspen, Colorado, where she resides. At the time, Stephanie would consider herself a "Chrystic" or a sort of New Agey "Christian Mystic." She laughs when she recounts the story of getting on stage at this event with scores of concerned citizens representing the anti-vax or anti-mandate community. She took the microphone and told the community of her plight, fighting to protect her son. Let's just say a few f-bombs were involved! Rather than being struck down by lightning or threatened by one of the cowboys in the audience, she was wholly embraced, and soon thereafter, she rededicated her life to the Lord Jesus Christ amidst the company of a kind, passionate, and soulful group of community organizers and political dissidents up in the mountains.

Among this community, there are several former high-ranking military officers, doctors, and influential folks who are well-known in the Aspen mountains. Although Stephanie took the stage in order to raise awareness for her legal battle to keep her son safe from the gene mutating vaccine, which was arduous and soul-crushing, as well as financially devastating, what she found were like-minded friends and a spiritual awareness that she never encountered in the otherwise self-indulgent New Age movement, where she'd been active the previous decade.

Within a week of the rally, Stephanie became tapped into a private network of what one might call "freedom fighters" around the country. Within a few months, her small publishing company became the chosen provider of services for some of the highest profile political dissidents and medical freedom fighters. During her recent career, her company has celebrated several *Wall Street Journal* bestselling books and has published such renowned thought leaders as Dr. Vladimir Zelenko and Brent Hamachek, The Wellness Company, Foster Coulson, Dr. Richard Amerling, Dr. Heather Gessling, Dr. Harvey Risch, Dr. Peter McCullough, Dr. Jana Schmidt, and Dr. Jen Van De Water, as well as many other frontline doctors, anti-pharma influencers, and political whistleblowers such as Colonel Ret. John Mills and former Wisconsin State Senator Frank Lasee. All of these beautiful souls, and more, were the gifts in referrals from that gracious audience at a tiny church in the mountains. The community there didn't give Stephanie a fish, but they gave her the opportunity to earn her own way to pay off her legal bills by doing great work for great people who were aligned with her values. By God's grace, she did, indeed, protect her son from the shot.

On August 8th, Stephanie was returning from a camping trip, mostly out of cell service, in the San Juan Islands, where she and her son were hoping to see Orca whales. Almost immediately when she returned to the continental U.S., her phone blew up with messages from friends who lived on Maui. Stephanie lived on Kaua'i several years ago and has maintained relationships with several people on the Big Island, Kaua'i, and Maui.

She learned that one friend had left work in Lahaina around 3:00 p.m. and would surely have burned to death if she had not decided to drive through police barricades that were routing cars back onto Front Street during the fire, where many of those people met their untimely death. Stephanie was horrified to hear about the woman's desperation to simply get on the highway to safety and the police barricades she had to barrel through to save her life. She then learned that the alarms hadn't gone off and that this woman friend had watched her employer in the car behind her almost become engulfed in flames before she jumped into the water, before spending the next eight hours out in the ocean. The woman shared a story that with cell phones down, her only communication during the horrific hour she spent trying to leave town was conversing with a picture of her grandson that was on the sun visor in her car. She felt like the picture spoke to her and said, "You need to get out of this town immediately, if you ever want to see your grandchildren again."

Because Stephanie has been a professional writer for the majority of her career, as friends shared stories about their experiences in the fires, she began taking notes and trying to put together pieces based on what she heard. She was already skeptical of everything around her after the Covid-19 events, so it was all she could do to begin an investigation as a service to her loved ones in Hawaii.

In October of 2023, she published *Burn Back Better*, a book that was written mere weeks after the fire, detailing some of the most important questions surrounding the Lahaina fires; it was a response to the media blackout and First Amendment violations going on in Maui at the time.

As Stephanie details in *Burn Back Better*, the original Lahaina investigation that addresses the "first" wave of questions people had just weeks after the fire, she points out that instead of enjoying our First Amendment rights to freedom of the press, instead we experiencing the following:

> *There were innumerable tons of boulders mysteriously ready on August 9th, ready to block people from taking pictures of the "burn zone" from the bypass over Lahaina;*

> *Although news crews were not allowed into the 'burn zone,' some intrepid reporters such as KITV's Jeremy Lee made do with hopping on a boat and reporting from the ocean, seizing his First Amendment rights for himself;*

> *A $3M fence referred to as a "dust screen" blocked anybody from seeing the burn zone, cleanup efforts, nor entering the area to search for friends, neighbors, family, pets, or take pictures of their homes.*

Boulders were placed on the bypass above Lahaina on August 9th
Nobody was allowed to stop to take pictures.

Image courtesy of Stephanie Pierucci. January, 2024 on "the bypass"

This book digs much deeper into some of the questions from the original book, and brings many more pieces of evidence that weren't covered in the original book to light. We have been careful not to "repeat" information from the first book so that this book can expound upon the original investigation. If you would like a copy of *Burn Back*

Better, you can visit Amazon or purchase at a bulk discount rate for your community by emailing Publishing@PierucciPublishing.com.

Shane Buell

Shane Buell grew up in Fort Wayne, Indiana, a couple houses down from a family who originated from Lahaina, Hawaii. As a child he became entranced with Star Trek, and by twelve years old he had a fascination with science, including Unified Field Theory and understanding the fundamental forces of the universe.

Another popular story series at that time was Star Wars, which brought awareness to the capabilities of directed energy. It's funny how art imitates life, eh? It was also during this time that Shane learned that technologies are often not disclosed to the public for about fifty years after they're developed. This opened up a world of possibilities to Shane, who wondered what technologies he hadn't yet discovered, and if he'd even be alive when today's technologies were unveiled.

However, when he observed the melted rims and glass during the Paradise, California fires, he wondered if timelines had begun to intersect and he was seeing "undisclosed" technologies being used in real time. To most of our readers, this now seems abundantly clear, almost an open and shut case. The Paradise fires were, for many, the first alarm that was sounded. When friends of Shane's posted pictures of homes being burned with nothing around them, he came to the conclusion that directed energy was clearly being used.

On September 8, 2020, Shane was watching a Live YouTube stream from Dutchsinse, "the earthquake guy." During that Live, the YouTuber streamed images from the College of DuPage website that captured a beam through an infrared satellite image. Beams show up on the near infrared spectrum that aren't visible to our naked eyes. This linear beam of higher temperature was visible to everybody watching the Live stream. It appeared to travel from an origination point above a national refuge in Oregon and terminated at one of the fires in California.[13]

You've seen photos of "beams" and probably, like your authors, thought they were fake. Sometimes you have to see it to believe it... or

---

13   https://www.youtube.com/watch?v=nDnzPkuJiX0&t=377s

totally disprove it. Due to the infrared image, Shane became a believer. When a friend of his in Northern California shared images of melted glass, and Shane learned that the melting point of glass was far higher than a brush fire, closer to 2,700–2,900 degrees Fahrenheit, he became devoted to digging deeper into the Paradise rubble.

When an old friend from the Lahaina "Kamaka" family posted about Lahaina on August 9th, he saw many of the same anomalies that he noticed in Paradise. He learned that people were jumping into the water and that the entire town had been burned. Quickly, he surmised that Lahaina's was not a normal fire. He immediately suspected the use of directed energy, but didn't jump to conclusions.

Thankfully, the fires on Maui in 2023 provided far more evidence than in Paradise or other suspicious fires. This might be due to the denser population as well as the number of eyewitnesses with cameras and cell phone video.

Like Pierucci and Derwin, Buell relied primarily on Eric West to courageously report from the ground on Maui when all other major news networks were censored or limited to filming outside the miles of fencing that was immediately erected around Lahaina, supposedly as a way to prohibit dust and debris from blowing outside of the burn zone. Although Buell scoured mainstream news sources, Eric West's coverage on the Hawaii Real Estate YouTube Channel[14] was far more informative than all the rest of the coverage combined. He was coming up regularly and readily in searches until he was suppressed by YouTube.

The interview between West and "Fish" was a pivotal moment in Buell's investigation; firing him up while breaking his heart. It was seeing Fish and hearing of people being routed into the "rotisserie" on Front Street that compelled Buell to make Lahaina his new mission.

It was shortly after Buell had set this sacred intention to devote time and effort into justice for Lahaina that he had what he calls a "sort of esoteric spiritual experience."

Buell admits that he isn't overtly spiritual online and it feels vulnerable to share the vision he had. But with a little arm-twisting, we were able to get it out of him.

---

14   https://www.youtube.com/@hawaiirealestateorg

"The August 8th Lion's Gate"
September 2023

The August 8th Lion's Gate happened, when factions of rich and powerful globalists committed the democide of the Hawai'ian native capitol of Lahaina, Maui, in collusion with the billionaires on the "other side" of the island and their Blackrock, Vanguard, and Carlyle oligarchies who are stealing the land from the natives for their "AI Smart City concentration camp pilot program."

Those Bastards road-blocked every exit out of the city to safety, corralling and boxing people in towards the path of the fire. Then they ran those people in circles in a sort of "roundabout rotisserie" while nuking them with DEW "space lasers".

I realized that sharing this truth would be making an extraordinary claim, which requires extraordinary evidence, and that the burden of proof is certainly on me, but that "burden" was rather seen as a responsibility I gladly will assume, one which excavated a buried call for me to "light my own fire within" and "carry the torch" of truth.

That Lions Gate was a huge awakening for me, and it was rough at first, but now I can hang ten and surf these waves of chaos. I'm having what I would call my "Second Seal" activation from the Lahaina, Maui fire and everything it has led me to. I'm conducting an in-depth investigation into it, and was up all week working on it. I kept skipping two nights of sleep and then sleeping on the third. After six days of that I was finally finished, but was definitely getting delirious at one point.

I kept seeing something out of the corner of my eye, and figured there might be spirits or something, even though I had just saged. So, I turned on my desk lamp to hopefully stop seeing dark figures and silhouettes in the corners of the room with my peripheral vision. While facing my monitor, the lamp began to fade in and out at a slow but steady pace, but whenever I turned my head to look, it stopped doing it. So this time, I kept my face forward towards my monitor and it started doing it again, but this time I looked with only my peripheral vision, not even turning my eyes, just shifting my awareness to that side.

I caught sight of a young Hawai'ian girl in traditional ceremonial attire, waving at me trying to get my attention with her hand passing in front of the lamp, but there was no fear. All I felt was peace, love, and joy. She was then accompanied by an older man who seemed very wise, and they began cheering, singing, and chanting to me in Hawai'ian. It was so beautiful that I had what I can only describe as "tiers of joy." Not tears, but "tiers," as the joy came in waves or layers, revealing itself to my conscious mind as levels of understanding to what seemed incomprehensible.

The girl and wise older man seemed to be cheering me on for the work I've undertaken, which has led to a revitalized spirit, passion, and purpose. My oversoul seems to have personalities that incarnated through that particular ancestral lineage, and some of those memories are still accessible to me, so that event seems to be a type of "sign" that activated some sort of latent, epigenetically "sealed" gifts for me. No matter where you place your faith, we all have a calling and I pray that you answer yours when you receive it.

*

Since that September revelation and vision, Shane has learned that as often as it whispers, his well-attuned intuition now more often yells at him, guiding him toward the questions he asks and answers he seeks. He began running a Facebook investigation, posing questions to the hive and allowing his audience to contribute as fellow citizen journalists. As many of our readers may have found, there were more questions than answers in those first few months after the Lahaina fires.

For the purpose of inspiring this audience to see how far Buell has come from his initial investigation until today, here is a screen capture of his original investigation.

Shane Buell
September 8, 2023 · 🌐

...

"TOWARDS THE DANGER"

Today is the the 1 month anniversary of the democide of the Hawai'ian native capitol of Lahaina Maui by the billionaires on the rich "other side" of the island who are stealing the land from the natives for their AI smart city concentration camp pilot program. Those billionaire Bastards roadblocked every exit from the city and corralled people into the fire, then ran them in circles in a roundabout rotisserie while nuking them with DEW space lasers. Extraordinary claims do require extraordinary evidence, and the burden of proof is certainly on us, but this "burden" is really just a hidden call for us to "light the fire within" and "carry the torch" of truth.

I've compiled all of the sources I can site, with zero embellishments. If there's any claim, rumor, or speculation that has not yet been sourced, I state it plainly and ask for your help in locating those sources, especially any videos, time stamps, and authentic photos that are relevant, such as the graphs or charts of the intentionally overloaded electric grids at the precise times the fires started. For example, the Kula fires, the upcountry fires, and the first Lahaina fire all began at 6:30am on 8/8, the exact moment that power was restored to the grid. If we can see how much power was flowing, it might help nail down another data point and build a case. You never know what's relevant until something actually corroborates or can be proven with evidence, so keep an eye out for any people, places, things, and events that may seem irrelevant or unrelated at first, because almost nothing actually is, especially when the fact checker smokescreen is a sure-fire way of calibrating when you're over the target.

Of the many survivor testimonies, there's only one that doesn't seem to confirm or corroborate, where a boomer tries to claim the County of Maui sent him an evacuation push notification via text to his phone, while both Charter Communications and Hawaiian Telecom were down, which sounds kinda suspicious to me and is probably a false report intended for damage control and plausible deniability by those in charge. The only evacuation notices were County of Maui Facebook posts, when there was already no phone, no internet, no power, no sirens even, and no water? Yeah, the "Water Nazi" Manuel at the Commission on Water and Resource Management, who declined water to Lahaina firemen, was already reassigned to a different unspecified position within the Department of Land and Natural Resources, per the Honolulu Civil Beat. But then again, the major shareholders of the utilities on Hawai'i are the corporate oligarchies of Blackrock, Vanguard Group, and the Carlyle Group, so collusion should be no surprise here, it's "par for the course". Remember that "Too many coincidences is evidence of no coincidence at all." - Jason Breshears, ARCHAIX

I will also be providing pictures, videos, exact locations, makes and models of each specific "non-photo blue" car that survived, and the order in which they survived, as well as the specific locations of boats anchored out to sea that also burned, so stay tuned. So far I've seen too many blue, cars, houses, trashcans, and even shirts and paper pamphlets, to list here, but they are all being placed on the updated maps, which are posted in the map comments.

Eric West of the Maui Real Estate YouTube channel has been a godsend during this obviously un-natural disaster. When the fire happened, he hit the trails on his dirt bike with 4K GoPros and drones. He was able to get in and collect footage of the entire Ground Zero area, house by house, and blue car by blue car, which turned out to be good for more than just surveying the damage to life and property, but the damage to liberty as well. He is taking great risks, both financial and personal, and has lost his job with his old real estate company and been harassed by police for the truth he began sharing after the sacred town of Lahaina was wiped off the map as part of a land grab for the diabolic plans of narcissistic billionaires with no regard for the sanctity of human life with their bloody land grabs. He is documenting everyone and everything that happened in the early moments, to preserve the truth so people can know what's really going on, and what we can do about it. He's doing it, and we can to. No matter where you place your faith, we all have a calling and I pray that you answer yours when you receive it. Ho'oponopono, Aloha, and Mahalo!

Included is an investigation white board that will get updated over time. Feel free to edit it and add your own data points, but be sure to share with the rest of the class! Here's the link to the original map taken from web:
https://duckduckgo.com/?q=Lahainaluna&t=brave&iaxm=maps...

I plan to continue to update this post with a Timeline, tons of links, videos, lawsuits, lists of legit relief efforts, (Not FEMA or Red Cross), lots of blue cars, burning boats anchored at sea, quotes, notes, source requests, songs, poems, and all things Aloha! And just for the record, the info I have has been uploaded to multiple people and they have the credentials to my social media, so if anything happens it's not gonna prevent the story from getting out.

Timeline:
(Coming soon)

Source requests:
Can anyone verify the number of firefighters dead at 10, or is this just another rumor?

Can anyone verify the boomer who allegedly got an SMS text notification from Maui County to evacuate, when the phones, power, and internet companies all shut down? (Kinda sus)

Does anyone have a picture of the Hawaiian Electric repair truck that was blocking the highway at Hokiokio road?

Legit relief efforts:
World Central Kitchen:
https://duckduckgo.com/?q=world+central+kitchen&t=brave

https://lookout.co/.../lahaina-maui-wildfire-surfing...

Maui Legal Preservation Fund
(LEGAL PROTECTION FUND TO PRESERVE LAND OWNERSHIP & PREVENT GOVERNMENT OVERREACH):
https://www.mauilegalpreservationfund.org/

Maui Strong Fund:
https://www.hawaiicommunityfoundation.org/.../maui-strong...

Compiled spreadsheet of the REAL list of survivors, missing, and confirmed dead:
https://docs.google.com/.../1WAA1iFGIOT7H3xJcr5a.../htmlview

Maui police chief John Pelletier was the Las Vegas false flag handler:
https://www.reviewjournal.com/.../las-vegas-police.../

The Water Nazi
https://freepressers.com/.../equity-obsessed-hawaii...

Hawaiian Electric controlled by Vanguard and Blackrock:
https://www.wallstreetzen.com/stocks/us/nyse/he/ownership
https://finance.yahoo.com/.../ownership-structure...

Fact check, on something the governor actually said about AI smart cities, he just said it somewhere else. (Link coming soon as well)
https://apnews.com/.../fact-check-hawaii-governor...

Maui's Smart city concentration camp pilot program:
https://sashalatypova.substack.com/.../maui-plans-for-a...

List of scheduled AI Smart Cities:
https://spring.smartcitiesconnect.org/about/cities.html

The globalists land grab of the globe, starting with Maui:
https://brucecain.substack.com/.../the-maui-fires-and-the...

The "Big Black Biden Barricade" (Policed by Blackrock and Vanguard):
https://townhall.com/.../black-curtains-surrounding-the...

Maui's Space Force mountain DEW. (AMOS):
https://afresearchlab.com/.../air-force-maui-optical-and.../
Space Force's sister site for DEW, the Starfire Optical Range (SOR) at Kirtland Air Force base.
https://www.kirtland.af.mil/.../directed-energy.../

List of lawsuits:
Hawaiian Electric (Vanguard/Blackrock)
https://www.cnn.com/.../busi.../maui-fire-lawsuit/index.html

Charter Communications and Hawaiian Telcom (Carlyle Group):
"Verizon Hawai'i was sold to The Carlyle Group and our name changed to Hawaiian Telcom."
https://www.hawaiiantel.com/aboutus/Our-History

Note 1: Don't forget to save ALL photos in .png format for higher quality images.
Note 2: FEMA gets $1300/night hotels, while victims get $700 one time, if their lucky after jumping through hoops and red tape.
Note 3: nothing blue burned...

Quotes:
"It was a choreographed disaster." - "Fish"

"The fire was going INTO the ocean! The best way to explain it was a continuous bomb going off. There was boats on fire 50 yards out, so even in the ocean, at THOSE points, we were STILL getting burned, at points we didn't even know where land was." - Mike Cicchino (They got burned over 50 yards out into the water, at points where they didn't even know where land was...)
https://www.youtube.com/watch?v=WaTJ9yk38g4

West Maui: "Half the world does not know how the other half lives.
The "other side" of Maui: "Half the world does not know how, the other half lives."

Videos:
Forensic Arborist says it's not natural. He proposes microwave DEW's, but we know laser DEW's were also used, as evidenced by the undamaged "non-photo" blue (which is non-interactive with light) cars that were directly adjacent to cars that melted into puddles:
https://www.youtube.com/watch?v=Bs3o3z0G8tw

Firefighter testimony: "Streams of smoke started coming from the steering wheel." "The glass windshield began bubbling, so we had to abandon the vehicle."
https://www.youtube.com/watch?v=89vCT3_7VBg

Eric West interviews "Fish" about the roadblocks:
https://www.youtube.com/watch?v=easMHBYdpJo
https://www.bitchute.com/video/hJXjpa6daC35/

Eric West's epic 4K footage of ALL of Lahaina.
https://youtu.be/7PSYNqZqAVs?si=FTytCeCXh90WUAW1
BitChute:
https://www.bitchute.com/video/hXPZ0QxbPXLL/
(Odysee link coming soon, just in case)
(Does anyone use Hive?)

Blue cars:
Blue Chevy Silverado 1500:
https://www.youtube.com/watch?v=6ToLyKh9EPs&t=235s

Blue Jeep Grand Cherokee:
Sitting perfectly fine, almost on top of a single puddle of 3 other cars in industrial park by the levee.
https://youtu.be/6ToLyKh9EPs?si=PU0R1oWiZJqHBfjB

Blue car in Kahoma village by the town homes (BC3 - 3rd laser miss)
(Link coming soon)

Non-photo blue color, non repro blue, is non-interactive with light:
https://en.wikipedia.org/wiki/Non-photo_blue

Songs:
Eiffel 65 - Blue (Da Ba Dee):
https://www.youtube.com/watch?v=68ugkg9RePc

"Against the Wind"
https://www.youtube.com/watch?v=2vRsEC65NTA

"Night of Fire"
https://www.youtube.com/watch?v=SRbhLtjOiRc

Don McLean - "American Pie"
https://www.youtube.com/watch?v=PRpiBpDy7MQ

Prophetic native Hawai'ian poem:
https://www.huapala.org/La/Lahainaluna.html

Other prophecies:
1st seal broken: 3/17/2020 (Covid)
2nd seal broken 8/8/2023-2024 (DEW democide)
3rd seal (Coming 2028)
4th seal (Coming 2032)
5th seal (Coming 2036)
6th Seal, the Phoenix: (Coming May 15th, 2040)
7th Seal, Nibiru (Coming 11/1/2046)
https://www.youtube.com/watch?v=k_UDht_KOEc

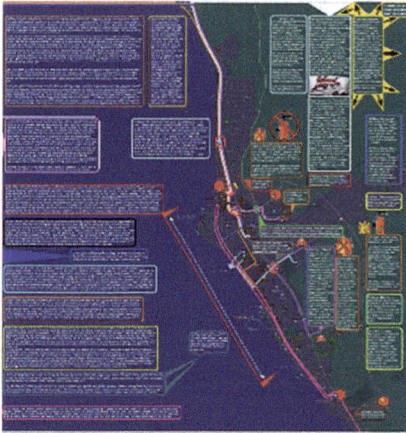

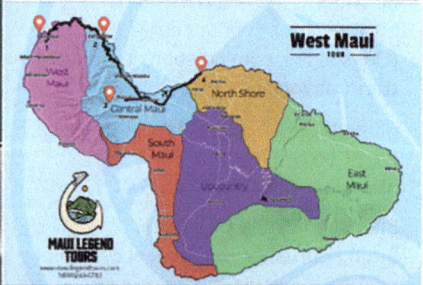

After posting on Facebook, Shane continued to diligently research. Some of the original sources in the preliminary Facebook investigation turned out to be inaccurate, such as the legitimacy of the Maui Strong Fund, or the timing of the Kula and Upcountry fires originally cited from Lahaina survivor Jeremy Baldwin from Wahikuli. Shane counted all the answered questions, and even the discovery of inaccurate information, to be gains because every piece of information, once confirmed or denied, led him to the truth. He followed each of the above links and decided to post an article on Wordpress. Some of his theories weren't fully fleshed out, and due to his commitment to only spreading information that he has triple-fact-checked, he hesitates to share the article until it can be fully updated. Nevertheless, a 200-page article was born. He did nothing for three months but eat, sleep, and drink Maui, he says. After he published his investigation on Wordpress on December 8th, he sent the article to Eric West and eventually to Traci Derwin. Within a few weeks, Traci Derwin asked him to appear on her "Brush Junkie" show.

While Buell didn't enjoy the process of writing, he does enjoy sharing information verbally. When Traci saw how he ignited and inspired her audience, he began helping her manage the barrage of emails she was receiving, including countless tips and rabbit trail links that they had to carefully categorize as "relevant to the investigation" or "interesting but leading us away from Maui."

Traci and Shane originally connected because of Shane's interest in the pictures she had of crafts flying above Lahaina during the fires, the "helicopter picture" that a friend in Alaska had found and sent to Traci. At that time and throughout even today (ten months post-fire at the time of this writing,) the crafts flying over Lahaina intrigued many but confused nearly everybody. Shane dove into the helicopter issue and had a good idea of what the crafts were, and where they originated.

Shane was positive when asked about the onslaught of emails Traci's channel was receiving. "For months I was digging for information, but now it was coming into my inbox. I didn't feel intimidated by some of the lengthier investigations. After having spent decades researching "conspiracy theories," I quickly ascertain what's relevant and what's best saved for a more thorough, global investigation. Traci and I have been 100% Lahaina-focused. We're not trying to save the world, but to save the world we will start by focusing first on Lahaina."

Buell was encouraged by how many people, like him, intuitively knew that something was "off" with the Maui fires. Since Traci has two young children and a part-time job, he was excited to help sort through the tidal wave of incoming information to find the needles in the haystack, not allowing the outlandish theories or unverified information to make it on Traci's channel, which has made "Brush Junkie" one of the most respected authorities on the Maui fires by residents on the island as well as viewers worldwide.

Among the most common theories from the community was the theory that China was involved in the Maui fires. This didn't pan out after Traci and Shane dug deeper. It's ultra "American" to look toward another country as the enemy, but the suspicion of Chinese involvement ultimately didn't pass inspection. For instance, China doesn't care about Lahaina. Sadly, many nefarious U.S. actors do. It's commonly known that documents ranging back many years illustrate that U.S. political representatives and documents have pegged Maui for what we can best describe as an "AI-powered Carbon-Neutral Smart City." There are enough stakeholders vying for that future that we have no reason to look towards China. The bad U.S. actors, sadly, are keeping us busy enough... for now.

China shows up to observe war games, indeed. U.S. personnel know that China is present and watching, but they aren't involved, even as their view is unobfuscated. For instance, Exercise Talisman Sabre took place until August 4, 2023 in the Pacific. Chinese ships and satellites were indeed present in an observational capacity, but not participating. China gets close enough to observe, but if satellites were involved in the incineration on Maui, they weren't Chinese, to our knowledge.

Although this book could be 200 additional pages with the amount of information that Shane has uncovered, we have kept it intentionally short and laser-focused (no pun intended) so that we will only reveal information that we've cited, sourced, verified, and triple-checked. That said, we aren't perfect, and we encourage you to tear apart any argument or evidence we present that you might have another perspective or purview of. You can always email Publishing@PierucciPublishing.com with your questions, comments, concerns, and, of course, conspiracies.

The Second Book Is Born

After Stephanie returned from a trip she took to Lahaina where she worked alongside engineers and other experts in the community to dig into some of the physical anomalies of the fire, she returned to Colorado knowing that there had to be a second book; *Burn Back Better* didn't scratch the surface of what happened on August 8th. It laid the foundation, asked the right questions, but it was specifically designed to explain immediate events. There needed to be more answers to the questions posed and evidence revealed in *Burn Back Better*.

In Lahaina, during January of 2024, she was invested in collecting footage and more data for her upcoming documentary, Sound The Alarm, which she is co-producing with award-winning documentary filmmaker Matt Weinglass. The group knew that if they were going to collaborate with other authors on a second book and, eventually, the documentary film accompanying this book, that they would need to align with responsible citizen journalists and investigators; not just YouTubers desperate for clicks. Traci Derwin was the undisputed choice, and her chief researcher Shane Buell was icing on the cake. They proved to the community both on Maui as well as internationally that they are a trustworthy source of information regarding the fire and, alas, the aftermath.

The three authors you've just learned about come from three unique corners of America, with varying and sometimes even opposing views on everything from politics to religion. However, the three of us have one thing irrefutably in common: a love for the people of Hawaii and a sacred call of duty to continue investigating and reporting on the fires, which sadly were not well-reported on by our American mainstream media.

Undoubtedly, we have all had our moments of trepidation and the temptation to return back to our "safe," normal lives. Stephanie encountered threats from disgruntled residents following her most recent trip to Maui and admits to periodically getting an eerie feeling in her house at night while sometimes fantasizing about painting her roof blue. However, at the end of the day, when you encounter something as meaningful as seeking justice for Lahaina and helping the people of

Hawaii stave off what appears to be an almost inevitable *land grab* on that island, you muster the courage to keep going everyday.

In *Sound The Alarm*, these three intrepid authors will continue the *Burn Back Better* investigation in three parts. Part One will investigate the many anomalies we've uncovered through our research and through the team at MauiCommunityInvestigation.com, where at least thirty citizen journalists have been collecting images and videos pertaining to the burn and the events leading up to it that caused historic Lahaina to incinerate. In Part Two, we'll explore the human actors who facilitated the *land grab* we're now seeing. Part Three explores the plans the government has in store for Maui, as well as the carbon-copy events taking place in other parts of the world.

In the conclusion of this book, the authors lay out *their* blueprint for reclaiming Hawaii, as well as other parts of the world that have been incinerated in order to move out locals and resurrect these lands as globalist mini-empires, sort of like sustainable Disneylands, where they look pretty on the outside but there are tunnels of poorly-treated, underpaid staffers working, slaving away with very little sovereignty underneath the surface. In short, the world will behold a handful of the most beautiful prison camps conceivable, if we don't immediately stop the World Economic Forum (WEF), United Nations (U.N.), and the World Health Organization (WHO).

Throughout these chapters, we'll look at things that happened before, during, and after August 8th that will make you scratch your head. Beware, if you go down this rabbit hole, there's no turning back. The following pages are not meant to shock you or compel ill-will toward the government. Rather, they're designed to help ignite a desire to create change in you. In Part Three of this book, we'll help you learn what steps you can take, alongside the authors, to seek justice and reverse course on the *Land Grab* that seems inevitable. Stay hopeful with us. It's not too late.

Throughout this book, we will continue to remind you of the brave efforts at www.MauiCommunityInvestigation.com (MCI) where we would like you to immediately stop and sign a petition on the homepage to join thousands of other men and women who are demanding an open, transparent, unbiased and public community investigation and hearing. If you're on Maui, it is likely you've seen one of their posters hanging in public places. Yep, we already asked you to do that in the

Intro. But if you put it off because you wanted to keep reading, here is your second formal invitation (and request.)

The MCI team has a vast network of investigative journalists, Maui citizens and eyewitnesses, engineers and arborists, and other experts working to put together a cohesive analysis of the fires based upon thousands of pieces of evidence that they have gathered.

Social Change, Community Organizing, Political Reform $20.00 US

STOP Corporate Rule for Profit and Domination
PULL the Dynamic Trigger for Systemic Change

Our global society is facing unprecedented change termed "The Great Reset" and "The New Normal," while being herded into a more stringent Corporate Rule. However, we have a choice as to what we reset into. MAUI COUNTY, HAWAII, has shown the way to rapidly and peacefully shift our governance by educating and engaging the local community. This uplifting change process is well-illustrated by its successes, using the grassroots strategy to focus on the trigger that puts communities on the road to the Common Good and a bright future.

"Paul Deslauriers' exciting and motivating action manual – *Reclaim Paradise* – is not about launching protests that go nowhere with today's politicians. It is about replacing them with your elected lawmakers starting at the local and county level where "the 99% have a strong say... all the way to the top."
—**Ralph Nader**

Paul Deslauriers is an organization development consultant with 36 years' experience. As director of the political action organization, the Maui Pono Network, in 2018 he helped usher in a Progressive majority in Maui County, Hawaii, for the first time in 125 years. Big-money corporations in 2020 came back with a vengeance, outspending the grassroots group by forty-three times. However, voters selected 14 of the 16 candidates and charter amendments endorsed by the Maui Pono Network. Paul also coordinated 287 grassroots groups that were focused on government system change. He has consulted for a wide range of industries, restructuring over 100 businesses to function at their optimum potential.

NRG
Visit ReclaimParadise.org

$20.00
ISBN 978-0-9773855-4-4
52000>
9 780977 185365

"I have never read a book like this on civic engagement. If there exists a better book to light this path to electing good public officials, let me know."
—Ralph Nader

RECLAIM
Paradise
RESET FOR THE COMMON GOOD

Maui County's Shift from Corporate Rule to Home Rule, and the Template for Global System Change

Paul Deslauriers

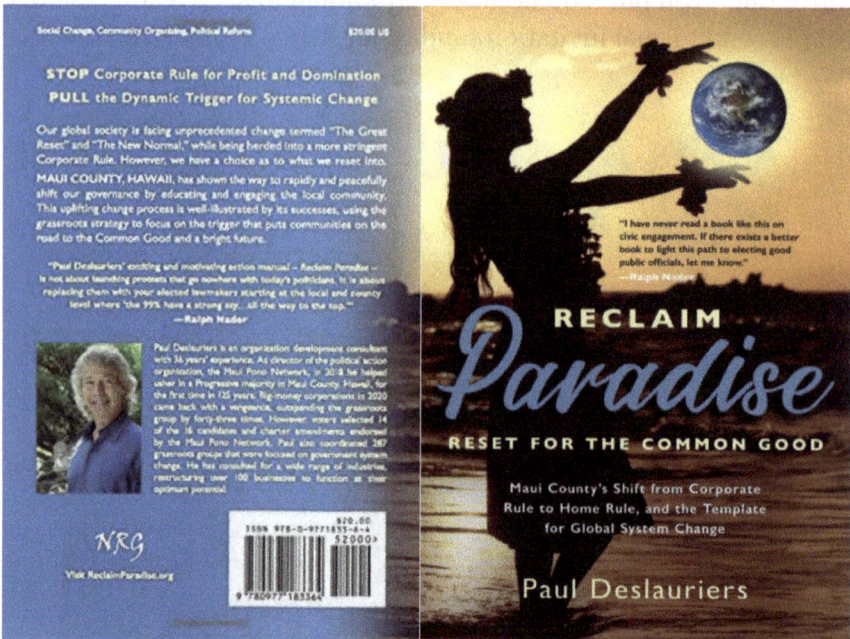

The MCI team is spearheaded by Paul Deslauriers, author of *Reclaim Paradise: Maui County's Shift From Corporate Rule To Home Rule,* and *The Template For Global System Change*, of which Ralph Nader said, "I have never read a book like this on civic engagement. If there exists a better book to light this path to electing good public officials, let me know." Deslauriers is joined by MCI co-founder Bruce Douglas, organizer of the Maui Earth Day festival for the past 20 years and engineer and founder of Mandala Eco Homes based out of Maui.

According to State officials, the Lahaina fire destroyed roughly 2,200 properties and caused more than $5.5 billion in estimated damage. We celebrate the people who survived by ignoring police blockades and those who have been working to find the truth, even though the media has been blocked out and the organization in charge of an investigation is shrouded in controversy... which you'll learn about later.

This book is our contribution to the fight against the New World Order because we believe that all nations and their people are sovereign and worthy of retaining their unique cultures and identities without being forced into homogenized, AI-driven work and dwellings.

Having already worked on the front lines of the fight for medical freedom before pouring her life and resources into helping Maui, somebody once asked Stephanie, "Aren't you ready to quit... or at least take a break from all the fighting for a while?"

"There'll be plenty of time to rest on the other side. As long as we are alive on this earth, there will be evil, and darkness never sleeps. The same demonic entities that inhabited evil men and women over many millennia are alive today. And so, for that reason, since darkness's fight against the human spirit will never rest, nor will I."

The authors hope that you, too, will help in the fight against darkness. And hopefully, one day, we will see Justice For Lahaina.

Mahalo for your prayers and support.

Shane Buell, Traci Derwin, and Stephanie Pierucci

CHAPTER THREE:
The Case For Arson

Before diving into this chapter about the weather anomalies on and around August 8th, which range from potential directed energy weapons to unmitigated brush at a potential arson point on the west side of Maui, we would like to make it clear that we have dedicated all of our time for months to this work, not to nab corrupt globalists or wrangle up bankers to be put behind bars. Rather, it's because people died unnecessarily on Maui, and more will die in other parts of the world, if we do not take time to look at the evidence and wake up to what is happening.

Our authors believe that what happened on Maui **will** happen in other parts of the world and already **has** happened in other places, which we'll dive into later on in this book. That is why this chapter is so critical. Once you see this "playbook" for incinerating land in order to take it over by the state, you'll see the writing on the walls in your community. God willing, you will thus be able to protect your own family.

Pay close attention to some of these anomalies and ask yourself the following questions:

1. Is this "anomaly" a potential "hazard" where I live?
2. Is this "anomaly" evidence of a random probable event, or a series of improbable and statistically unlikely events all occurring on the same day or within the same period of time?

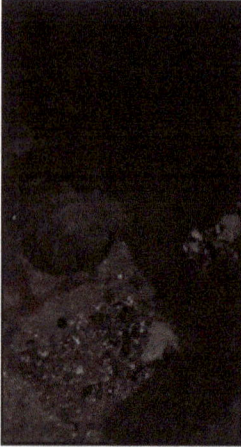

As he walks through the streets of Lahaina with another survivor searching for friends, all five of whom perished, Kahokule'a Haiku illustrates fourteen hours of footage from the streets of Lahaina during the fire. Nobody came to help and out of respect to the deceased, he has not yet disclosed the vast number of bodies that he saw perished as he walked through Lahaina, which was silent but for the sound of the town crackling as a backdrop to his film.

Graphic Courtesy of Pierucci Publishing
with Images Captured on Video by Kalokule'a Haiku

In the 54-minute video documentary entitled *Winds of Change* by Kalokule'a "Hoku" Haiku, released April of 2024, you will see that the morning after the fire, when he emerged from the parking garage under which he hid, there were no sirens, no police, no fire, no Army, no Navy, no National Guard, and no Coast Guard. Yet, there were many bodies in the water, and potentially *hundreds* of people were pulled out or able to climb to shore safely and survive. Where were our first responders? Hawaii is the location of our Navy! And yet... during and directly after the fire, there was nothing but silence.

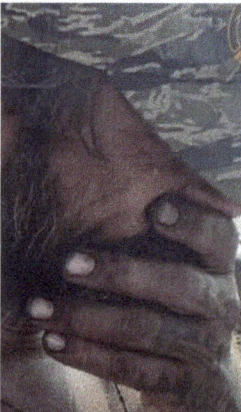

Kahokule'a Haiku, above, is a miraculous survivor. He shows on video that even 14 hours after the fire began, there were no officials present to help the victims nor any attempt being made to save any one or thing. On the right, an Anonymous video contributor walks through Lahaina on Aug. 9th. He seems to be the only person around. We will not link to his full video until the families have identified their loved ones and we have received their support.

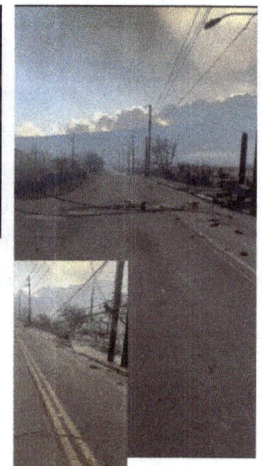

Kahokule'a Haiku, morning of August 9th, Lahaina

It is our suspicion that the reason Lahaina was a veritable ghost town during the fires, despite the close proximity to help (and water to fight the fire), is because it was intended to burn to the ground, plain and simple.

Throughout this chapter, we'll look at a handful of the things that happened before, during, and after August 8th, that will make you scratch your head. Beware, if you go down this rabbit hole, there's no turning back. The following pages are not meant to shock you or compel ill-will toward the government. Rather, they're designed to help ignite a desire to create change in you. Throughout this book, we'll help you learn what steps you can take, alongside the authors, to seek justice and reverse course on the *Land Grab* that seems inevitable. Stay hopeful with us. It's not too late.

Images from Glenn Pascual, courtesy of Eric West, an intrepid citizen journalist and Maui resident you can find on YouTube at https://www.youtube.com/@hawaiirealestateorg

Some survivors spent eight hours in the water; there was no coast guard and no navy to rescue these victims. Sadly, many bodies were retrieved from the water past the point of rescue...

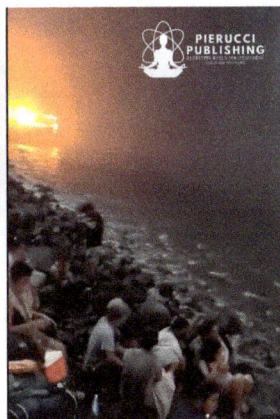

Dry Brush

One of the first anomalies that compelled researchers on Maui to suggest that this fire was orchestrated is the fact that brush had not been properly mitigated on Maui. In the following image, you'll see how many public and private landowners are responsible for cutting dry brush and grasses on West Maui[15]. In 2017 and 2018, Maui

---

15   https://rumble.com/v4c0ibq-the-maui-fires-6-months-later-with-paul-deslauriers-and-bruce-douglas-thl-e.html

experienced fires caused by dry brush and grasses that had not been properly cut. When not tended to, these grasses become like tinder, allowing fire to start and spread rapidly.

Image taken from The Homeless Left episode #32, "The Maui Fires 6 Months Later"[16]

One thing that's important to note, however, is that there isn't a lot of fuel in these brush fires. They'll take off fast, but they'll likely also burn out fast, since the brush is almost instantly burned up.

Potential Points of Arson

Now let's look at why this "brush" issue is relevant to our quest. In their investigation, the Maui Community Investigation has uncovered three potential points of arson. They consider these points to be "proof positive" that the fires were intentionally started in areas where brush was not mitigated. In the image below, you'll see those points on maps, including one that shows the arson points on both sides of the bypass.

---

16   https://rumble.com/v4c0ibq-the-maui-fires-6-months-later-with-paul-deslauriers-and-bruce-douglas-thl-e.html

Many have questioned how the fire could have seemingly "jumped the highway."

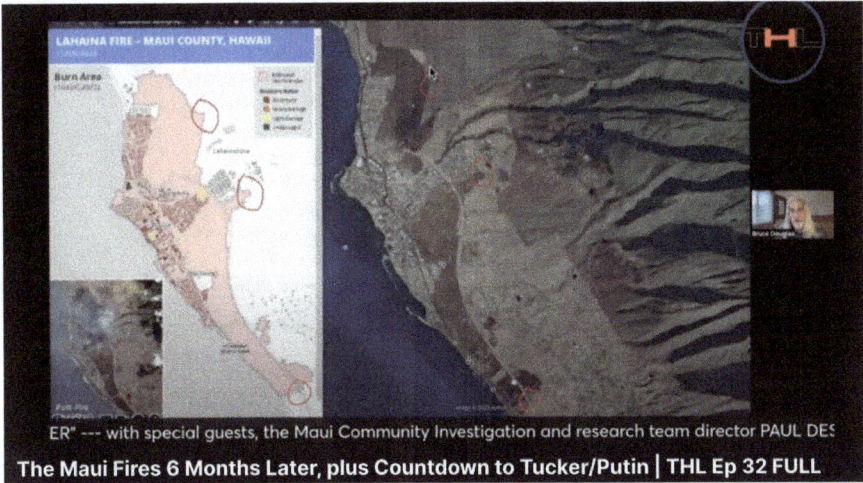

The Maui Fires 6 Months Later, plus Countdown to Tucker/Putin | THL Ep 32 FULL

The Maui Fires 6 Months Later, plus Countdown to Tucker/Putin | THL Ep 32 FULL

From the two points in the above image, you can see where the fire may have started and where the wind blows down from Laniopoko toward Lahaina. That's where the fire began and then incinerated Lahaina, from right to left, from the perspective of that image. From this next image, you can see where the burn began in the brush on both sides of the highway, traveling toward Lahaina.

Non-Tribal Approach to News --- Subscribe now at www.rumble.com/c/TheHomelessLeft or www.Yo

From the ground, you can see high brush all around and a clear ignition point that was likely carried by wind toward Lahaina.

Below, you'll see a third place where an electrical fire occurred the morning of August 8th, just below an electrical substation, marked by the red circle in this image. The location of this fire provides plausible deniability that the electrical substation caused the fire, but it also raises the possibility that the fire was ignited by somebody physically starting the blaze.

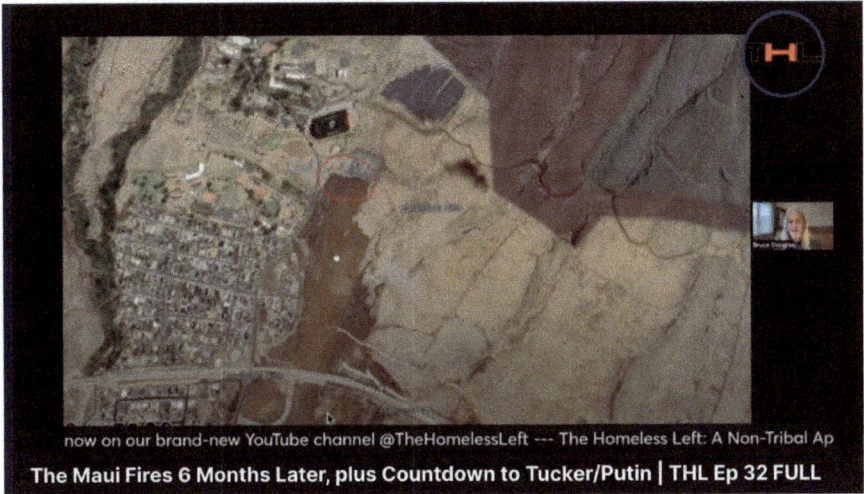

now on our brand-new YouTube channel @TheHomelessLeft --- The Homeless Left: A Non-Tribal Ap

The Maui Fires 6 Months Later, plus Countdown to Tucker/Putin | THL Ep 32 FULL

Yet another place where a fire started was on the north side of Lahaina, as shown in the image below.

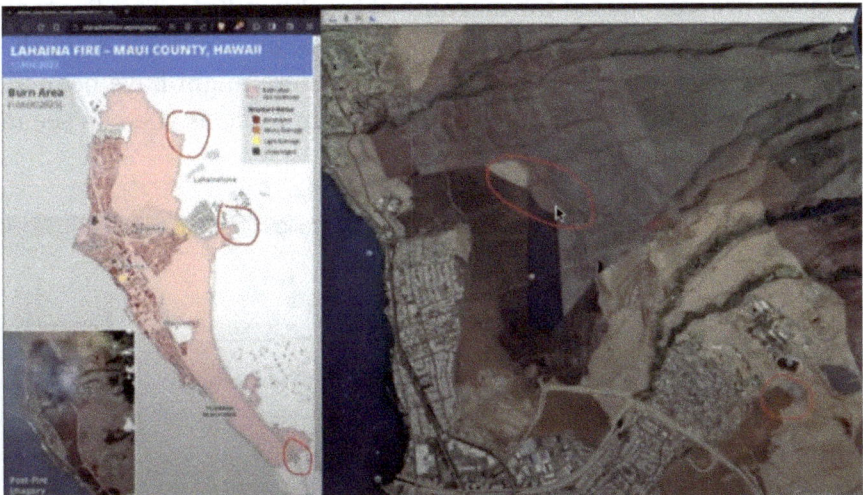

As of this book being written in the summer of 2024, it is anticipated that the Hawai'ian Electric Company (HECO) will take the blame for the fire. However, they will want to see this evidence that the fire began in a place that had absolutely no power lines.

You'll see in the following image that there are no electrical lines along this road; it's a bare road. This is another place that would have been ideal for somebody to start an arson fire, with the winds coming down from the mountains and blowing toward Lahaina.

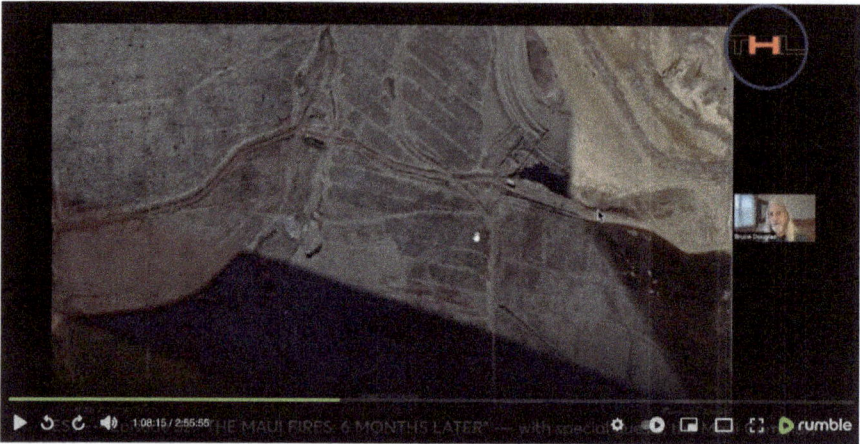

Another fire was started the morning of the 8th in Kula. This fire took all the firefighters, even those from Lahaina, up to Kula to fight the fire up there. It's fairly clear to see where there might have been an arson point in the brush that burned trees in Kula, as you can see in the image below.

This supposed "wildfire" left more questions than answers.

The Weather (Manipulation?):
Missing Satellite Images on August 8th

During research on the NOAA website, using the images provided by the "GOES-18 West" weather satellite, there are multiple views looking at the Hawai'ian Islands, and we can see below the different types of readings, measurements, and weather patterns that the satellite took photos of. The state of Hawaii is in all of these images.[17]

Now, after searching for archive images of Dora in "2023 Pacific storms," the fifth one down is Hurricane Dora. Toward the bottom of this page, there are four data entries for August 8th. When observing the loop of Hurricane Dora, we can see that the outline of the state of Hawaii is not in any of these loops or images.[18]

---

17   https://www.star.nesdis.noaa.gov/GOES/sector.php?sat=G18&sector=hi
18   https://www.star.nesdis.noaa.gov/GOES/floater.php?stormid=EP052023

With further investigation for Hurricane Dora in the archives, we ended up finding an archive of Dora on a Colorado weather website. It uses the same imagery from the GOES-18 West satellite. There are entries for Dora's imagery, and there's eight entries per every 24 hours. So that's one image every three hours in a 24 hour period. However, when we scroll down to August 8th, the day of the Lahaina fire, there are only two entries.[19]

---

19 https://rammb-data.cira.colostate.edu/tc_realtime/archive.asp?product=16kmgwvp&storm_identifier=ep052023

When scrolling to the bottom of the page, we created a loop to see what the timeline would display. Drawing attention to the bottom of the timeline, where it has the date and time stamps, all data entries are in UTC time or military time. Right when it gets to the 8th, there is a quick jump. Upon further analysis, you'll see it goes from around 18:10 UTC time on the 7th to 18:10 UTC time on the 8th, then to 21:10 UTC time, then it goes to the 9th at 00:10 hours. So there are 21 hours worth of images missing from this loop. What happened to these images? We're under the impression that somebody doesn't want us to see something here.[20]

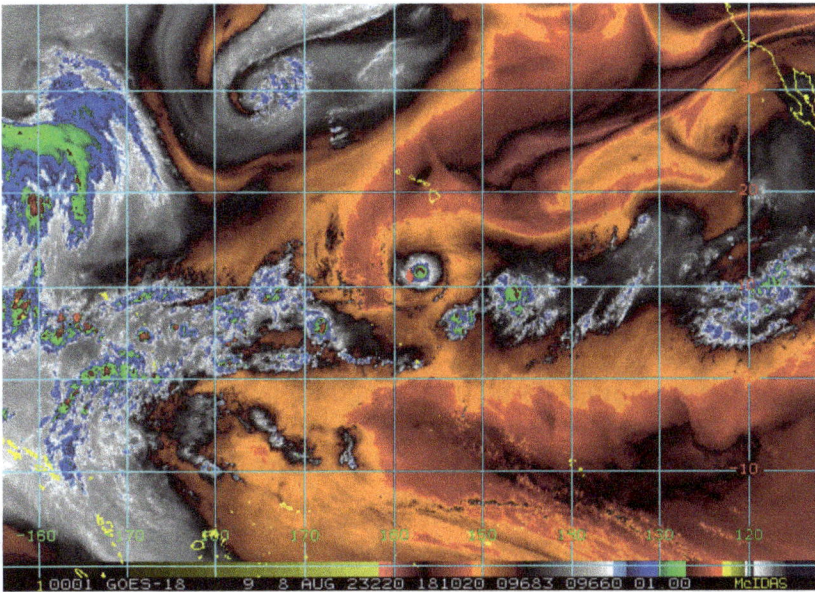

The main point of putting this together is there is a gap. There is a gap where there are no satellite images available to see. Normally, every three hours, there should be an image, totalling 8 images per 24-hour period. However, starting on the day of the 7th at 6:10 p.m. and continuing until the 8th at 6:10 p.m., there is a lack of images. We do strongly feel that they were taken down from public view. To understand why these images were scrubbed from the record, we will

20 https://rammb-data.cira.colostate.edu/tc_realtime/loop.asp?product=16kmgwvp&
    storm_identifier=ep052023&starting_image=2023ep05_16kmgwvp_202307312110.
    gif&ending_image=2023ep05_16kmgwvp_202308222110.gif

look at research from Bruce Douglas on the wind and weather patterns seen the day of the 8th.

Bruce Douglas is a longtime Hawaii resident who has studied wind, hurricanes, and weather anomalies for fifteen years. Bruce has been featured in the documentary "What in the World are They Spraying," and also has a background in engineering. Mr. Douglas spoke to a nationwide audience at the conference "Consciousness Beyond Chemtrails" and at the "Conscious Life Expo," among others. His videos on engineered hurricanes can be reviewed at www.MauiSkyWatch.org where he has included scores of links and information about projects that he supports or has contributed to as an opponent of Geo-Engineering, as well as information about how we can stand against Geo-Engineering, namely by either running for office or voting our current corrupt politicians out.

After the Lahaina fires, Douglas co-founded Maui Community Investigation[21] with longtime friend Paul Deslauriers to investigate and document the causes of the Lahaina fires, the repository of data we mentioned in the introduction of this book. With the evidence that Deslauriers and Douglas have gathered in the months since the fire (nearly eight at the time of this writing), they have acquired confirmation from five former fire chiefs and captains who have all confirmed that they do not think the August 8th fires were natural.[22] Among the most important anomalies that have tipped off these fire experts is the weather events before, during and after the fires.

After studying satellite images from the days leading up to and after the fires, Douglas learned that the clouds took an odd, linear formation the day before the fire in Lahaina. They began to form in straight lines toward Hawaii.[23]

If you've ever seen somebody create a vibration on a plate with sand, causing it to take linear shapes and patterns according to the vibration, that's a phenomenon called "cymatics." If you study the clouds pictured in the image below you'll easily see the resemblance to sand being vibrated on a pan or plate, as shown in the video in the footnotes.[24]

---

21   www.MauiCommunityInvestigation.com
22   https://rumble.com/v4c0ibq-the-maui-fires-6-months-later-with-paul-deslauriers-and-bruce-douglas-thl-e.html
23   https://www.ssec.wisc.edu/data/geo/#/animation?satellite=goes-west&end_datetime=latest&n_images=all&coverage=fd&channel=13
24   https://rumble.com/v4c0ibq-the-maui-fires-6-months-later-with-paul-deslauriers-and-bruce-douglas-thl-e.html?start=2885

Bizarre clouds seen by Douglas, August 7th

On August 7th, the clouds over Maui were also lined up against the trade winds, which travel from the northwest and head southeast. Trade winds don't affect the continental U.S. They are air currents that are closer to the earth's surface which blow from east to west near the equator, as illustrated in the image below.

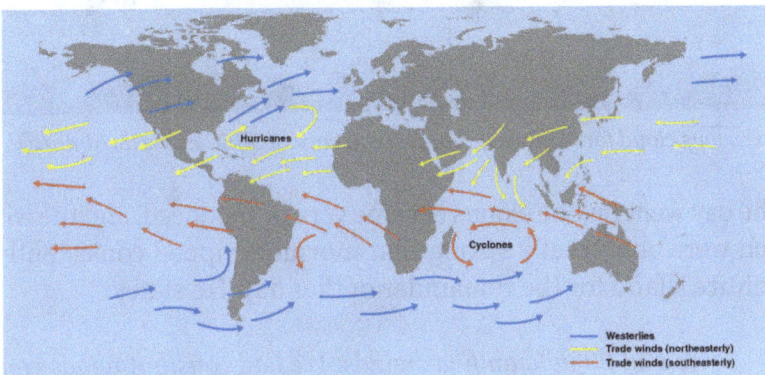

The trade winds blow from east to west near the equator. Credit: NASA/JPL-Caltech

Trade winds are fairly predictable winds; the morning is calm on Maui and the afternoons will experience a cooler trade wind.[25]

On August 8th, Bruce sat on his front porch on Maui's North Shore and clearly witnessed the "perfectly formed, long tubes of clouds" mentioned above, coming toward him. He didn't need to study images from satellites to know that something odd was afoot.

Based upon satellite images he shared with us below, the clouds that headed for the Hawai'ian islands actually stopped; they didn't go beyond the islands. On the other side of the islands were fairly normal, puffy clouds, as you'll see in the following image.

Curious cloud formations on August 8th care of SSEC.wisc.edu/data/geo

As the day went on, the clouds became very pronounced, and the winds, which were abnormally strong that morning, ripped consistently on the entire island for the remainder of that day. He states:

> *"We had 30 mile an hour winds. We had constant winds coming at us on the 7th. There was a strange white haze across the island, too, that was coming in as well. I wondered, 'What is that white*

25   https://scijinks.gov/trade-winds/

haze?' Well, I didn't see any signs of reflectivity in it. Now, it could be phosphorus or sulfur that doesn't reflect. I don't know what that white haze was. I'd never seen that, I'd never seen clouds line up.

Then, on the morning of the 8th, the clouds are still lined up. It's a little different reflection in the patterns, so you don't see it exactly the same. The weather changes and doesn't go past. But take a look at Lahaina town right there. This cloud shows these winds are coming from the north west, and this right here shows that they're actually in, you know, the shadow of the West Maui. You know, Lahaina, typically, has very few winds. The hurricane was 500 miles to the south of Maui moving away from the islands".[26]

Here's where Douglas's eyewitness report gets downright suspicious...

"On the afternoon of the 8th, there were clouds lined up in a perfect line, creating the wind coming at us. But for some reason, Maui is all blocked off by this black line out of it. [in the image below]

Conveniently, we don't have a record of that. It's blocked out. These black lines do appear across the screens randomly. It's curious that this happened exactly the moment when Maui was having the fires. On the morning of the 9th, the weather is back to normal patterns."

In the image below you'll see the black line across the satellite image on August 8th. You'll also see the bizarre cloud formations that were heading to the Hawai'ian Islands, the "cymatics" nature of the lines.

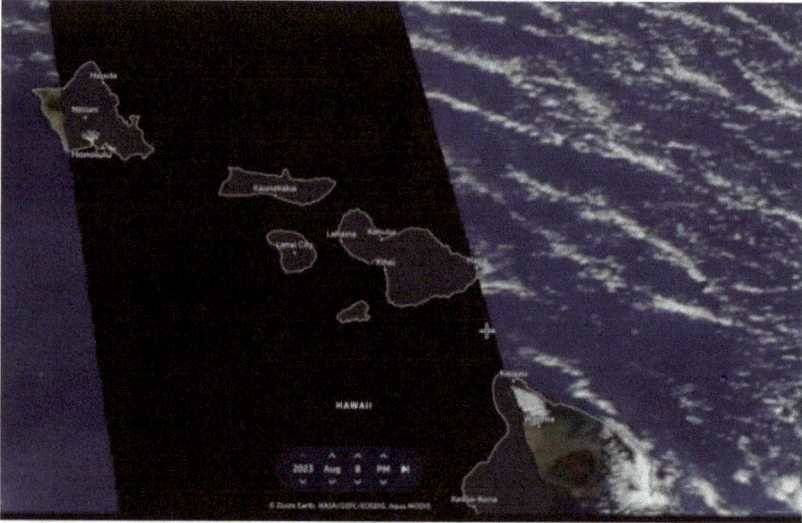

This example shows the satellite "blackout" at 8 p.m. during the fire.[27] [28]

Bruce captures these cloud formations over the course of several days leading up to the fire. In the images below you'll see fairly normal clouds on the 5th and 6th of August, 2023.

August 5th, a.m.

27   https://youtu.be/78Det47pZq0?si=JrCvO3IPqfqf9G5u Timestamp 33:40
28   https://www.ssec.wisc.edu/data/geo/#/animation?satellite=goes-west&end_datetime=
     latest&n_images=all&coverage=fd&channel=13

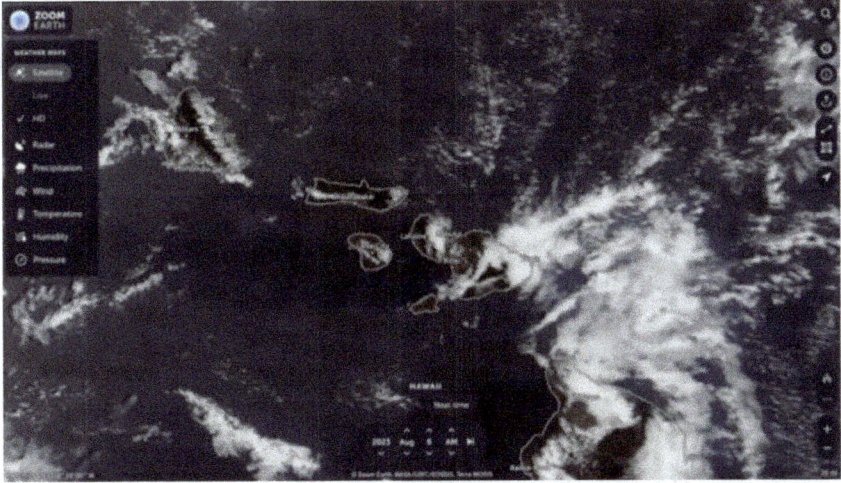

August 6th

It was on August 7th that we see the clouds beginning to take the "wave-like" patterns that Bruce Douglas describes having seen from his home on the north side of Maui, where the cursor is located in the image below.

Image showing the wave patterns forming in the clouds. Cursor represents approximately where Bruce Douglas was located at his home when he noticed the bizarre cloud patterns.

By the afternoon of August 7th as seen in the image below, you can see the well-formed wave pattern in the clouds that began on the morning of the 7th. The winds, according to Douglas, had started to rip fiercely from his location on the north side of Maui.

August 7th, afternoon

In another image just below, you'll see normal cloud formations except for the top right of the image where the cymatic style lines of clouds appear to approach the Hawai'ian Islands but then, mysteriously, stop at the islands.

Hurricane Dora was far south of Maui, at least 500 miles according to meteorologists and satellite images. Photo courtesy of Bruce Douglas on Rumble.[29]

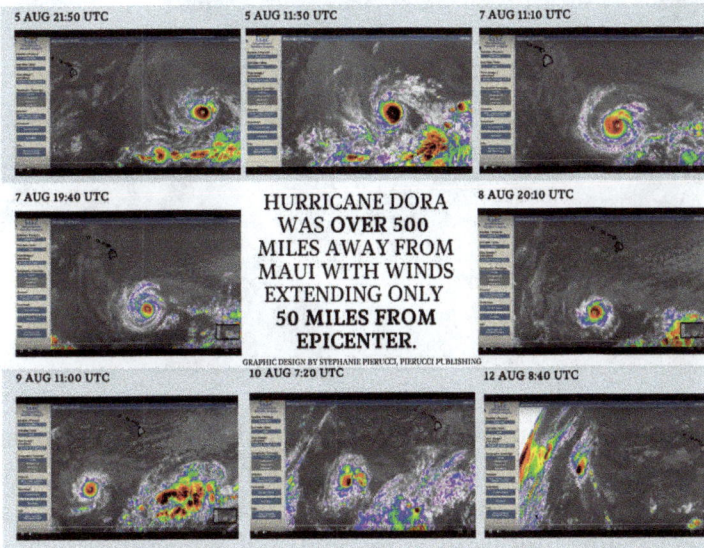

The path of hurricane Dora on Aug. 8th. Image taken with permission from a video by Bruce Douglas at www.MauiCommunityInvestigation.com/videos

---

29 https://rumble.com/v4c0ibq-the-maui-fires-6-months-later-with-paul-deslauriers-and-bruce-douglas-thl-e.html

The day after the fire on August 9th, the clouds were back to normal, as seen in the image below. On August 9th, although there is still a black line over the satellite images, the clouds no longer appear to have been generated through a sort of wave generator. To be fair, these "blackout" lines do periodically indeed happen on these satellite images. However, to say that it isn't curious that there was a blackout precisely during the fire would be plainly naive. Could it have been an accident? Absolutely. Could it have been intentional? Indeed, it could have been. It is because of these outstanding questions that the team at Maui Community Investigation along with many others (some of whom choose to remain less in the public eye due to fear for their safety and/or lives), that a transparent public investigation by the people, not by Underwriter Laboratories, is required to get to the truth.

The image below comes from a video made by Bruce Douglas that shows the clouds coming toward Hawaii in waves and disappearing once they "hit" the island. In the image you can even see where the Kula and Lahaina fires were, as marked on the image by bright orange blazes.

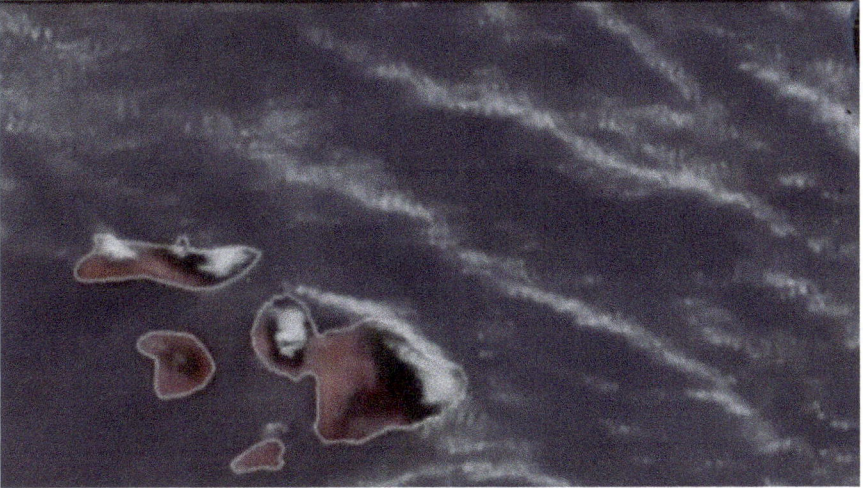

Screen capture of a video by Bruce Douglas that shows the waves of clouds approaching the Hawai'ian Islands and stopping once hitting the islands.

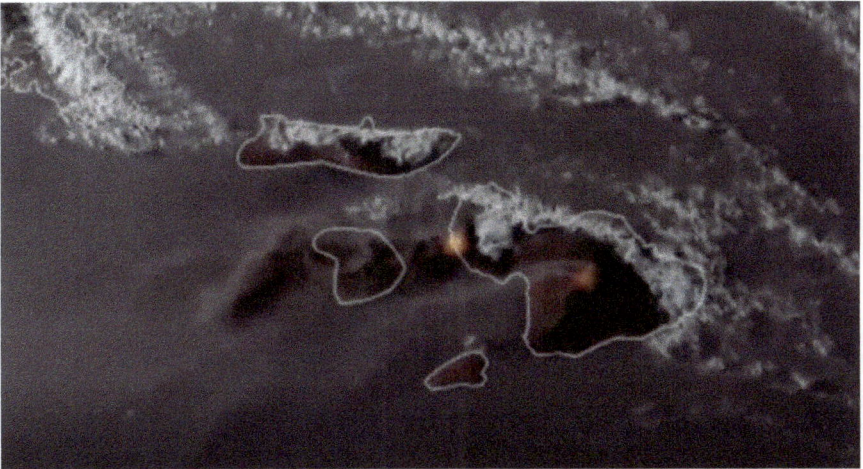

The Lahaina fire (left orange blot) and Kula fire (right orange blot). Photo courtesy of Bruce Douglas.

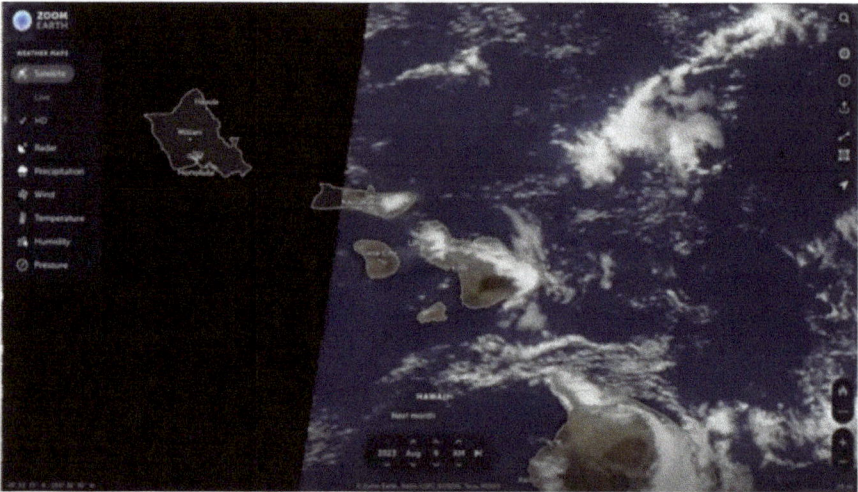

The following image shows something Bruce Douglas indicates he hasn't seen in 15 years of watching weather; you seem to see the focal point of the wind being generated. The clouds have symmetry; they aren't random in any way.[30]

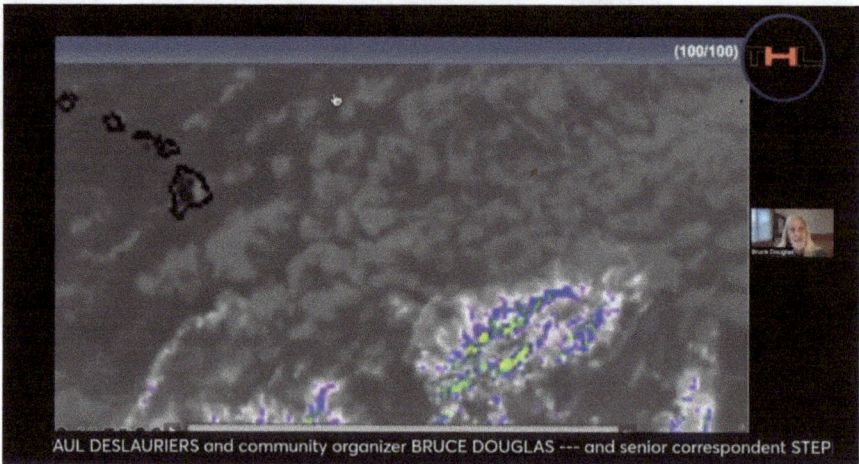

---

30   https://rumble.com/v4c0ibq-the-maui-fires-6-months-later-with-paul-deslauriers-and-bruce-douglas-thl-e.html?start=3053

As the following image shows, the wind storm had just enough power to hit the islands, but not to go past it.

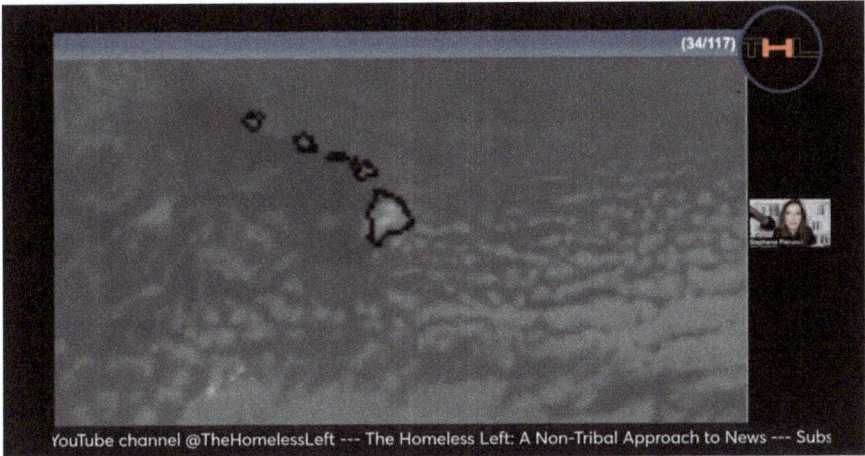

CHAPTER FOUR:
Playing God With the Weather

Does the government, military, or even private corporations have the ability to alter the weather? The simple answer is yes. Those with enough money and power have been able to change the weather for decades. Congress passed the National Weather Modification Policy Act on October 13, 1976.

Original documents housed at the White House Records Office legislation case files, at the General R. Ford Presidential Library[31]

---

31   https://www.fordlibrarymuseum.gov/library/document/0055/1669610.pdf

The bill states, "It will direct the Secretary of Commerce to conduct a study, which would include a review and analysis of research efforts and needs in weather modification technology, which would include an assessment of the potential economic importance and legal, social, and ecological implications of expanded weather modification activities. It will include the formulation of options for a model regulatory code for domestic weather modification activities[32]."

In the following image, you can see the ionospheric heaters in Alaska from the High-frequency Active Auroral Research Program (HAARP) antennas[33]. These ionospheric heaters bounce ions on the ionosphere through high frequency radio waves[34]. The ions are where the ozone layer is, high in our atmosphere.

Weather modification technology bounces frequencies on that ionosphere and actually heats up the ionosphere in a certain area. The molecules move faster in the region you're aiming the energy at, and it raises it up and creates a low-pressure cell down below it. Through that, you can guide windstorms and other weather by creating low-pressure cells.

Remember the lines of clouds? Those cymatic patterns illustrate what weather modification technology can do; they can also create a

---

32   https://www.fordlibrarymuseum.gov/library/document/0055/1669610.pdf
33   https://www.kirtland.af.mil/Portals/52/documents/AFD-111103-026.pdf
34   https://doi.org/10.17226/18620

low-pressure, raise it up, and then suddenly turn it off, and it is like a drumbeat coming down. When you have a drumbeat going up into the atmosphere, that creates an ionospheric heater, which can create an aerosol. Then, you can interact with ions in the aerosols directly. They can be turned off and on, creating a low frequency down below. It affects the clouds below and even steers hurricanes and other weather storms by creating a low-pressure cell and following it around. They can spin it as well. HAARP is the most powerful ionospheric heater on the planet; and it's a well-known phenomena among scientists.

Thursday, February 8th @ 12:00pm PST | 3:00pm EST --- Episode 32: "THE MAUI FIRES: 6 MONTHS L

Photo Courtesy of "The Homeless Left" podcast on Rumble[35]

This isn't just in Alaska; it's all over the world that we have these antennas. The newer technology includes mini-domes that can be mounted on ships.

35 https://rumble.com/v4c0ibq-the-maui-fires-6-months-later-with-paul-deslauriers-and-bruce-douglas-thl-e.html

According to Douglas, these large ionospheric heaters are the "old school"
technology[36]

We certainly have the technology to alter the weather, as the world learned in April of 2024 when synthetically created rain storms that may have contributed to massive flooding in Dubai. According to a Brave Browser search:

> *Dubai, along with other parts of the United Arab Emirates, uses a*
> *weather modification technique called "cloud seeding" to address*

---

36   https://rumble.com/v4c0ibq-the-maui-fires-6-months-later-with-paul-deslauriers-and-bruce-douglas-thl-e.html

water challenges in the country. Cloud seeding aims to enhance rainfall by introducing certain chemicals into clouds, which can potentially lead to more precipitation. However, experts suggest that while cloud seeding may have enhanced rainfall, it is not solely responsible for extreme weather events like floods. The UAE continuously monitors its atmosphere using weather radars to implement cloud seeding[37].

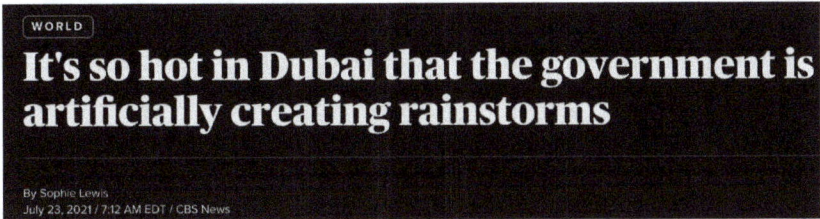

WORLD

It's so hot in Dubai that the government is artificially creating rainstorms

By Sophie Lewis
July 23, 2021 / 7:12 AM EDT / CBS News

According to their patent, "With the advent of smaller mobile arrays, Artificial Ionospheric Mirrors will no longer be limited to polar regions."[38] [39]

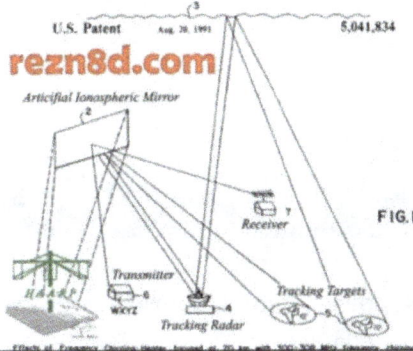

With the advent of smaller mobile arrays, Artificial Ionospheric Mirrors will no longer be limited to polar regions. A new technique called the Ionospheric Current Drive (ICD) [13] will allow HAARP-like heaters along the equator to create ELF waves and tiny Artificial Ionospheric Mirrors called **"Super Small Size Field-Aligned Scattering (SSS FAS) mirrors."**

Photo Courtesy of www.Rezn8d.com

37 https://search.brave.com/search?q=dubai+rain+weather+modification&source=desktop
38 https://climateviewer.com/2014/10/22/haarp-boat-ionospheric-heaters-go-mobile/
39 http://www.ipr.umd.edu/sites/default/files/documents/Papadopoulos%20.pdf - "Mobile HF Sources Research & Applications" Physics of Ionospheric Modification, Theory & Laboratory Experiments, Dennis Papadopoulos – Gennady Milikh, University of Maryland, College Park, AFOSR MURI KickOff March 12, 2014

The National Oceanic and Atmospheric Administration (NOAA) Central Library states, "In the late 40s and 50s, many deemed the deliberate or the inadvertent alteration of atmospheric condition human activity, also known as weather modification, as a promising science of the future."[40] The U.S. government has been studying weather manipulation since the 40s and the 50s, and the National Weather Modification Policy Act of 1976 was passed in the 70s.[41] This isn't just in Alaska; there are antennas all over the world; and newer technology includes mini-domes that can be mounted on ships.

A company called Weather Modification Inc. has this statement on their homepage, "When most people look up, they see clouds. WE SEE POTENTIAL."[42] Douglas says, "It's not a secret. It's all out there. It's called ionosphere heaters. It's for heating up the ionosphere—the upper atmosphere and the ionosphere. It takes a huge amount of power and aims it to a small area."

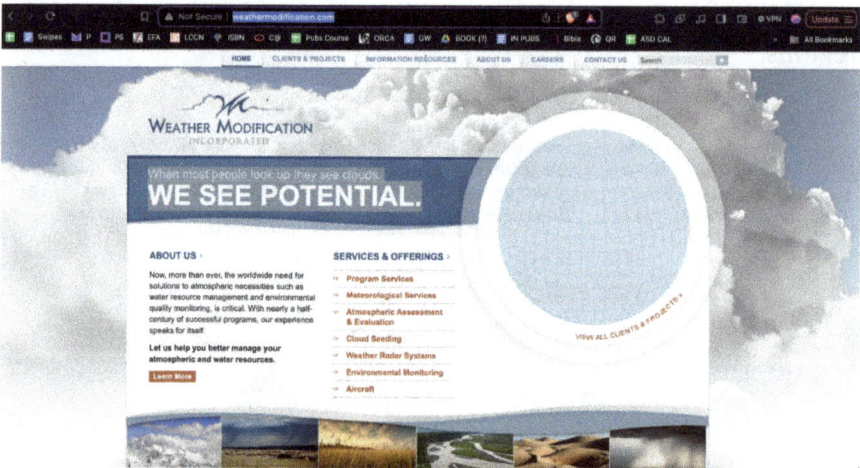

HAARP was the most powerful ionospheric heater in the world in 2015 before it was shut down. However, the new technologies work together in synchrony across the world. When you have different heaters aiming at the same part of the ionosphere together, you can create extremely powerful events in the ionosphere.

---

40   https://wpo.noaa.gov/
41   https://www.congress.gov/bill/94th-congress/senate-bill/3383/all-info
42   http://www.weathermodification.com/

There is an ionospheric heater in Peru, which is still in use today, as shown below. It's as big as the array in Alaska. It takes a powerful hydroelectric dam and pumps it into these arrays to aim huge amounts of power to manipulate the weather. They're everywhere now, which is easier to accomplish since they don't have to have big arrays; they can have much smaller types of devices that control the weather.

Photo Courtesy of www.Rezn8d.com

A new technology called Ionospheric Current Drives will allow HAARP-like heaters along the equator to create Extra Low Frequency (ELF) waves. ELF waves create the vibration—the up-and-down vibration—that manipulates the weather.

In fact, there is even a HAARP dome in the Honolulu Harbor, with enormous power generation capacity and massive capacitor banks to hold a charge, so that they can put pulses out in big bursts. Local military personnel call it the HAARP Dome because there is a big dome on the top. It's said that a billion dollars were invested into its construction, and it's periodically seen at Pearl Harbor as well. According to Douglas, this is a weather modification device that's mobile and acts out of the Pacific Ocean.

A mobile HAARP dome seen in Honolulu Harbor

However, to the public, the dome is portrayed as a defense system there to detect missiles. It's even called the "Sea Band X-Band Radar-1."[43] However, according to "Hawai'ian Public Radio," the 75-person crew is composed of defense contractors,[44] with zero uniformed military personnel. According to Hawaii News Now, it can detect ballistic missiles and determine if they're real or fake.[45]

---

43   https://www.mda.mil/global/documents/pdf/sbx_booklet.pdf
44   https://www.hawaiipublicradio.org/local-news/2019-08-14/go-inside-the-pearl-harbor-golfball
45   https://www.hawaiinewsnow.com/story/6797888/floating-white-dome-at-pearl-harbor-protects-nation/

Missile Defense Agency History Office
7100 Defense Pentagon
Washington, D.C., 20301 - 7100

1 May 2008

Approved for Public Release
08-MDA-3447 (16 MAY 08)

At this time it is interesting to mention a company called Weather Modification Incorporated. Per their website, "Weather Modification, Inc., has a wide range of services to provide knowledge, data, equipment, and capability at any phase in your project. We can also tailor a program to meet your specific objectives and manage it from beginning to end."[46]

> *"Our talented scientists, researchers, project managers, technicians, and pilots have the expertise you need to carry out an efficient, effective weather program."*

Fortunately, there's an app called "SkyGlass" that can track airborne flights by their call signs, and can even identify and keep track of the

---

46   http://www.weathermodification.com/program-services.php

flight paths of planes belonging to companies like Weather Modification Inc.[47] Even more fortunately, there's an ex-military YouTuber named "Monkey Werx US" who does almost daily updates on their flight paths, as well as those of military aircraft.[48]

On March 14, 2024, a YouTuber by the name of Dutchsinse reported on how NOAA denies the existence of weather modification on one hand, while on the other hand ironically demands that weather modification companies report their activities to them.[49] The weather modification project report from the NOAA states:

> *The Weather Modification Reporting Act of 1972, 15 U.S.C. § 330 et seq. requires that all persons that conduct non-Federal weather modification activities within the United States or its territories report such activities to the U.S. Secretary of Commerce at least 10 days prior to and after undertaking the activities. Failure to report can result in fines of up to $10,000.*

Activities subject to reporting.

(a) Weather modification activities are defined as: 'Any activity performed with the intention of producing **artificial changes in the composition, behavior, or dynamics of the atmosphere'** (see 15 CFR § 908.1). The following, when conducted as weather modification activities, shall be reported (see 15 CFR § 908.3):

1. *Seeding or dispersing of any substance into clouds or fog, to alter drop size distribution, produce ice crystals, or coagulation of droplets, alter the development of hail or lightning, or influence in any way the natural development cycle of clouds or their environment;*
2. *Using fires or heat sources to influence convective circulation or to evaporate fog;*
3. *Modifying the solar radiation exchange of the Earth or clouds through the release of gasses, dusts, liquids, or aerosols into the atmosphere;*

---

47   https://www.aviarlabs.com/skyglass
48   https://www.youtube.com/@MonkeyWerxUS
49   https://www.youtube.com/watch?v=FiDHtOpWWcE

4. *Modifying the characteristics of land or water surfaces by dusting or treating with powders, liquid sprays, dyes, or other materials;*

5. *Releasing electrically charged or radioactive particles or ions into the atmosphere;*

6. *Applying shock waves, sonic energy sources, or other explosive or acoustic sources to the atmosphere;*

7. *Using aircraft propeller downwash, jet wash, or other sources of artificial wind generation;*

8. *Using lasers or other sources of electromagnetic radiation; or*

9. *Other activities undertaken with the intent to **modify the weather or climate, including solar radiation management activities and experiments.***" [50]

Weather modification is real and it's happening all over the world, whether or not people will admit or research this fact. It affects our lives, crops, and everyday lifestyles. But here's the real question: How much of a role did it have in these unnatural "wildfires" in Lahaina? As this book was written, Dubai had an unnatural flood. On the ABC News website, on April 17, 2024, there was an article entitled, "Dubai sees severe flooding after getting 2 years' worth of rain in 24 hours." The article stated,

> *Over a half foot -- 6.26 inches -- of rain was recorded in the United Arab Emirates city between 10:00 pm local time Monday and 10:00 pm local time Tuesday, according to the Dubai Meteorological Office. Dubai receives 3.12 inches of rain per year on average, according to the World Meteorological Organization, meaning two years' worth of rain fell in 24 hours.[51]*

The weather can be weaponized.

Is that what happened in Dubai?

---

50   https://libguides.library.noaa.gov/weather-climate/weather-modification-project-reports
51   https://abcnews.go.com/International/dubai-flooding-heavy-rainfall/story?id=109321601

Image in Dubai taken from a video on AP News[52]

Ben Livingston, The Father of Weaponized Weather

Retired Air Force Lieutenant and commercial cloud seeder Ben Livingston, "The Father of Weaponized Weather," was interviewed by Alex Jones for "PrisonPlanet.TV," at which time he claimed, "I was the first person to ever seed a cloud with the intention to cause it to do military damage."[53]

Livingston continues:

> *I got interested in weather modification when I was a farm boy. I never could understand why the clouds weren't bigger and had a little more shade when I was chopping at cotton. I got into the Navy and managed to get into meteorology school, and I think that's where I learned most of my physics. I was assigned to the Typhoon Squadron in Guam where I served for 3 years as a flight meteorologist and meteorological engineer.*

---

52   https://apnews.com/article/uae-oman-rains-flooding-fatalities-7bf3881efbea998dfa4c1e
     d8d538217c
53   https://www.youtube.com/watch?v=-sZl2qsqK18

From there I came back for additional schooling at Texas A&M University down at Kingsville, and from Kingsville they sent me to the Hurricane Hunters Squadron in Jacksonville Florida. That squadron of course had just become involved in Project Stormfury, so when I reported to that duty station as a meteorological engineer I was immediately designated the military member of the Stormfury Advisory Board, who were doing a lot of testing work over the test range in China Lake California where we dropped cloud seeding flares, or silver iodide generators, in the clouds to see what the reaction was. It was there that I learned for sure that you could change a cloud by the amount of silver iodide put into it and where you put it.

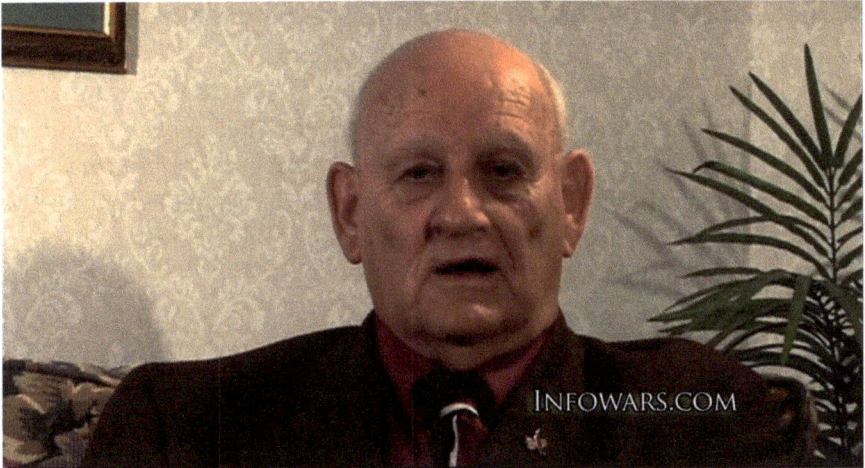

Livingston goes on to state:

These clouds (seen below) were located up in the southern part of north Vietnam, and we needed to make rain down on the Ho Chi Minh trail, but there weren't any clouds around. This was the end of the monsoon season, but there were a number of these small clouds that barely reached the freezing level, and by putting a small amount of silver iodide in there we got them to collect and start to build. And as they built, we just worked on the largest tower in the group until in a very short time we had clouds that made 14 inches of rain.

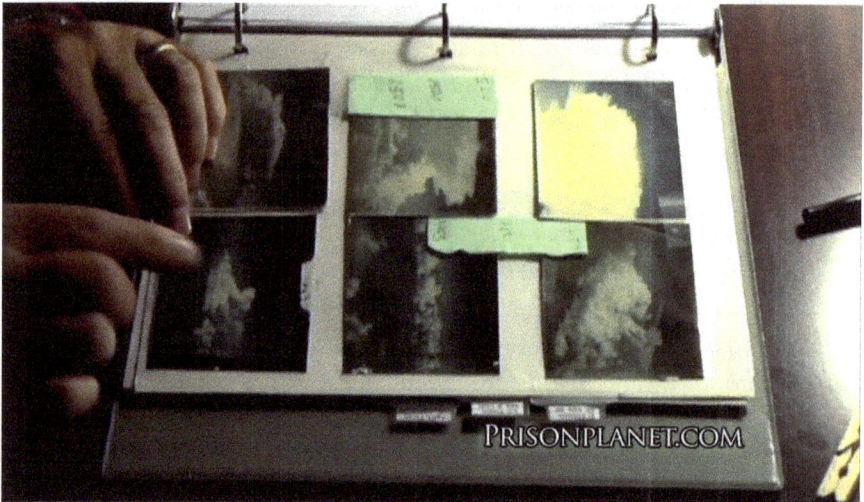

This cloud here (in the images above), from the time it started raining until it quit, put out a little bit over 14 inches of precipitation. It just washed all the roads out, and there was a bridge attached to a mountain that they had bombed and couldn't get rid of, but this heavy rain washing down that river took that bridge out. This was on October 13th.

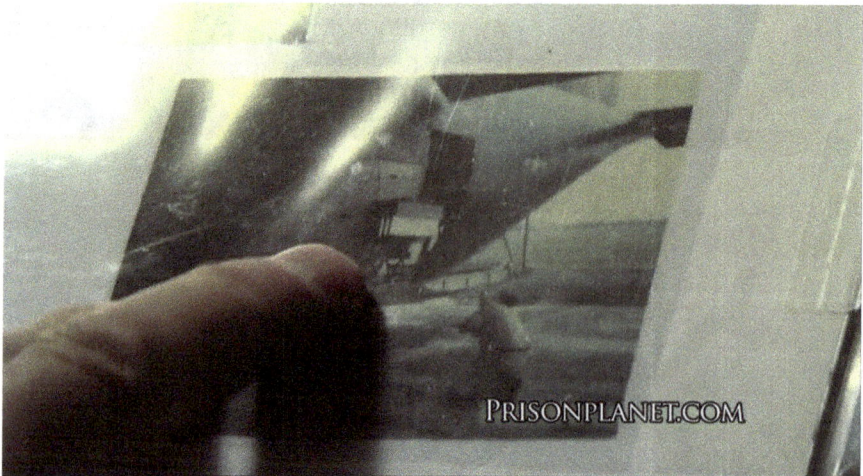

"These are cloud seeding suspension units on the side of C-130s as you can see. These dispensers held 52 units."

"And under here on this F-4, we had these camouflaged."

"And these were our own airplanes, the airplanes I had in my commercial cloud seeding business. We built the flares into the wings of our airplanes so they caused as little resistance, or drag, as possible."

Image of Project Stormfury, taken from the National Weather Service Heritage website.[54]

Per Livingston:

> *I was cleared for top secret, eyes only. I was as high as you could get. We were the first ones to fly into hurricanes for the purpose of modifying them, if you will. That was Project Stormfury. I began to be extremely confident that we could do whatever we wanted to with a hurricane. Project Stormfury had been going on since 1961, and they had already done 2 experiments, one in '61 and '63. Well, when I was there in 1964, I wrote the plan and started to have a track and mission for every flight that was on the hurricane cloud seeding experiments, so we had documentation for everything. Operations of Project Stormfury were very positive...*

> *Some wanted to continue hurricane reduction and the other part did not want to. It was a political football, and there were people who wanted to do more peer research and less applications and engineering that wanted to kill Project Stormfury, so they built up*

---

54   https://vlab.noaa.gov/web/nws-heritage/-/almost-science-fiction-hurricane-modification-and-project-stormfury

an artificial barrier that prevented hurricanes from ever qualifying to be experimented on or seeded for damage reduction. NOAA research people came up with data that suggested that if a hurricane went through a certain little geographical area, where there was no history in 100 years of a hurricane that had been through that area had ever reached land, so they made it a requirement that the storm must go through this area, I call the area of improbability, before it would qualify for hurricane damage reduction attention. So after about 10 years, no hurricane went through there and the people, that is the scientists, who didn't want to spend money on aircraft reconnaissance decided it's just too expensive, we can't wait any longer. So they killed the project altogether. I am terribly disappointed that the government has decided a long time ago not to do the hurricane damage reduction anymore...

...I was asked to start to put together a top secret operation to go to Vietnam to see if we can't make it rain more over there as a military operation. All the roads over there are dirt roads, and when it rains it causes a lot of problems so that during the monsoon season there was so much rain and water in the roads that the trucks couldn't move very freely. Our mission was to make it rain during the dry season. On that particular day, the clouds were very small, there just weren't any real big thunderstorms or anything like that. But I picked a cloud that was sitting out essentially by itself with a number of small clouds. I'm talking about clouds whose tops were somewhere near the freezing level but not high enough to really grow, and I nurtured one of those clouds until I finally got it well past the freezing level, and then it developed a lot of convective activity and it started sucking clouds in and it just started building up and building up. I took a series of pictures I call the "41 minutes". By the end of 41 minutes we had flown up to 65,000 feet and we still couldn't reach the top of the cloud, so we knew we had a barn burner there. And by the next morning, we had washed out everything, and did a lot of damage to people and all that sort of thing, but it was real success as far as blocking the roads off....

...We actually began the 3rd or 4th of September, and by the 13th of October we had a couple of storms that had actually washed out

bridges, and the results were so successful that I was called down to Saigon to brief the Air Force and Army generals down there. They suggested that I need to go make this report to President Johnson back in D.C. They were excited about it, but they had no authorization to use this as a military weapon system. I was there in a very top secret classification as a "research project". That way we were able to conduct the mission without the international community being apprised of what we were doing and how we were doing it. It was kept top secret for a long time. It was first reported that this was going on in 1972. That's the first time that congress ever heard about it, so you can see it was not something everyone knew about for a long time. That same project went on through 1972 when we got out of Vietnam, but the Air Force was still doing it.

Weather Warfare: Pentagon Concedes 7-Year Vietnam Effort

On 20 March, several high-ranking officials of the Department of Defense (DOD) told members of the Senate Foreign Relations Committee in detail about a $21.6 million 7-year program of cloud-seeding to induce rain over the trails of Laos, North Vietnam, South Vietnam, and Cambodia. There had been persistent allegations that the military was carrying out such operations in Southeast Asia. Their briefing, therefore, constitutes the first public description of weather modification techniques as a weapon of war.* Senator Claiborne Pell (D–R.I.), who asked for the briefing, recently released the text of it, of which excerpts follow.

The use of rainmaking as a weapon of war has long been a subject of controversy among weather scientists and arms control experts. Some of the scientists have objected that military use of weather modification will inhibit international cooperation in the atmospheric sciences. Their work, they add, should be used for humanitarian ends such as increasing the world's food supply. Some arms control experts fear that weather modification indiscriminately hurts noncombatants and enemy troops; they also argue that U.S. use of it in Vietnam could lead to proliferation of this relatively simple weapon to other countries.

In any [event?] to Pell is far and away the most complete statement DOD has made to date of its role in weather warfare. [Even

former DOD Secretary [...] hedged on the issue (3 [...] While it furnishes ma[...] some other information [...] For example, there is [...] cussion of whether age[...] DOD have engaged or [...] weather warfare—yet t[...] ligence Agency (CIA [...] have started Vietnam [...] with a rainmaking pro[...] in 1963. There is some [...] ongoing National Secu[...] view of weather modi[...] but no statement of D[...] future military weath[...] programs. Finally, the [...] that they succeeded in [...] to 7 inches of rain in [...] is not supported with [...] that civilian scientists [...] verifying it. Hence t[...] that weather modificati[...] tactical weapon" is no [...] Most of the presenta[...] [...]nant Colonel E[...] [...]hiefs of Staff. O[...] men were: Dennis J. [...] Assistant Secretary o[...] Asia and Pacific Affair[...]

*Weather Modification, hearings before the subcommittee on Oceans and International Environment, Committee on Foreign Relations, U.S. Senate (Government Printing Office, Washington, D.C. 1974).

I was the acting commanding officer at the Corona Naval Weapons Research Center. My main contribution at Corona was to write a plan for weather modification controls for the whole world. At any given time, we could send a number of airplanes with the materials and dispensing equipment we had and probably control the weather all the way around the world.

At the time Project Stormfury started, Dr. Simpson was the head of the U.S. Weather Bureau, and with the funds being made available for Project Stormfury, they created a new entity of government, called the National Hurricane Research Center, and Dr. Bob Simpson was the director of that group. He is preeminent, along with his wife Joanne, who was the head of Project Stormfury for the two years I worked with her." (How ironic that the National Hurricane Research Center itself was originally created and funded out of a weather modification project!)

A number of people, scientists if you will, didn't necessarily endorse applications and engineering in these storms. They demanded that a 3rd party investigate all of what Stormfury had done. Stanford University was the institution that did the study of the activity that Project Stormfury had done. In summary, the results of the Hurricane Debby experiments seemed so positive that many individuals believed the project should go operational, seeding major hurricanes that threatened any landmass. A team of scientists at Stanford Institute did a decisional analysis on all past seeding events, including the ones in 1961 and 1963, and Dr. Matheson from Stanford University, the head of the research institute, reported that the government may have to accept the responsibility for not seeding, and thereby exposing the public to higher probabilities of severe storm damage and higher death tolls."[55]

coverage was less than optimum, analyses of radar reflectivity sequences also supported the hypothesis showing an "eye" expansion after seeding [Gentry, 1970], consistent with the predicted results.

The results from the Hurricane Debbie experiments seemed so positive that many individuals believed the project should go operational, seeding major hurricanes that threatened land. A team of scientists, at Stanford Research Institute at Stanford University, did a decision analysis on all past seeding events (including the Esther and Beulah experiments). Dr. James Matheson of that group, reflecting their views, stated, "We claim they should consider seeding now, if a big hurricane comes straight for Miami". These scientists said "The Government may have to accept the responsibility for not seeding and thereby exposing the public to higher probabilities of severe storm damage and possible higher death tolls". [Pothier, 1972].

However, scientists involved with the project, although encouraged by the results, were much more cautious. Dr. Robert Cecil Gentry, Director of Project STORMFURY at the time, responded that:

---

55   https://youtu.be/-sZl2qsqK18?si=V4msSIBkFpT5Z8Jj&t=1679

Since 1947, the government has used the excuse, logic, or reasoning, that liability is the killer for weather modification. In Ben's opinion, the main reason for why the government didn't follow through with this operation was given as legal liability. He said:

> *Even if a well supported theory of hurricane modification existed, the potential legal aspects of weather modification on this scale argue strongly against any such efforts. Just a few of the many possibilities include; (A) The storm is not modified at all but some perceive that it is, get hurt, and sue the modifiers. (B) The storm is modified according to theory but still does significant damage, and some people blame the modifiers on the damage, even though the modification actually reduced the overall damage and impact. (C) Third, the modified storm produces winners and losers and the perceived losers sue. For example, what if soon after seeding, the hurricane abruptly changed course? The people affected by the new course might well blame the modifying effort and sue...*

> *...If you study the situation you may learn, and very diabolically so, and you don't like to believe this, but there's a possibility that the economics of it verify the fact that there's so much damage done that the construction industry in general all over the US benefits because the cost of materials goes up. So the insurance company may or may not gain from having damage reduction take place, and as far as the energy industry is concerned, we all know that they get their money back almost immediately by increasing the price of their product, and it's not unheard of to believe that the actions performed by FEMA or the government is not a sure fire way to buy votes, so there may not be any political or economic motivation on the government or major industries part to reduce the damage of hurricanes."[56]*

---

56   https://youtu.be/-sZl2qsqK18?si=V4msSIBkFpT5Z8Jj&t=1679

The White Haze

Another concerning observation many Hawai'ians reported to the Maui Community Investigation group and others was the "white haze" on the island on the day of the fires, which is clearly visible in cell phone photos that have been circulating online, as you can see in the examples below.

Photo on the left, a normal day on Maui. On the right, a white haze on August 7, 2023. Photo courtesy of Bruce Douglas as shared on "The Homeless Left" on Rumble.[57]

---

57   https://rumble.com/v4c0ibq-the-maui-fires-6-months-later-with-paul-deslauriers-and-bruce-douglas-thl-e.html

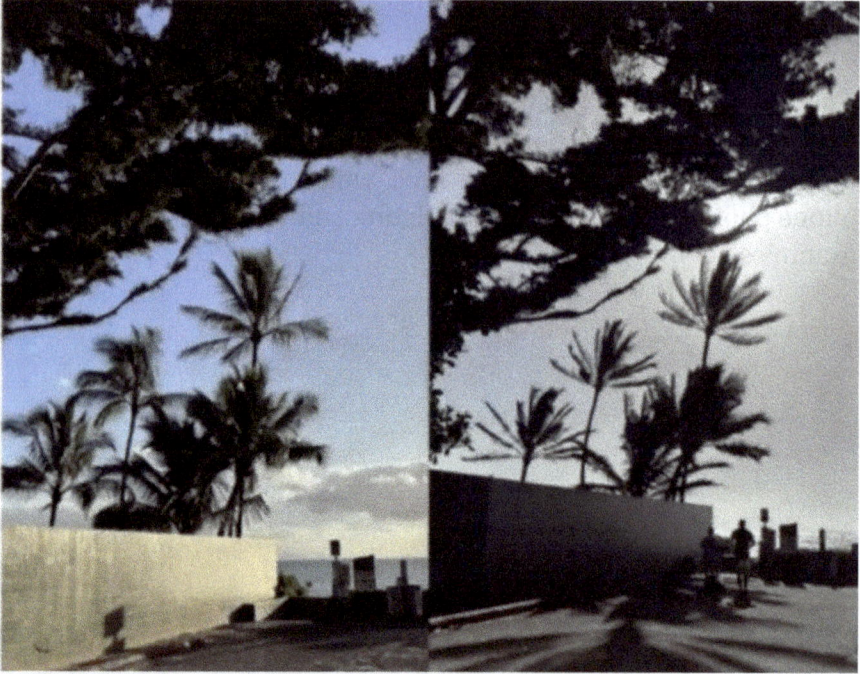

In this image, you see a normal day on the left and the white haze on the right on August 7, 2023. Photo courtesy of Bruce Douglas as shared on "The Homeless Left" on Rumble.[58]

The image below shows what a Doppler radar, which sees lower level clouds, picked up on the 7th, 8th, and 9th of August, 2023. In the first image on the 7th, you'll see a weird haze that had traveled since at least August 1st, according to a video created by Douglas, coming from the coast of California toward the Hawai'ian islands. On the 8th, you see it directly over the islands. On the 9th, it passed the islands.

---

58   https://rumble.com/v4c0ibq-the-maui-fires-6-months-later-with-paul-deslauriers-and-bruce-douglas-thl-e.html

Doppler Radar shows haze, Hawaiian Islands with red circle

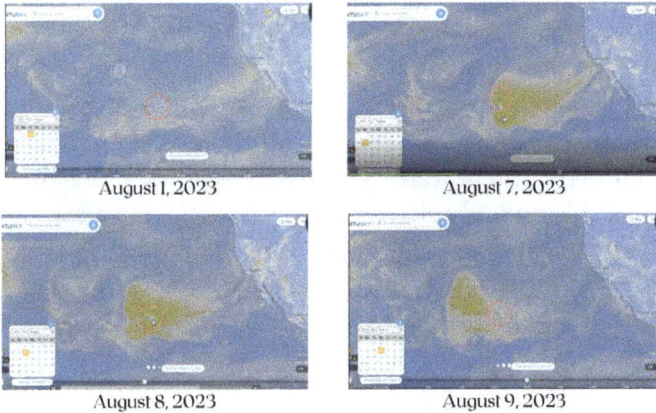

August 1, 2023

August 7, 2023

August 8, 2023

August 9, 2023

Douglas says that the "white haze" didn't contain reflective particles, such as nano-aluminum, which you might see in aerosols. In fact, Douglas admits it has him scratching his head. Some have suggested the haze could have been an accelerant, but there is little evidence to confirm this.

Another bizarre occurrence before the fires were "wind funnels" over the ocean on the morning of August 8th. Douglas took the images below on the morning of the 8th on his phone, while on the highway near Lahaina, looking out toward Molokai. Many of these wind cyclones were seen in various locations off the coast of Maui.

"Wind Funnels" seen the morning of August 8, 2023

Images Courtesy of Bruce Douglas as shared with "The Homeless Left" podcast on Rumble.[59]

---

59   https://rumble.com/v4c0ibq-the-maui-fires-6-months-later-with-paul-deslauriers-and-bruce-douglas-thl-e.html

On the 7th of August, the north and south shores of Maui were experiencing strong winds, but they had calmed down significantly on the 8th. On the 8th, however, the West side of Maui, where the firestorm occurred, was having crazy winds that moved in multiple directions. One of the most curious anomalies during the fire were citizen reports that there were huge gusts of wind moving one direction and then would suddenly change course and blow in a totally different direction. This is atypical of a hurricane, as hurricanes typically have sustained forceful winds that don't change direction. And as we've covered, Dora was far enough away to be considered irrelevant.

CHAPTER FIVE:
Infrastructure Failures

Among the many failures on August 8th were the infrastructure failures; which we will outline for you now. First, there was no cell phone service prior to the fire. Without cell service, it was harder for victims of the fire to communicate with one another and identify for one another how to get to safety, how to retrieve children, or even the location of vulnerable family members and neighbors. Losing cell service during a disaster can result in unnecessary loss of life. Surprisingly, some members of the community were able to briefly gain service, and curiously Mr. Haiku, as featured earlier in this book, was able to "Facebook Live" for a brief period during the fires. In the ongoing investigation, these rare glimpses from cell phone footage were, at times, all the world had due to the media blackout that was enforced during and after the fires.

Another infrastructure failure includes the absence of electricity starting around 3:00 a.m. on the 8th of August, before the initial fire took off. In addition, there was no water to fight the fires, an issue still shrouded in controversy. Ironically, although there was water magically available around the big box stores, there was hardly any water at all around the residential areas. If you visit Lahaina today, you'll see that Safeway, Starbucks and McDonalds remain untouched and open with a virtually leveled, incinerated town all around them.

One detail among many for the "arson" theory on August 8th is not only the rampant infrastructure failures, but also the fact that a Kula fire around 6:35 a.m. on the east side of Maui created enough pandaemonium, chaos, and confusion to provide plausible deniability for some of the other infrastructure failures.

The image below shows where the fires were on August 8th. The Kula fire was about forty miles away from Lahaina.

The following image shows a fire that began at around 6:35 a.m.

By 9:30 a.m. or so, that fire was put out, but it reignited at 2:55 p.m. farther down from that original fire, the trajectory of which is shown in the image below.

Sirens

Burn Back Better goes into detail about the fact that the sirens on Maui were not sounded, and this detail is our book's namesake. We'll take a sentence to briefly remind those who haven't read *Burn Back Better* yet that Hawaii is home to the most sophisticated siren system in the world."[60] The island of Maui has 80 alarms just in and around Lahaina. On the Hawaii Emergency Management website, it states, "the all-hazard siren system can be used for a variety of both natural and human-caused events; including tsunamis, hurricanes, dam breaches, flooding, wildfires, volcanic eruptions, terrorist threats, hazardous material incidents, and more.[61]

---

60   https://a.co/d/iw9fBJp
61   https://dod.hawaii.gov/hiema/all-hazard-statewide-outdoor-warning-siren-system/

Two alarms are pictured below. This incredible alarm system was never turned on to warn vulnerable residents of Lahaina, some of whom were taking an afternoon nap and perished due to there not being any sirens nor alarms.

On August 8th, Herman Andaya served as Maui County's Emergency Management Agency (MEMA) Director, and Gaya Gabuat his administrative assistant. Their insidious texts are detailed in Chapter One of this book, commonly referenced as the "LOL OK" texts that downplay the severity of the fires with Gabuat texting Andaya, "PIOs are funny. There are 3 of them and they look scared and overwhelmed. I think they need a hug lol to calm down."[62]

Further investigation into the correspondence between Andaya and Gabuat during the fire indicate they never corresponded with the consideration of sounding the sirens.[63] Anybody who has lived on the Hawai'ian islands for a number of years has likely heard these sirens being sounded for practice. The most common reason for sounding the sirens are for hurricanes or tsunamis. However, text messages traditionally go out to the public giving details as to what the sirens are being sounded for so that the public understands if the alarms are being tested or if there is an actual emergency. If the internet had been working in Lahaina during the day of the fire, we feel certain that people would have known that a dangerous fire was on its way to the city center. The fact that these world class sirens were not sounded served as a red flag to many people on and off the island that there was something unordinary about the fire. Why the sirens weren't used to protect the people doesn't merely seem negligent, but murderous.

---

62   https://www.kitv.com/news/texts-show-herman-andaya-constantly-engaged-warned-mayor-and-state/article_66227314-ff1e-11ee-afd8-537843b27e82.html

63   https://ag.hawaii.gov/maui-wildfire-investigation-resources-page/

Police Blockades

Among the most bizarre anomalies during the fire is what Shane referenced in Chapter Two as the "human rotisserie," wherein police barricades blocked people from exiting the burn zone, which meant certain death for many people. Those who escaped beyond the barricades had a chance at surviving. Those who circled back in as the police directed faced an absolute inferno. The police blockades which maximized the death toll is the second big "alarm" to many people on and off the island that the intention of this fire was maximum damage and death to the people of Lahaina, including tourists, children, and the elderly.

Simply stated, those who survived were those who didn't follow the police instruction. The image below was delivered to the Maui Community Investigation team by a man named "Spider" who survived the fire by sheltering in a place that did not incinerate.

The next two photos, also provided by the Maui Community Investigation team, show people managing to survive even though there were explosions going off all around Maui. In Stephanie's trip to Lahaina, she saw dozens if not scores of propane tanks intact in the burn zone. These tanks are designed not to explode, which invalidates the theory that the explosions going off were from propane tanks, a common source of fuel on the island. If the propane tanks weren't exploding, as they are designed to (not) do, then what was exploding?

Undamaged Buildings

During the August 8th fire in Lahaina, the destruction was almost unimaginable, which you'll see in the Photos section at the end of this book. At least one-hundred people are confirmed dead and many citizens and even one legislative official believe that the number of deceased exceeds 1,000, even over 1,500. The fire damaged or destroyed 2,207 structures to our knowledge and according to the best reports. Eighty-six percent of that which was exposed to the fire was classified as residential. In this former capital of the Kingdom of Hawaii, 2,170 acres were consumed in a largely blue collar small business epicenter. It is said that there may be many more people who perished who were not registered, many of whom were migrant workers.

Oddly, as you'll see in the image below, many of the big box stores and hotels survived, even if those buildings were situated in what was otherwise the "middle" of the fire.

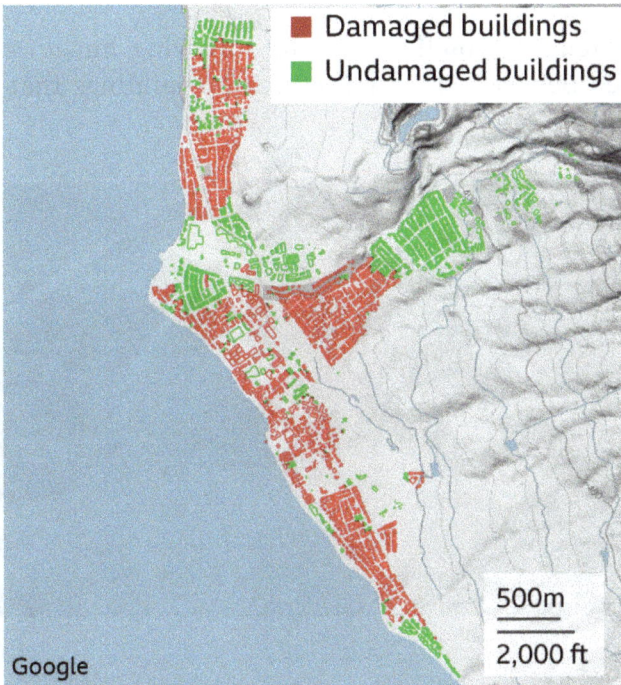

Source: FEMA/ESRI, data published 12 Aug   B B C

A smoking gun, so to speak, during the Lahaina fire is the presence
of structures that survived in the middle of complete devastation, as
you'll see below.

Some of them, as you'll see in the following image, were even
sandwiched between other structures or buildings that were not
incinerated.

The following image shows an aerial view of a structure that survived with everything surrounding it having been turned into white ash (a phenomenon we'll discuss later.)

According to experienced fire captains, there is a tendency for older construction to burn first because they are often made of wood and other flammable materials. Those residences tend to be closer to the beach, so it's no wonder that most of the shore line was destroyed. Factors such as the amount of clearing around a building can affect the damage done to properties, but newer construction tends to be more flame resistant and made of materials that are less flammable. Due to the extreme destruction, it is not always known which properties had cleared their yards or upgraded to less flammable materials. Nonetheless; many structures, old and new, did get burned to the ground.

It's nevertheless interesting to note that the fire seemed to burn hot enough to melt many materials that wouldn't traditionally burn during a real "brush fire," and happened to "skip" over many structures that, whether made of wood or synthetics, would surely have at least partially burned or shown severe damage. The fact that undamaged structures show no evidence of being close to a fire that may have exceeded the temperature required to melt glass within a few feet of them is curious and fuels discussion of directed energy weapon usage.

Kaleo Manuel & The Absence of Water...

"Where was the water?" is one of the first and most important questions residents and observers of the Lahaina fires asked. An interview we appreciate is with Representative Elle Cochran on the "Roseanne Barr Podcast" from February 29, 2024. Cochran was born and raised in Lahaina with a family from Oahu. Cochran and her husband live on Maui in Lahaina just below Lahainaluna High School. She had taken a nap when the fire started and woke up to the smell of smoke; she noticed that her neighbors were missing when she woke up and drove to the end of her street. She called the fire chief, who was allegedly off the island on the mainland, and asked what was happening, and if she needed to evacuate. He stated, "why?" He wasn't even aware that there was a big fire, and at that time it was around 4:00 p.m. Cochran recalls that the first thought she had was that there were people in those homes down there dying; fireballs were landing "all around" her and the roads were gridlocked. Thankfully, Cochran drove onto the Lahaina bypass, but she was devastated to see the entire Lahainatown in flames before her eyes.[64]

In the same interview, Barr asked Cochran if she was shocked at how "ill-prepared" Maui County was. Due to what Cochran recalls as

---

64 https://rumble.com/v4gf3yf-no-water-coming-out-of-fire-hydrants-lahaina-rep-elle-cochran-the-roseanne-.html

"hurricane lane," she was, indeed, shocked at how ill-prepared Maui was, particularly with regards to water.

"We are public servants. The people who pay taxes, that's our salaries... that's who we ought to be beholden to," says Cochran on the podcast, who also reminded viewers that she liquidated her 401k in order to get elected on the grassroots level. We the authors feel the need to mention Cochran, her campaign, her successful election, and her commitment to Hawaii with grassroots efforts because it's a glimmer of hope and light in this otherwise dark story of a corrupt Hawai'ian government.

"Water is key... and I don't know why they're not talking about it... they need to reallocate," states Cochran. She heard constituents state that they'd love to rebuild, but they have no water. There is allegedly more than enough water, but it's not allocated to the people nor to new construction and housing. The water Lahaina needed wasn't there during the fire. And post-fire, the water isn't being reallocated to help the people rebuild.

That said, the question still stands: "where was the water?"

Water, stated Cochran, is a public trust. Nobody should "own" water. It falls from the sky, fills aquifers, but then it's allocated to things like golf courses and directed away from the people. On Maui, more than the corporate entities' "fair share" is being taken. Thanks to Lahaina's fires on August 8th, the entire world is now able to hold Maui County accountable for diverting water to golf courses and hotels. Lahaina's water was diverted about a hundred and fifty years ago to plantations; but Lahaina used to be called the "Venice of the Pacific." Canal street, Cochran points out, used to be a proper canal, in fact. However, the fallow grass grew and became fuel for the fire, particularly if the cause of the fire was in part due to arson, as we mentioned in Chapter Three.

The main scapegoat for there being "no water" is former Department of Land and Natural Resources (DLNR) Director Kaleo Manuel, who is blamed for the water not coming out of fire hydrants. Days after the fire, a scathing video was played by multiple news media outlets of a speech he made about the sacredness of water in Hawaii, citing water as "an earthly manifestation" of gods.[65] In the video, he made several rightfully off-putting comments about how water should not be a right but a thing that should be revered.[66] In every sense, his tirade embodied the essence of gaslighting and blame shifting, according to your authors.

As one might imagine, those who watched this video were outraged because they knew Manuel's actions were the reason no water came out of the hydrants. In fact, the video of Manuel was recorded many months before the Lahaina fires on October 12, 2022 at the "Malama One Water For Hawaii 2.0/UH Better Tomorrow Speaker Series."

Curiously, this video did not become widely shared on mainstream media until August 16, 2023, one day after Manuel was reassigned to a new position with the Maui government. This suggests that the video was released as part of a smear campaign against Manuel.

Video of Kaleo Manual from the "Better Tomorrow Speaker Series"

However, the original video was filmed on October 12, 2022, 10 months before August 8, 2023. He wasn't being interviewed about the fires when he made statements about the water; these statements were made *before* his devastating decision to withhold the release

---

65   https://rumble.com/v3a3s37-obama-appointee-asshole-turned-murderer-shut-water-off-to-maui-m.-kaleo-man.html

66   https://youtu.be/2GsMMgz1ibo?si=tcOP2kc0Ovh7KG-Q

of water needed to fight the August 8th fires. Manuel stated, "we've become used to looking at water as something which we use, and not necessarily as something we revere, something that gives us life."[67]

On her channel "Brush Junkie," Traci created two videos with details about the water diversion mishaps, including thoughts following Manuel's resignation two months after he was reinstated to his post as commissioner following the fires. On August 15th, the day before the scathing video with Manuel was released, he was assigned a different post. Eventually, Kaleo Manuel resigned; that resignation happened around late December of 2023.[68]

Residents of Lahaina pointed out that their tap water, water from their hoses, and water in fire hydrants were all cut off; this order came from much higher up than Manuel, to our understanding. It is our logical assumption that Kaleo Manuel has been made a scapegoat for something that was, for all intents and purposes, above his pay grade.

After her original video about Manual went viral, Maui Land Company sent Traci a detailed letter supporting Manuel, stating that Manuel was a well-respected member of DLNR and had been an advocate for water rights for the people of West Maui. A copy of the letter can be read on Traci's youtube video on Manuel.[69]

Additionally, unnamed citizens sent Traci thoughtful emails questioning the theory that Kaleo Manuel was guilty of "murder on Maui" by refusing to turn water on or diverting water in any way. Maui City Council members voted 7 to 2 to have Manuel reinstated, which also suggests that Manuel was not guilty of intentionally refusing to release water. In short, we think that Manuel, like so many other hardworking citizens and officials on Maui, was made to be a scapegoat when the "Better Tomorrow Speaker Series" video was released the day after he was originally temporarily removed from his post as Director with DLNR or reassigned to another position.

---

67   https://www.youtube.com/watch?v=EWh978uT-nA
68   https://www.youtube.com/watch?v=6krq7xAPKvc
69   https://youtu.be/2GsMMgz1ibo

Water Rights - Kaleo Manuel, West Maui Land Co, and Alexander & Baldwin   Inbox ×

unnamed.client ‹unnamed.client@proton.me›   Fri, Aug 28, 8:41 AM
to me ▾

Hi Traci - A few weeks ago I would have never thought I'd be writing this email. Your videos on YouTube about Maui are some of the few that I feel are telling the truth, while providing history and perspective. After watching your latest video, I wanted to reach out and see if you might consider covering the topic in the subject of this email? I believe it's important for people to understand - as researching it really opened my eyes to how the people of Maui and Hawaii have been treated by the government before this tragedy in Lahaina even took place.

Like many others around the world, I've watched in horror the events unfolding in Maui. I've grown frustrated seeing citizens of Maui being the ones providing relief to survivors, while our government does nothing. When I heard on the news about Kaleo Manuel prioritizing "equity" over releasing water immediately for the fires' I was disgusted. What kind of person would prioritize water equity over saving peoples lives? That was the narrative we were told, and is the narrative most news organizations have been telling us.

The story we are told by Gov. Green and West Maui Land Co is that Kaleo Manuel restricted water supply for hours, which led to firefighters running out of water at a critical time. If that was the case, and he holds responsibility for water being shut off to Lahaina - then why are residents of West Maui fighting for Kaleo Manuel to get his job back?[2]

It is now purported that the water release would have only filled water reservoirs for West Maui Land Co - none of the water in question could ever have made it to county facilities or fire hydrants in Lahaina.[3] The fire hydrants in Lahaina likely lost pressure when electricity went out.[4]

I've learned that both the water infrastructure and rights in Maui are, for lack of a better word...complicated. Complications stemming from the history of plantations on the island. More accurately, complications stemming from Hawaii being taken over and Hawaiians being stripped of their land. For the past 30+ years, it seems there has been a struggle for water rights, with Hawaiians and the everyday citizens of Hawaii on one side; and the state, property developers, and corporations on the other. A

It is now purported that the water release would have only filled water reservoirs for West Maui Land Co - none of the water in question could ever have made it to county facilities or fire hydrants in Lahaina.[3] The fire hydrants in Lahaina likely lost pressure when electricity went out.[4]

I've learned that both the water infrastructure and rights in Maui are, for lack of a better word...complicated. Complications stemming from the history of plantations on the island. More accurately, complications stemming from Hawaii being taken over and Hawaiians being stripped of their land. For the past 30+ years, it seems there has been a struggle for water rights, with Hawaiians and the everyday citizens of Hawaii on one side; and the state, property developers, and corporations on the other. A perfect example of the imbalances at play was a story where just a few years ago local families were told to limit their showers to 5 minutes and cut back on watering their land, while hotels and golf courses were given an almost unlimited amount of water.[5] The overdrawing of water by property developers for decades was a major factor of the mostly arid vegetation that fueled the fires.[2]

Now that the fires have subsided, Gov. Green has suspended portions of the water code allowing property developers greater supplies of water...essentially rolling back recent rulings from the Supreme Court in favor of water rights activists.[2] It amounts to millions of gallons of water per day, while the water usage for fire suppression is in the tens of thousands of gallons when needed. Not surprisingly, it's a lucrative deal for property developers, as they also sell back the water to the county at 2-4x the cost of their leases.[6]

Although I might be on an entirely different end of the political spectrum as Kaleo Manuel, I can only conclude he was a scapegoat. It seems that every step of the way, the government has tried to place blame on others without accepting their own culpability. When they aren't pointing fingers, they are denying events even occurred. It's unacceptable. The people of Maui deserve better.

Thank you for hearing me out. I hope you will consider covering this topic at some point, providing your insights and perspective. I look forward to seeing your future videos.

All the best,

X

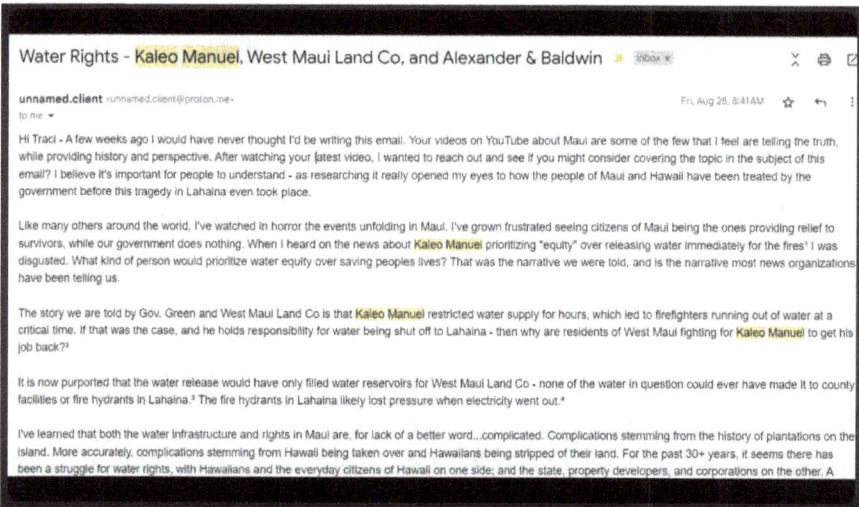

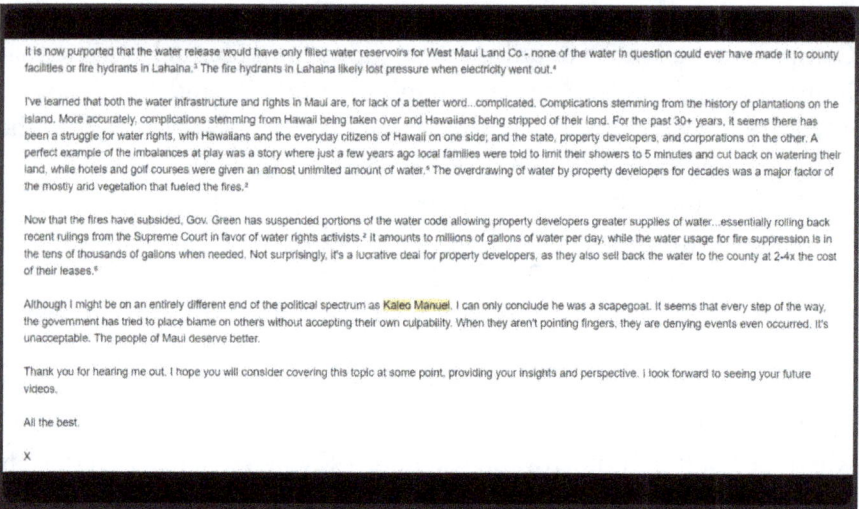

There have been many excuses about the lack of water to fight the fires. Why wasn't water airlifted to fight the fire, for instance? Some theories suggest that the wind prevented air lifting water.

Another excuse for the lack of water is the fact that taro farmers refused to release water on the day of the fires, but there is no proof of this that we can find. For those less familiar with native agricultural cultivation, most types of taro need a large amount of water to flow through the crops.

As a child, Traci used to visit the Waihole taro farm and "stomp" in the taro patches, which were covered with about a foot of mud, making taro a difficult crop to cultivate without consistent running streams. Taro used to be the native Hawai'ians' main source of starch-served with fish, pork, or on its own. It was made by smashing the taro root with a stone and turning it into a paste.

In short, as far as your authors can find, Kaleo Manuel did not have sole authority to shut down the water during a natural disaster. Shortly after these scathing videos were released to the public, Manuel was reassigned to a different department.

On October 6, 2023, Maui Council member Keani Rawlins-Fernandes led the commission to reinstate Manuel to his previous position as director of DLNR. This decision had to be approved by the Maui County Counsel, but he was given his old job back only to resign a few months later. His reasoning was that he would only have been a roadblock to the department, which was taking a different path than he would choose to take.[70] Manuel is currently the Director of Water Resources for Kamehameha Schools according to his Linkedin profile.

Another reason for the lack of water to fight the fires is the theory that the water pumps did not have power. However, under normal circumstances there are backup generators to allow for water flow. Something else your authors have considered is that the energy technology used to burn the town could have penetrated the pipes and made them unable to deliver water. There is evidence of this happening to a metal culvert at the Emerald Plaza.

Until a brave official comes forward, we may never know exactly what was going on with the water; but it is our strong belief that Manuel certainly did not "turn the water off". In addition to Manuel, other resignations have come from Nani Medieros and Harman Andaya. Medieros was the Chief Housing Officer on Maui, about whose work you can read in *Burn Back Better* as she was part of a commission developed by Governor Josh Green to support affordable housing which came under attack following the suspicion that Green intended to erect housing projects "at any cost" when a mid-July 2023 "Emergency Proclamation" was signed, which is also thoroughly detailed in *Burn Back Better* by Stephanie Pierucci.

---

70 https://youtu.be/6krq7xAPKvc

CHAPTER SIX:
Bizarre Burns and Fire Behavior

Stephanie admits that after her first book, in which she took a very skeptical approach to directed energy weapons theories, she received a fair bit of mail and correspondence stating, in essence, "look at the white ash, lady! That's a dead giveaway for directed energy weapons!"

That is why your authors have paid more special attention not to types of "lasers" or "weapons," but to some of the details about the Lahaina fires that would suggest use of directed energy.

White Ash

Many experts say that white ash is a dead ringer for energy weapons. For the level of incineration to occur, as is depicted in the following image, it must be extremely hot—much hotter than a typical brush, building, or house fire.

Photo Courtesy of The Maui Community Investigation

Despite the presence of white ash, somehow there are trees still standing, as the following image illustrates.

Photo Courtesy of the Maui Community Investigation

Bruce Douglas and Paul Deslauriers heard many reports similar to the one Stephanie heard on Maui wherein a man located his parents' car and when he went to touch their bodies, they disintegrated into ash before his eyes. The authors of this book have seen images of bodies that we chose not to share, as we're waiting on forensic evidence from the investigation team on Maui. If you have any information, photos, or videos to submit to the Community Investigation, please send them to MauiCommunityInvestigation@gmail.com or call 808-264-3536.

Most notably, the images of deceased bodies we've seen from the fire looked like they'd been microwaved from the inside rather than burned from the outside. One image that has already circulated widely on the internet and has recently been corroborated as a valid image from Lahaina, as it was also filmed by Kahokule'a Haiku in his documentary (which we mentioned in a previous chapter with a link to his YouTube channel,) shows a man with braided hair lying face down with his body being singed from the inside out in many places, but his hair still intact. Other videos show bodies with abdomens burned by hair, alas, still intact.

These images are evidence, according to the experts, of potential plasma waveguide technology. There are many images of people with their hair intact or animals with their fur intact, but the inside of the body looks to be incinerated.

"Blue" Items Don't Burn?

There were a curious amount of items and structures that survived and were blue, which propelled many theories online of blue light, blue helmets worn by the U.N., and celebrities "painting their roofs blue."

Oddly, several plastic items also did not burn and were recovered after the fire, as the following image illustrates. Plastic doesn't have as much density to it, which may further corroborate the plasma waveguide theory.

The plastic playground at the Children of the Rainbow Preschool was untouched.[71]

The following image shows a before and after aerial view of an area that illustrates the white ash. Note that the blue building was burned; it was not somehow saved due to its blue color.

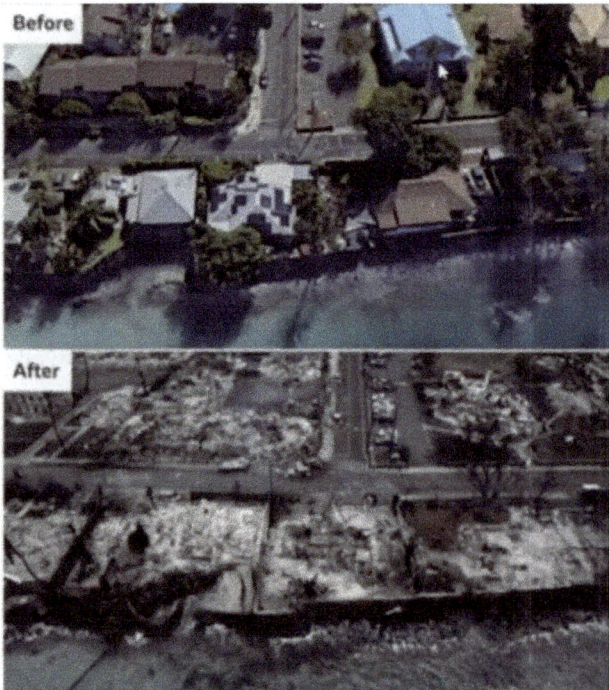

We toggle back and forth on this whole blue laser theory. Stephanie dispelled it as a myth in her book *Burn Back Better* and remains skeptical. However, it's important to note that according to experts, lasers can be programmed for different frequencies. Each color has a different frequency. Tommy Bahama's blue umbrellas did not burn at all when the entire place around them turned to ash. The umbrellas were left fully intact. Stephanie proposes that if the "blue laser" theory were real, these umbrellas would probably have been removed immediately; and considering 2,207 structures burned in the fire, it's nothing extraordinary that a small fraction of the "blue" items were spared.

The infamous "Tommy Bahama" Umbrellas in Lahaina
Photo Courtesy of Stephanie Pierucci, January 2024

Nevertheless, since this is an investigation designed to compel the reader to ask questions, it's interesting to note that research reveals that different colors react with different frequencies, some being immune to different frequencies; which would explain why some items might not have burned. However, Stephanie doesn't see much compelling evidence that lasers were used in this fire, especially when you consider the higher likelihood that plasma waveguide technology was, perhaps, the more likely directed energy weapon in these fires.

The following image was originally taken from a video on TikTok[72] which has since been removed, but there is still a Rumble video that shows the same phenomenon.[73]

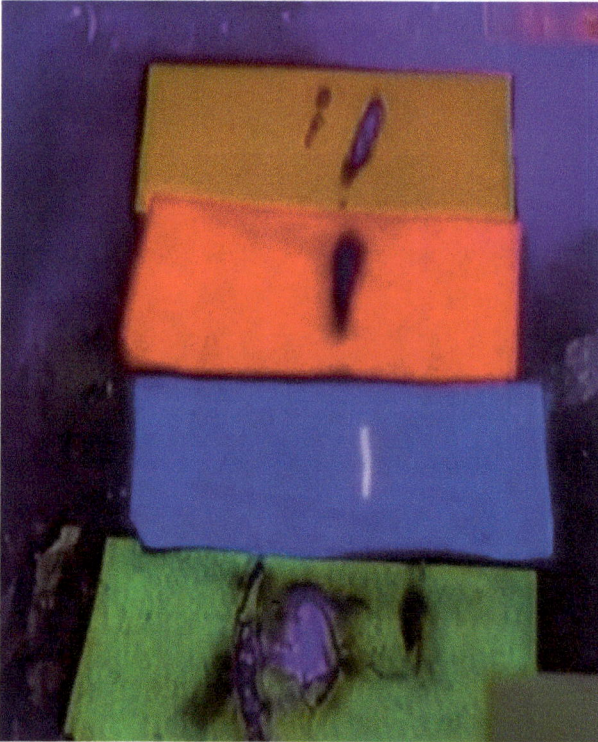

Lasers can be programmed for different wavelengths. Each color has a certain wavelength and can absorb or reflect laser light. The image above shows a laser burning through all the colors except blue because the laser is a blue light so the blue color doesn't absorb it; it reflects it.[74]

72   https://youtu.be/_fa2sQ7_gIA?si=MypaiwrCecodz0OH
73   https://rumble.com/v3bsris-blue-lasers-supposedly-dont-burn-conductivity-leading-towards-the-un-blue-h.html
74   https://rumble.com/v3clib2-blue-lasers-to-destroy.html

In an interview called, "Why do we need different coloured lasers?" on TheNakedScientists.com website from October 9, 2018, Chris Smith interviewed physicist Jess Wade. Wade answered, "The color of the light determines the energy that the laser light will have. So you can use a really high energy laser, a kind of ultraviolet or a blue laser, or a lazy infrared laser.[75]

According to Wikipedia, in 1996, Japanese inventor Shuji Nakamura,[76] invented the first low-power blue laser. He received the Millennium Technology Prize awarded in 2006,[77] and a Nobel Prize for Physics along with Professor Isamu Akasaki,[78] and Hiroshi Amano[79] in 2014 for this invention.[80]

There is a laser available to the public called, "The World's Most Powerful Blue Handheld Laser: A Legit 7 Watts INSANE Laser Power." The description reads: "7.5 Watts 455nm laser diode we use in 'the striker' is currently the most powerful blue laser diode on the market. It ignites paper and wood almost instantaneously! You will not even have to pinpoint focus the beam!" If this is on the market, that means there are even more powerful weapons used in the military.[81]

Joe Biden spoke at a press conference after the Texas fire. Luckily someone filmed it and here is what he said, "If you fly over these areas that are burned to the ground, you'll see that among twenty homes that are totally destroyed, one home is just sitting there because it had the right roof on it."[82]

Biden mentioned the roofs again when speaking with someone after the conference where he said, "Have you noticed when you fly over in a helicopter those places with good roofs, they didn't burn." He has shared an important insight that all people need to pay attention to. In a later chapter you will learn about the U.S. military researching direct energy weapons since the 1950s, and possibly earlier.[83]

---

75   https://www.thenakedscientists.com/articles/questions/why-do-we-need-different-coloured-lasers
76   https://en.wikipedia.org/wiki/Shuji_Nakamura
77   https://en.wikipedia.org/wiki/Millennium_Technology_Prize
78   https://en.wikipedia.org/wiki/Isamu_Akasaki
79   https://en.wikipedia.org/wiki/Hiroshi_Amano
80   https://en.wikipedia.org/wiki/Blue_laser
81   https://www.sanwulasers.com/product/7wblue
82   https://youtu.be/e2W79s1uv-s?si=XMwnUI6mAEHlxKu5&t=109
83   https://rumble.com/v4kp9g2-texas-wildfire-3rd-largest-fire-in-state-history.-lasers-beems.html

Here's an interesting fact. The military for the United Nations wear bright blue helmets. Why would a military force have such a bright color worn on the heads of their soldiers?

The answer was found on the Dag Hammarskjold Library website, in an article entitled, "What is the origin of the blue helmets worn by UN peacekeepers?" Here is their answer:

> In 1956, the UN Emergency Force (UNEF)[84] was established as the first UN peacekeeping operation. Troops from different countries wore their national uniforms and added distinctive UN arm bands and shoulder patches to identify them as UN peacekeepers. According to the UNEF I Background website, "The blue beret and helmet were created by Secretary-General Hammarskjöld during the formative days of UNEF". Urquhart writes, "What was needed was distinctive headgear easy for a distant sniper to recognize. A UN-blue beret seemed to be the answer.[85]

They must not be worried about snipers fighting for the other side. Going back to the Maui fire, you see that wood burned more efficiently if it was in direct contact to metal. To your authors, it seems odd that a "wildfire" had a hard time burning wood...

---

84   http://peacekeeping.un.org/sites/default/files/past/unefi.htm
85   https://ask.un.org/faq/209615

Vehicles

Thanks to the reporting of some Maui local citizens, most notably Eric West,[86] The world watched in horrified stupors as images emerged of cars burned in odd ways... and in odd places. In the following image you'll see that one vehicle incinerated next to another that didn't even have melted tires. Note that nearby transformers in this image appear to be fine.

Bruce Douglas reminds us that with the way lightning and energy weapons work, they seek out something with mass, just like lightning doesn't hit the ground, but it will hit a tree or a car or building. It seeks out something with density that will be the grounding point for the energy. In the same way, a car has an intense amount of energy; the engine block is the most dense part of the car, so the energy will want to concentrate there either with lightning or energy weapons.

In the following image, you'll see that the back of the cab is relatively untouched, but the portion of the vehicle with the most

---

mass was destroyed. In fact, aerosol cans in the door of the vehicle appear to be fine. Even stranger, the following image shows that the adjacent house and light brush on the fence is fine. This image was taken approximately during the third week of August. The vehicle is on asphalt; the back of the truck and the hut behind it are untouched. What's more, the gas tank in the back of the vehicle did not ignite the truck. The amount of gas in the carburetor of the car isn't enough to melt the vehicle, let alone steel.

*Image courtesy of the Maui Community Investigation interview with
"The Homeless Left" on Rumble*

For steel and glass to melt, you need extremely high temperatures. For the type of damage shown of melted steel and glass in the following image, you'll need temperatures up to 2,700 degrees. A normal brush fire, however, would only reach 1,500 degrees. It could melt aluminum at 1,200+ degrees, but a building, brush, or house fire wouldn't get to 2,500 or even 2,700 degrees, requisite for steel and glass to melt. The following images show bent steel as well as melted glass with brush nearby being fine in some cases.

Image courtesy of the Maui Community Investigation interview with "The Homeless Left" on Rumble

Image from Paula Ramon / AFP Via Getty Images 8-12-23

Offshore Boats

How could a fire burn vessels 200 yards off shore? This is yet another smoking gun from the August 8th fire. People along the shoreline reported many explosions happening in rapid succession.

Image courtesy of the Maui Community Investigation interview with "The Homeless Left" on Rumble

Image courtesy of the Maui Community Investigation interview with "The Homeless Left" on Rumble

*Image courtesy of the Maui Community Investigation interview with "
The Homeless Left" on Rumble*

*Image courtesy of the Maui Community Investigation interview with
"The Homeless Left" on Rumble*

Image courtesy of Cammy Clark via "Maui Now"[87]

What could create that level of destruction to boats that were offshore like that? Over fifty vessels? With many exploding? It defies the logic that embers ignited these boats. Perhaps that could have happened to a few, but not all fifty vessels.

The Maui Trees

When the Maui Investigation Team showed the following images to fire captains and fire chiefs in their expert network, they, too, confirmed that this type of fire and the surviving structures was not normal. Again, when you see the buildings that were reduced to white ash and then a number of trees survived, you have a "directed energy weapon" smoking gun, as the following images illustrate.

---

87   https://mauinow.com/2023/09/02/mission-set-up-to-remove-fire-caused-marine-debris-destroyed-vessels-from-lahaina-harbor-waterways/

Post Lahaina Fires, 2023. Photo Courtesy of the Maui Community Investigation

Post Lahaina Fires, 2023. Photo Courtesy of the Maui Community Investigation

The following image shows another tree that was burned inside out in Lahaina off the main highway where branches and other twigs that would have ignited like tinder remain intact. Note that the tree bark in the following image is untouched, but the tree is hollowed out.

Post Lahaina Fires, 2023. Photo Courtesy of the Maui Community Investigation

Post Lahaina Fires, 2023. Photo Courtesy of the Maui Community Investigation

Recall what Bruce Douglas shared about energy weapons burning items at their base when you see the following images of trees that are burned inside out, and Retired Captain Matt's explanation of how this is "not natural."

Post Lahaina Fires, 2023. Photo Courtesy of the Maui Community Investigation

This next set of images comes from a parking lot near Front Street in Lahaina about 7 months after the fire. You'll see many instances of the tree being burned at the root, but the fine branches around the trees remaining untouched. What's more, there is growth around the trees indicating that many of the smaller branches were not incinerated at the root. They're burned out from the core. The Maui Community Investigation team is committed to continuing to get samples from these trees, speaking to arborists, and analyzing samples of the trees for footprints of foul play.

Photo Courtesy of Maui Community Investigation on Instagram
https://www.instagram.com/mauicommunityinvestigation/

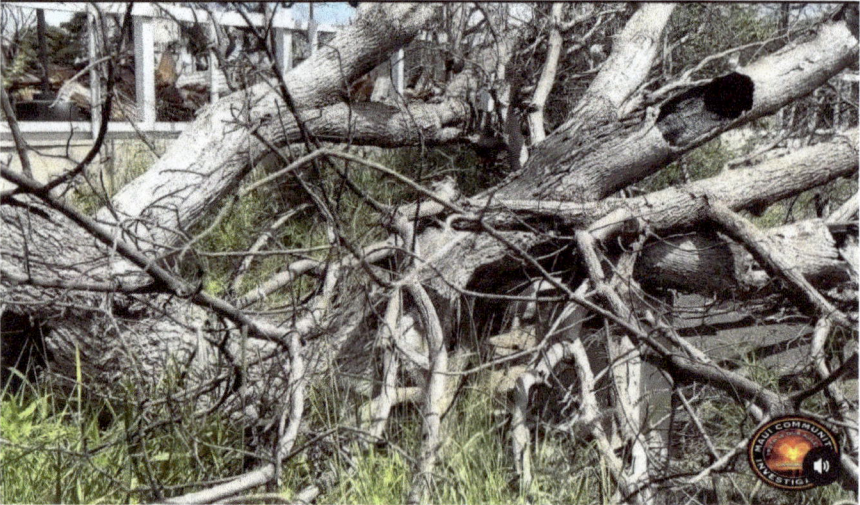

Photo Courtesy of Maui Community Investigation on Instagram
https://www.instagram.com/mauicommunityinvestigation/

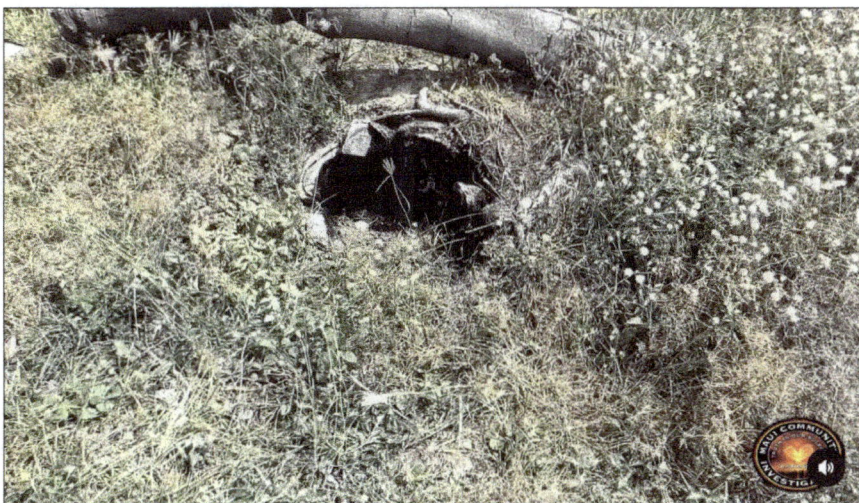

Photo Courtesy of Maui Community Investigation on Instagram
https://www.instagram.com/mauicommunityinvestigation/

Photo Courtesy of Maui Community Investigation on Instagram
https://www.instagram.com/mauicommunityinvestigation/

Photo Courtesy of Maui Community Investigation on Instagram
https://www.instagram.com/mauicommunityinvestigation/

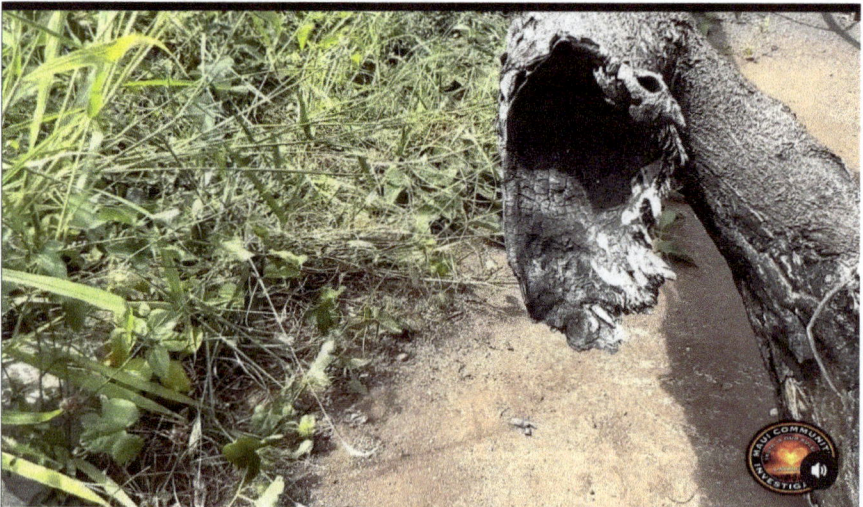

Photo Courtesy of Maui Community Investigation on Instagram
https://www.instagram.com/mauicommunityinvestigation/

Photo Courtesy of Maui Community Investigation on Instagram
https://www.instagram.com/mauicommunityinvestigation/

Is it possible that "sparks" or embers went into the trees to cause them to catch fire? Absolutely. But not likely.

Photo taken by Stephanie Pierucci
January, 2024

When cutting into the trees with a chainsaw, Bruce found that the trees had only burned about six to twelve inches from the base. That is consistent with plasma wave technology, as the energy, once again, goes to the base or the root of the tree.

Photo Courtesy of The Maui Community Investigation
www.mauicommunityinvestigation.com

CHAPTER SEVEN:
Who Would DEW This?

In Chapter Three, your authors covered weather warfare as one potential cause for the Lahaina August 8th fires. We also include Directed Energy Weapons (DEW) in that category of potential causes for the fires for a variety of reasons. Namely, the plausible deniability of geoengineering currently being passed off as "climate change." When Stephanie interviewed various representatives of the Lahaina community on Maui in January, she learned from many lifelong locals who stated that climate change was the reason for the fires. In fact, as your authors continue to interview people on Maui for the upcoming movie documentary for "Sound the Alarm," we continue to see that "climate change" is being used to gaslight citizens into thinking that "they" caused the fires with their plastic straws or disposable plastic cups. By focusing on energy and climate policy and gaslighting citizens into thinking they are the cause of the fires, the real criminals aren't just diverting attention away from themselves, but they're cashing in on it through a flood of funds to "sustainable" developments and initiatives.

Interestingly, many of the citizens we've spoken with recognize that the behavior of the August 8th fire was curious. Some even report that they or their friends saw things they would never have expected from a normal brush fire. Others claim they saw helicopters, fireballs, or lasers. In fact, we have never met a single soul on Maui who believes that the death toll is only 101 people, the official count at the time of this writing. Nevertheless, despite mounting evidence that there was nefarious activity at play, the community on Maui is either too traumatized, too exhausted and overwhelmed, or too brainwashed to invest a lot of time into this question of DEWs. Although many

Hawai'ians strongly believe the DEW theory, it's not popular to admit this in mixed company.

One of the most common theories about why objects were burned in bizarre ways is the theory of plasma waveguide technology, a type of directed energy weapon that works in tandem with microwaves. The technology we're referencing, according to Bruce Douglas, is not light, photons, nor lasers. This technology behaves very much like lightning. Lightning is a type of plasma, and directed energy weapons use plasma too. When lightning hits a tree, the energy comes down so that lightning concentrates at the base of the tree, as you can see the weatherman referencing in the image below.

TREE ON FIRE AFTER LIGHTNING STRIKE

IRES: 6 MONTHS LATER" --- with special guests, the Maui Community Investigation and research te

The Weather Channel, May 15, 2023
A St. Louis cemetery tree after being struck by lightning.

Lightning lights the base of the tree on fire. It travels downward and hits the ground, grounding out. This is when the tree catches fire at its base. With "lasers," you often see the light flashing. With plasma waveguides, you often don't see the light. Lightning is an extreme form of plasma hitting. We have harnessed that energy, according to Douglas, and made technology that is being used today in Israel, for instance, with energy weapons that can be mounted to a tank or a ground base. You can even mount these weapons to a drone. It's downright easy to start a fire with this technology.

Is this what we're actually seeing now, worldwide?

The Lahaina Pentecostal Church

The authors heard many people in our communities downplay the use of directed energy weapons in favor of theories of weather warfare until the "Lahaina Pentecostal Church" images came out. In fact, the final chapters of Stephanie's *Burn Back Better* quote Dane Wiginton, whom we'll discuss more later in this chapter, and his theories of weather warfare, as he blatantly states that there isn't enough evidence to suggest that DEWs were used in Lahaina, but that the behavior of the weather is a much better and more likely culprit for the incineration of Lahaina.

However, there are some compelling reasons to continue exploring the DEW theories. Namely, the Lahaina Pentecostal Church. The images of this church went fairly viral in the conspiracy communities because it appears as though a "laser" cut through the top of the church.

In the image below, you'll see that the southeast corner of the Lahaina Pentecostal Church appears to have experienced external electrical induction. This has been confirmed by fire behavior analysis, according to our reports. It doesn't take much to dispel the "directed energy weapon" theory when you realize that underneath the slice through the ceiling is a wire for a light fixture.[88]

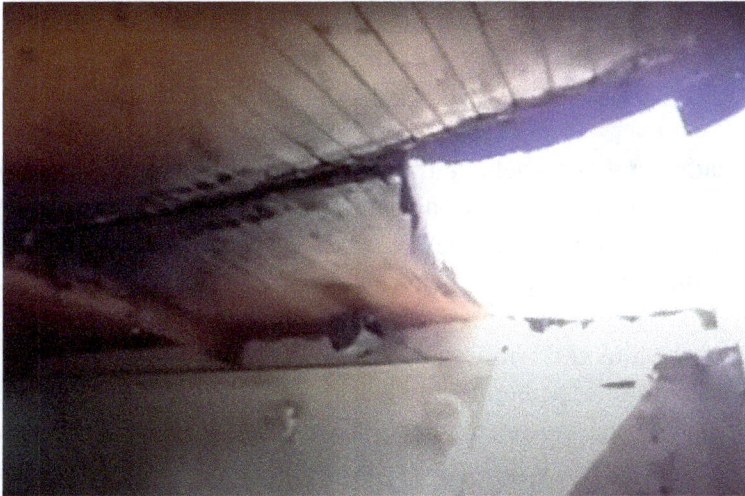

South half of ceiling, Lahaina Pentecostal Church

---

88   https://www.youtube.com/watch?v=_vNJRFRp07o

However, this ceiling in the southeast corner of the building appears to be the only area affected. In fact, the image below shows that the same wire and beam existed on the other side of the Pentecostal Church, but the incineration stopped about halfway through the ceiling of the church. The north side of the ceiling is intact, as you can see below. There isn't any trace of ash anywhere else in the church; the chairs, carpet, and even the walls appear to be fine without any evidence of smoke damage or burn.

South half of ceiling, Lahaina Pentecostal Church
Note that the north half of the ceiling is intact.

This leads experts to believe that the wire in the south corner of the Pentecostal Church served as a heating element that only burned what was touching it. It acted as if current was being induced through it from an external source of power.

Here's where this explanation gets odd. The electricity was shut off in West Maui and Lahaina during the early morning. There was no internet available to people in Lahaina, and there would have been no internal electrical power to surge through the ceiling of the Lahaina Pentecostal Church. It is for this reason that many believe that directed energy, specifically microwaves, were used during the Lahaina fire, for how else could electricity or energy be induced through the wires in the ceiling of this church?

During the Paradise fires in California as well as other fires in recent years, we have seen that flammable materials near metals are exposed to radiative infrared heat energy emitted from the resistive heating of nearby metals. The metals could be as miniscule as dust or as large as engine blocks. The nearby flammable materials will sublimate[89] into vapor or gasses or calcinate[90] into powder or stone, leaving neat piles of white ash or small beads of stone rubble.

However, in the next image you'll see on the floor of the Lahaina Pentecostal Church was found the wooden beam that housed the wire for the light fixture. It was clearly neither sublimated nor calcinated. Rather, the beam fell from the ceiling and stopped burning when it fell away from the metal wire. In the image above that shows a straight line burned through the south end of the ceiling but not the north end, you can see the path that the "energy" took when it propagated through the wire.

The Lahaina Pentecostal Church wooden beam, which fell from the ceiling on the south side of the church

Below the wooden beam, as seen below, you'll see something even more odd than the beam falling from the ceiling without burning. A close-up of the wire running along the ceiling, also below, illustrates that the

89 https://en.wikipedia.org/wiki/Sublimation_(phase_transition)
90 https://en.wikipedia.org/wiki/Calcination

wire or ceiling was burned, but nothing else flammable seemed to catch fire. However, underneath the beam is a podium with paperwork on it that didn't ignite, even though the wood laid right on top of them. We believe that the wood was no longer energized when it fell away from the metal wire, which is why it stopped burning when it fell, and why it did not carry enough heat with it to burn even the highly flammable paper on the podium in the church.

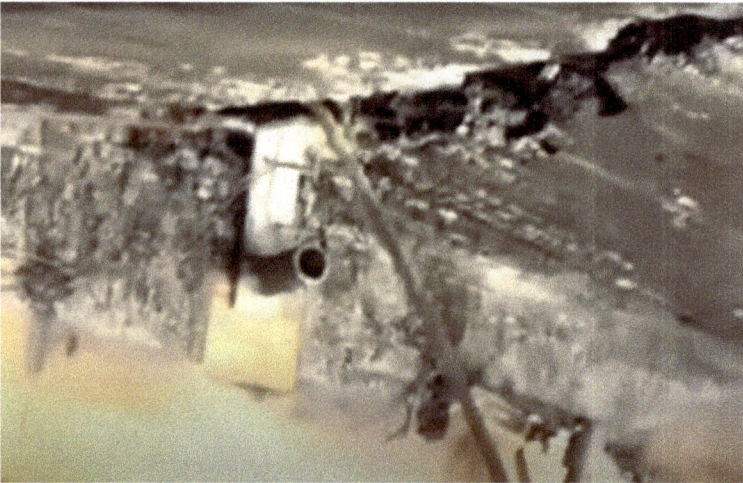

South half of ceiling, Lahaina Pentecostal Church
The wire was burned but nothing else flammable around it ignited.

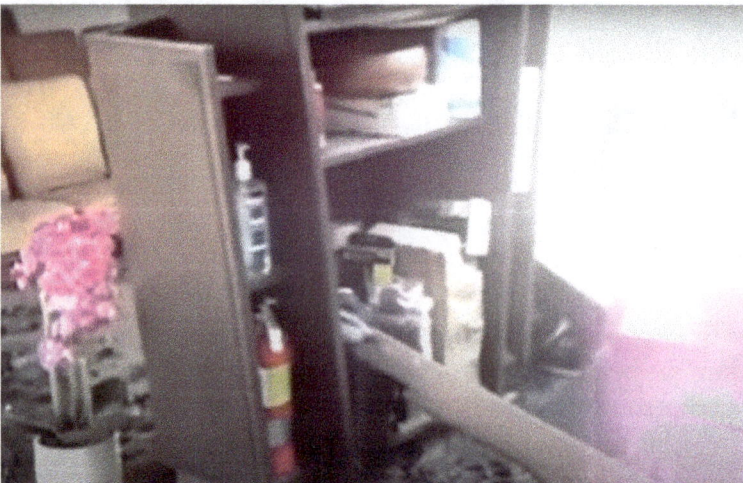

South half of ceiling, Lahaina Pentecostal Church
The wooden beam fell right onto and into the podium but didn't ignite the paperwork.

Directed Energy Weapons Were Developed... For Mankind's Safety?

The history of using directed energy as a weapon goes back much longer than fifty years, but for the purposes of this book we'll detail just the last few decades of clear "DEW" activity, starting with the development of the Defense Advanced Research Projects Agency (DARPA).

DARPA is a U.S. research and development agency established in 1958 by President Dwight D. Eisenhower that focuses on the development of emerging technologies for use by the military.

DARPA was officially launched in response to the Soviet launching of Sputnik. When the United States realized that the former Soviet Union had the ability to quickly take action on military technology developments, the United States went on the defense. DARPA launched with $520 million in funding and 150 employees within months of the launch of NASA.

Both NASA and DARPA are main characters in a wealth of conspiracies, not limited to both of them showing up in science fiction books or television in pop culture, but also due to NASA's blatant use of manipulation, theatrics, photo-shopping, and their ongoing PR campaign to be like the Disneyland of Space for both children and adults. Their PR campaigns target children as young as toddlers who have NASA sheets on their beds and NASA branded toys can be found at most retail stores and museums around the United States. Through this ubiquitous branding, NASA makes sure children never have time to question the "moon landing," the earth's shape or movement, the way planets and the sun move and spin, or even gravity itself.

When NASA launched, DARPA became focused on more "high-risk," "high-gain," and "far out" projects, according to reports from the book "Where Wizards Stay Up Late," by Matthew Lyon and Katie Hafner.[91] NASA became the Disney-like, kid-friendly technology organization for "space exploration" while DARPA handled more technology that was strictly related to war and/or defense.

---

91   Lyon, Matthew; Hafner, Katie (1999-08-19). *Where Wizards Stay Up Late: The Origins Of The Internet* (pp. 21,22). Simon & Schuster. Kindle Edition.

Forest Fire as a Military Weapon

Just over ten years after DARPA was formed, the agency sponsored a study by the U.S. Department of Agriculture's Forest Service titled "Forest Fire as a Military Weapon." A report concerning the study was released on June 1, 1970, and was archived by the Department of Defense Technical Information Center. The report was originally labeled "Secret," although distribution was authorized to the U.S. Government agencies and their contractors. It was unclassified by DARPA on May 10, 1983.[92] According to the report, forest fires were used as a weapon of war in Vietnam. "Forest Fire As A Military Weapon" reviews how the military might intentionally burn and destroy jungles and forests in Vietnam, particularly where monsoon is common and the ideal conditions to begin a forest fire come in short windows based on weather, season, and other conditions.

Sadly, the theories in this report were, indeed, materialized and enacted in Vietnam, massacring innocent people.[93]

Fires have been used as a weapon of war for a long time.

In the report "Forest Fire As A Military Weapon," the most effective methods of burning are analyzed, including details about aerial spraying, chemicals, weather conditions, and examples of potential global target cities. Below you'll see just a few images from the report, but the footnote contains a link to the entire 175 page document. [94]

---

92   https://apps.dtic.mil/sti/pdfs/AD0509724.pdf
93   https://zerogeoengineering.com/2022/forest-fire-as-a-military-weapon/
94   https://www.paperlessarchives.com/FreeTitles/ForestFireAsAMilitaryWeapon.pdf

June 1970 | U.S. Department of Agriculture — Forest Service
Authors: Craig C. Chandler, Jay R. Bentley
Sponsored by Advanced Research Projects Agency Order No. 818

For instance, on page 4 of the 175 page "Forest Fire As A Military Weapon" report, we read from the report "Summary:" [95]

> In 1965 the Joint Chiefs of Staff requested that the Secretary of Defense initiate research to determine the feasibility of measuring the flammability characteristics of forests and jungle growth, modifying flammability so that vegetation would readily support

---

95   https://www.paperlessarchives.com/FreeTitles/ForestFireAsAMilitaryWeapon.pdf

combustion and developing measures to destroy large areas of forest or jungle growth by fire. This research has been conducted by the Forest Service of the Department of Agriculture, under sponsorship of the Advanced Research Projects Agency through ARPA Order 818. The primary research attention was given to the flammability characteristics of jungle growth in tropical and monsoonal climates where forest fires seldom occur naturally.

June 1970

U. S.   Department of Agriculture — Forest Service

Sponsored by

Advanced   Research   Projects   Agency
Overseas   Defense   Research
ARPA   Order   No.   818

SECRET

SUMMARY

In 1965, the Joint Chiefs of Staff requested that the Secretary of Defense initiate research to determine the feasibility of measuring the flammability characteristics of forests and jungle growth, modifying flammability so that vegetation would readily support combustion, and developing measures to destroy large areas of forest or jungle growth by fire. This research has been conducted by the Forest Service of the Department of Agriculture, under sponsorship of the Advanced Research Projects Agency through ARPA Order 818.

Primary research attention has been given to the flammability characteristics of jungle growth in tropical and monsoonal climates where forest fires seldom occur naturally. Major consideration has been given to developing operational guidelines that utilize input data readily available to military commanders under field conditions. The following conclusions are directly pertinent to the JCS request:

Forest flammability depends on the amount of dead vegetation on or near the ground surface, the moisture content of this ground level material, and the weather at the time of burning.

Forest flammability can be greatly increased by killing all shrub vegetation, selecting optimum weather conditions for burning, and igniting fires in a preselected pattern.

Removal of overhead tree canopy requires the initiation of high intensity crown fires. In many climates, crown fires are unlikely to be achieved by any environmental modification technique. However, significant military damage can be produced by forest fires of lesser intensity.

Back to the modern day and Lahaina. We have now seen how agencies such as NASA and DARPA were developed and we understand that the Department of Defense was involved in projects that use fire to commit acts of war. It's clear that there have been decades of research on using forest fires as a weapon of war. An important question to ask now is this, "was Lahaina an act of war either of another country or global entity or corporation against the United States... or maybe even a United States business or corporate entity against their own brethren?

> *What business or entity might have benefited from the incineration of Lahaina?*
>
> *Why wouldn't, for instance, Disney want to create the next "Moana Theme Park?"*
>
> *Would some hotel chain or real estate development company want to build the next "Venice of The Pacific" tourist experience in Lahaina?*
>
> *Could it behoove the State of Hawaii to create sustainable tourism or sustainable development communities in order to impress their globalist pals at the WEF? (Read Burn Back Better if you want to see Josh Green buddy up to the WEF and why that's concerning for the people of Hawaii.)*

Dane Wiginton, activist, filmmaker, writer, and founder of "GeoengineeringWatch.org, states:

> *Vast portions of the planet are on fire. Fire behavior is unprecedented. Every year is worse than the last. Why? All official sources refuse to or are unable to offer any valid explanation for the increasingly catastrophic fires and fire behavior. Why not?* [96]
>
> *Is the military industrial complex insane enough to incinerate Earth's last remaining forests in order to achieve the objectives of the global controllers? The short answer is yes. The formerly classified U.S. military document titled "Forest Fire as a Military Weapon"*

---

96   https://www.youtube.com/watch?v=-nmL0aTXXoM

*is a truly shocking exposé of planned scorched Earth destruction.
The U.S. Forest Service actually participated in the research and
planning that went into this military instruction manual for
carrying out orchestrated forest fire catastrophes.[97] [98]*

"Forest Fire As A Military Weapon" is one of many other projects
created by the U.S. government that illustrates how capable they are
to enlist private non-military citizens and scientists to commit mass
murder for them.

"Star Wars" and The U.S. Government

In 1979, while Ronald Reagan was still the governor of California, he
visited the NORAD command base at Cheyenne Mountain Complex
to learn about their tracking and detection systems capabilities at the
time. Reagan was said to be anxious that although our military could
track attacks, they could not stop the attacks. There was technology to
illustrate where missiles were headed, but nothing in place to stop them.

Reagan allegedly felt that, in the event of an attack, this would place
him in a terrible position. Reagan would have to choose between an
immediate counterattack or scrambling to mitigate and clean-up an
attack against a U.S. target while also fighting to retaliate. In short, either
the U.S. is attacked and they focus on retaliation or they're attacked and
they focus on cleaning up post-attack.[99] There was no winning.

Presumably, Reagan brought these concerns with him to the White
House. On March 23, 1983, President Ronald Reagan announced the
Strategic Defense Initiative (SDI). In a nationally televised speech,
President Reagan famously said, "I call upon the scientific community
in this country, those who gave us nuclear weapons, to turn their great
talents to the cause of mankind and world peace, to give us the means
of rendering these nuclear weapons impotent and obsolete." [100]

Reagan's Strategic Defense Initiative, nicknamed the "Star Wars
Program," was a proposed missile defense system intended to protect

---

97   https://www.youtube.com/watch?v=-nmL0aTXXoM
98   https://www.youtube.com/watch?v=3aIqqvNnYYM
99   https://ahf.nuclearmuseum.org/ahf/history/strategic-defense-initiative-sdi/
100 https://www.thyquotes.com/nuclear-weapons/

the United States from attack by ballistic strategic nuclear weapons, including "intercontinental ballistic missiles" (ICBMs) and "submarine-launched ballistic missiles."

In 1984, the American Physical Society (APS) was asked by the newly-formed Strategic Defense Initiative Organization (SDIO) to provide some alternative concepts to a nuclear arms race and a military and strategic theory landscape that looked ominous, at best. Various concepts were put together, and the panel of experts included many of the inventors of the laser. In 1986 they presented their original report, which remained classified until early 1987 when it was released to the public. Unfortunately, it was released in redacted form, meaning that some information was missing or "blacked out" in order to protect information deemed unfit for public consumption by the government.

The report by the APS presented an analysis of every system under development to usher in more world peace by making nuclear weapons "impotent and obsolete," as President Reagan stated in his speech. Unfortunately, none of the systems were deemed ready for deployment as anti-missile systems, or at least not until "the next century." [101]

It is the belief of your authors that, just like with weather warfare, the "Star Wars" program was only alleged to be discontinued in order to advance its operations in the dark under the cover of plausible deniability, at least until the 2017 Tubbs Fire near Santa Rosa, California, introduced "unprecedented" fire behavior to the Fire Behavior Analysts at CalFire.[102]

High Energy Lasers

One of the advances made in the interim between 1987 and 2017 involved the combination of what were previously two separate systems competing with each other for directed energy contracts; high energy lasers (HELs) and high power microwaves (HPMs). On April 3, 2002, the patent shown below was issued for a device capable of "Microwave Transmission Using a Laser-Generated Plasma Beam [as a] Waveguide." [103]

---

101 https://apps.dtic.mil/sti/pdfs/ADA345227.pdf
102 https://youtu.be/-nmL0aTXXoM?si=2fdx_0Ff-BFxra76&t=27
103 https://patentimages.storage.googleapis.com/dc/02/c4/806b346d32d711/US6377436.pdf

US006377436B1

(12) **United States Patent**
Margolin

(10) Patent No.: **US 6,377,436 B1**
(45) Date of Patent: **Apr. 23, 2002**

(54) **MICROWAVE TRANSMISSION USING A LASER-GENERATED PLASMA BEAM WAVEGUIDE**

(76) Inventor: **Jed Margolin**, 3570 Pleasant Echo Dr., San Jose, CA (US) 95148-1916

(*) Notice: Subject to any disclaimer, the term of this patent is extended or adjusted under 35 U.S.C. 154(b) by 0 days.

(21) Appl. No.: **09/543,252**

(22) Filed: **Apr. 5, 2000**

Related U.S. Application Data

(60) Provisional application No. 60/173,148, filed on Dec. 27, 1999.

(51) Int. Cl.[7] **H01T 23/00**
(52) U.S. Cl. **361/230**; 307/149
(58) Field of Search .... 361/230, 231; 307/149; 372/1, 4, 9, 14, 15, 29.01, 109, 76; 250/396 R, 423 R, 424; 385/147; 342/54; 359/27, 34, 179, 188, 298, 299, 342, 349

(56) **References Cited**

U.S. PATENT DOCUMENTS

3,719,829 A	*	3/1973	Vaill 307/149
5,726,855 A		3/1998	Mourou et al. 361/213
5,930,313 A	*	7/1999	Slinker et al. 376/127
6,111,237 A	*	8/2000	Paustian 361/117

OTHER PUBLICATIONS

News Release: Los Alamos National Labortary, Aug. 19, 1996, "There's new light at the end of the tunnel for some laser–based technologies." http://www/.lanl.gov.
Product Announcement: Lawrence Livermore National Laboratory, "High–Average–Power Titanium:Sapphire Laser", http://www.lllnl.gov/IPandC/op96/05/5f–hig.html, No Date.
Company Information: Hardric Laboratories, Inc., http://www.hardic.com, No Month 1999.
Product/Services Announcement: Hardric Laboratories, Inc. "Beryllium Optics", http://www.hardric.com/page 4.html, No Date.

* cited by examiner

Primary Examiner—Ronald W. Leja

(57) **ABSTRACT**

A directed energy beam system uses an ultra-fast laser system, such as one using a titanium-sapphire infrared laser to produce a thin ionizing beam through the atmosphere. The beam is moved in either a circular or rectangular fashion to produce a conductive shell to act as a waveguide for microwave energy. Because the waveguide is produced by a plasma it is called a plasma beam waveguide. The directed energy beam system can be used as a weapon, to provide power to an unmanned aerial vehicle (UAV) such as for providing communications in a cellular telephone system, or as an ultra-precise radar system.

11 Claims, 23 Drawing Sheets

"Microwave Transmission Using a Laser-Generated Plasma Beam Waveguide"

J. Phys. D: Appl. Phys. **45** (2012) 265401 M Alshershby *et al*

Table 1. Conductivity and skin depth of plasma filament for different values of wavelengths of microwave radiation and different concentrations of free electrons.

N_e (cm^{-3})	$\lambda_{mw} = 3$ mm		$\lambda_{mw} = 1$ cm		$\lambda_{mw} = 6$ cm	
	$\sigma\ (\Omega^{-1}\,m^{-1})$	$\delta\ (\mu m)$	$\sigma\ (\Omega^{-1}\,m^{-1})$	$\delta\ (\mu m)$	$\sigma\ (\Omega^{-1}\,m^{-1})$	$\delta\ (\mu m)$
10^{15}	19.61	359	25.65	574	26.33	1.38×10^3
10^{16}	193.10	115	249.12	184	256.26	445
10^{17}	1.90×10^3	36.50	2.42×10^5	59	2.48×10^3	142
Copper 10^{22}	5.57×10^7	0.2	5.61×10^7	0.4	5.63×10^7	1

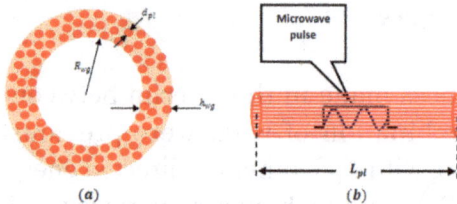

Figure 1. (*a*) Beam pattern and filament distribution after propagation and (*b*) schematic diagram of a cylindrical microwave waveguide formed by plasma filaments.

"Guiding microwave radiation using laser-induced filaments: the hollow conducting waveguide concept"

The purpose of the high energy laser is to ionize, or "charge" the air through which it travels. This creates a static electric trail of ions called plasma. This plasma trail is electrically conductive and, like other conductive materials, the charged air particles are capable of reflecting microwaves. When these lasers are arranged into a ring configuration (as seen above), they create a hollow cylindrical tube of charged air particles that can contain microwaves and guide them to the intended target, sort of like an air duct.[104]

This contains the microwaves within the virtually tubular form of the cylindrical beam and keeps them from spreading out in a cone like they normally would, as shown in the images below.

This can explain the unusual phenomena where microwave effects are observed in tightly contained areas that seem to prevent collateral damage to adjacent objects.

Figure 1. Illustrative Effects of HELs Versus HPM Weapons

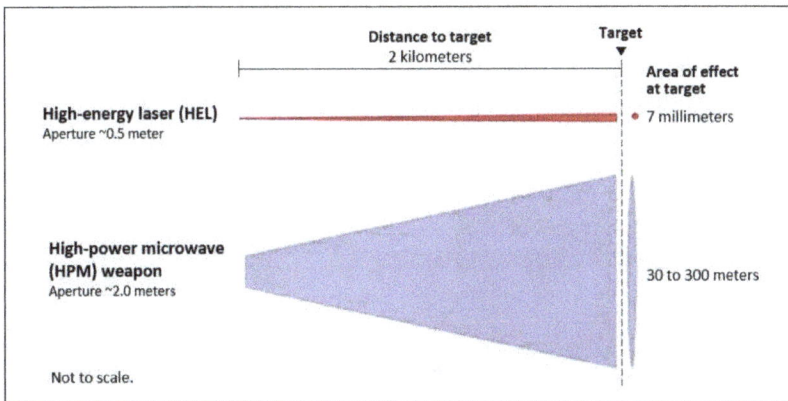

Laser-generated plasma beams can keep microwaves from spreading out like normal

About one year prior to the Tubbs Fire, the U.S. Congress coincidentally passed the "Directed Energy Weapons Systems Acquisition Act," on April 12, 2016. The Act was aimed at "the rapid acquisition of directed energy weapons systems by the Department of Defense, and for other purposes,"[105] as shown in the image below.

---

104 https://www.researchgate.net/profile/Mostafa-Alshershby/publication/241779808_Guiding_microwave_radiation_using_laser-induced_filaments_The_hollow_conducting_waveguide_concept/links/5deceb3c92851c83646cf154/Guiding-microwave-radiation-using-laser-induced-filaments-The-hollow-conducting-waveguide-concept.pdf?_tp=eyJjb250ZXh0Ijp7ImZpcnN0UGFnZSI6InB1YmxpY2F0aW9uIiwicGFnZSI6InB1YmxpY2F0aW9uIn19

105 https://www.congress.gov/114/bills/s2778/BILLS-114s2778is.pdf

The Directed Energy Weapons Systems Acquisition Act also states:

The Committee of Armed Services of the Senate noted in the report accompanying this bill that since the 1960s, the Department of Defense has invested more than 6 billion dollars in directed energy science and technology initiatives and that this committee is concerned that, despite the significant investment, the Department's directed energy initiatives are not resourced at levels necessary to transition them to a full-scale acquisition program.

II

114TH CONGRESS
2D SESSION

S. 2778

To amend title 10, United States Code, to provide for the rapid acquisition of directed energy weapons systems by the Department of Defense, and for other purposes.

IN THE SENATE OF THE UNITED STATES

APRIL 12, 2016

Mr. HEINRICH (for himself and Mr. INHOFE) introduced the following bill; which was read twice and referred to the Committee on Armed Services

A BILL

To amend title 10, United States Code, to provide for the rapid acquisition of directed energy weapons systems by the Department of Defense, and for other purposes.

1   *Be it enacted by the Senate and House of Representa-*

2 *tives of the United States of America in Congress assembled,*

3 **SECTION 1. SHORT TITLE.**

4   This Act may be cited as the "Directed Energy

5 Weapon Systems Acquisition Act of 2016".

6 **SEC. 2. FINDINGS.**

7   Congress makes the following findings:

8   (1) The Committee on Armed Services of the

9   Senate noted in the report accompanying S. 1356

The Directed Energy Weapons Systems Acquisition Act of April 12th, 2016

Our theory is that the Act was signed by Congress as an excuse for the Government to throw billions more dollars in tax revenue at the Directed Energy Weapons program, giving a virtual blank check to the men tasked with directing your investment from the Department of Defense, including Thomas Karr, James Trebes, and Frank E. Peterkin. These accomplices all work at the Department of Defense in the "Office of The Under Secretary of Defense For Research and Engineering (OUSD R&E).[106] Frank E Peterkin, the Principal Director at OUSD R&E, is responsible for coordinating directed energy development and implementation efforts across the Department of Defense. This includes developing and maintaining the Department of Defense roadmap for the development of directed energy weapons.[107]

How The U.S. Government Justifies DEWs

Without question, part of defense was creating a viable suite of offensive technologies and strategies ranging from "lasers" to ionospheric heaters used to manipulate weather a la "Forest Fires As A Military Weapon." In other words, the best defense is a good offense. The technologies listed on .gov and .mil websites for public viewing include many types and variations of directed energy weapons.

The U.S. Government Accountability Office states:

> Directed energy weapons—such as lasers—use energy fired at the speed of light. These weapons can produce force that ranges from deterrent, to damaging, to destructive.

> ...Directed energy weapons (DEW) use concentrated electromagnetic energy to combat enemy forces and assets. These weapons include high energy lasers and other high power electromagnetics—such as millimeter wave and high power microwave weapons. Unlike weapons that fire bullets or missiles, DEWs can respond to a threat in different ways. For example, they can temporarily degrade electronics on a drone or physically destroy it.

---

106 https://youtu.be/6gcZcuX47Cs?si=60u9kGzvnioUFhgj&t=988
107 https://www.ucf.edu/research/person/james-trebes/

Different types of electromagnetic energy have different properties. For example, the wavelength affects what the directed energy can penetrate—such as metal or human skin.

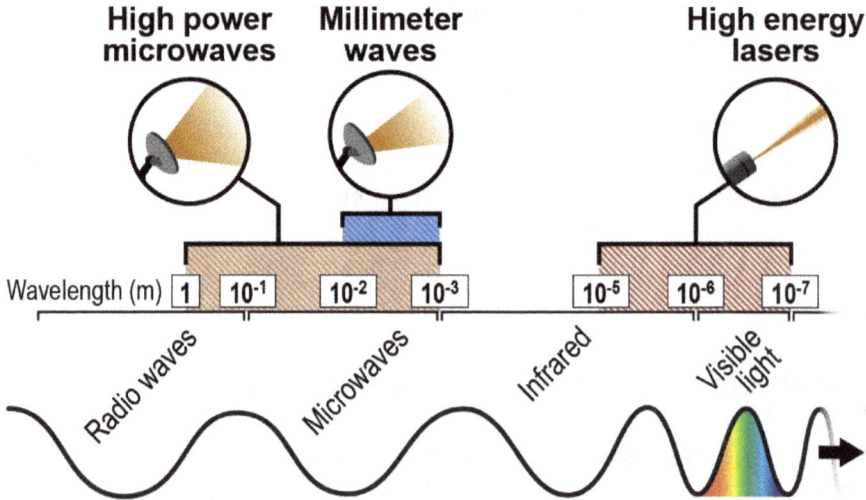

Source: GAO. | GAO-23-106717

"Location of directed energy weapons on the electromagnetic spectrum."
Photo courtesy of the U.S. Government Office of Accountability. GAO-23-106717

While DEWs use electromagnetic energy similar to everyday items, such as household microwaves, their output is vastly higher.

High power microwave weapons produce microwaves, which have longer wavelengths than high energy lasers and millimeter wave weapons. These weapons can produce more than 100 megawatts of power, which is nearly 150,000 times more powerful than the average household microwave. Like millimeter wave weapons, they can also affect multiple targets because of their larger beam size.

Each DEW can produce a range of effects from nonlethal to lethal, depending on factors such as the time on target, the distance to the target, and even the part of the target on which the DEW is focused. DEWs can use this range of effects to graduate responses to a threat. A graduated response could start with temporarily preventing use of an asset or its access to an area and increase to destruction of the asset if necessary.[108]

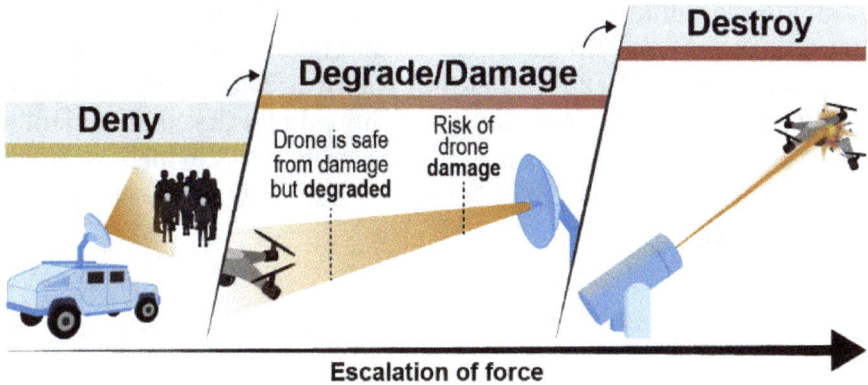

"Examples of graduated responses using directed energy weapons."
Photo courtesy of the U.S. Government Office of Accountability. GAO-23-106717

The image below shows a "Laser Weapon System" at the White Sands Missile Range in New Mexico.

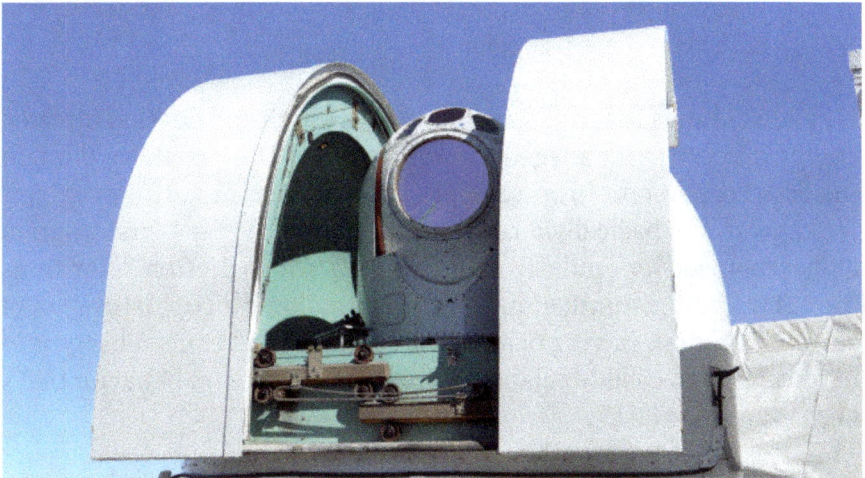

Demonstrator Laser Weapon System at the White Sands Missile Range, New Mexico

---

108 https://www.gao.gov/products/gao-23-106717

Because DEWs use energy fired at the speed of light, they're fast, cheap, and effective compared to missiles which are expensive, heavy, and have little to no margin for error. What's more, DEWs may have unlimited ammunition; they fire as long as they have power.[109] Weather conditions can limit the effectiveness and quality of DEWs, which is why you'll generally expect that they will be fired on a clear day. The U.S. Government Office of Accountability admits that there is still a question about the long-term health effects of DEWs, which concerns the authors for the people of Maui who may have been exposed to directed energy.

Regret

> The Defense Science Board Task Force on Directed Energy Weapon Systems and Technology Applications (the "Task Force") found that "directed energy offers promise as a transformational 'game changer' in military operations, able to augment and improve operational capabilities in many areas. The Task Force believes that the range of potential application is sufficient to warrant significantly increased attention to the scope and direction of efforts to assess, develop, and field appropriate laser, microwave, and millimeter wave weapons."[110]

If I hadn't known that they continued to research and develop directed energy in secret after allegedly discontinuing SDI, I would've thought the Task Force report to be a complete 180 on their part. However, now we know it was basically a rapid evolution of the Star Wars program at "warp speed", popularly called SDI II, which I often refer to as the "Star Trek" initiative due to the technological sophistication of current iterations having beams contained within beams. This type of hardware could easily explain the "unprecedented" fire behavior that's been seen since 2017.

---

109   https://www.gao.gov/products/gao-23-106717
110   https://www.congress.gov/114/bills/s2778/BILLS-114s2778is.pdf

CHAPTER EIGHT:
Carbon Copies of Maui

The 2024 Chile Fires

On February 2, 2024, Chile experienced the deadliest fire in their history. According to the Associated Press, 137 people were declared deceased as of May 2024 and 16,000 people were made homeless after what was called a "forest fire." The fire mimicked many of the same elements of other fires that screamed to have been manipulated or fueled with directed energy.

We suspect that the "real" perpetrators of the Chilean fire saw how rapidly word spread about the Maui DEW questions and allegations of foul play. In order to presumably find their own scapegoat similar to what Maui did to Kaleo Manuel, Chile named a volunteer firefighter of starting the fires and former employee of the National Forest Corporation with planning the event. Prosecutors indicated that the motive for Mondaca was to provide more work for firefighters, and that there may have been others involved. [111]

The fire in Chile began in the Lago Peñuelas National Reserve in the mountainous eastern edge of Viña del Mar. This beach resort town was famous for its Latin music festival. Nearby cities Quilpué and Villa Alemana were also affected by the fires, which spread in the dry weather with strong winds.

---

111 https://apnews.com/article/chile-forest-fires-arrests-ab431b293fe71d9c0e5b0381778b8ffc

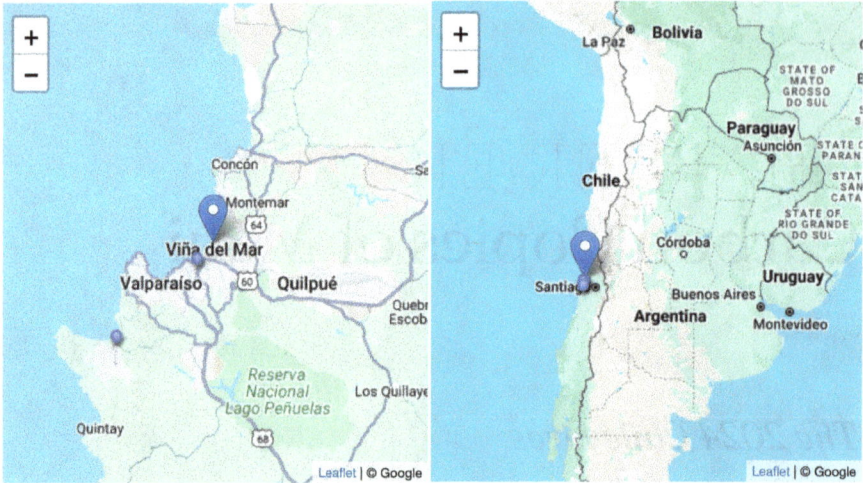

The fire caused the interruption of traffic on local highway Route 68 as well as F-718. Just 15 minutes after the fire began, at 3:25 p.m., a red alert was declared in Valparaíso Province due to a second fire that affected Las Docas road, south of Valparaíso. At 3:54 p.m., just 19 minutes after the second fire (and about 20 miles away), yet another fire was reported in Lo Moscoso, in the communes of Quilpué and Villa Alemana, directly upwind from the city of Viña del Mar.[112]

By 10:00 p.m., more than 15,000 acres of land had been affected by the fires.

It is due to the rapid near-simultaneous commencement of several fires in the same region that there has been rumor of foul play by arsonists and/or the aid of directed energy.

---

112 https://www.vinadelmar2024.sdewes.org/

The 2024 Chile fires in Viña del Mar, Lo Moscoso and Quilpué.

These three fires spread across an area of about forty miles and quickly encompassed the "Smart City" of Viña del Mar and even spread into part of Valparaíso.

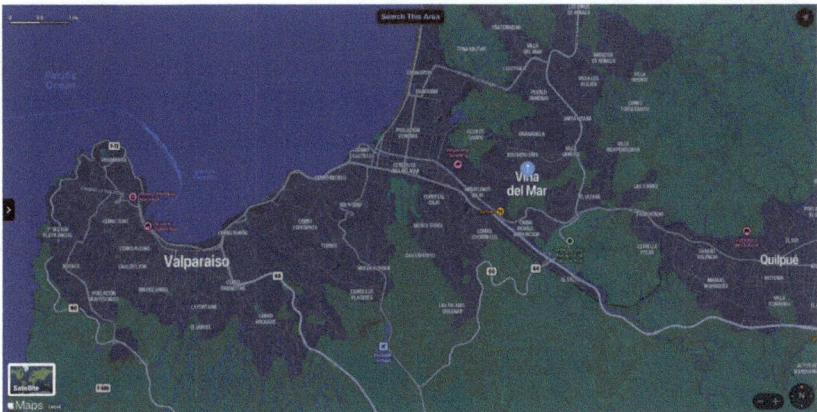

An "official" total of 131 people were killed in the fires, of whom only 35 had been identified at the time of this writing in summer of 2024. At least 14,000 homes were affected by the fires around Viña del Mar alone, while over 370 people were reported as still missing in that area.

Infrared map of Valparaíso. (Red is unburned vegetation, black is the burn scar)

The 2024 Chile fires revealed many similarities with the Lahaina Maui fire. These include:

1. Fires starting uphill and upwind from a densely populated area[113] that was slated for "sustainable" redevelopment and just hosted a smart grid conference a month prior[114];
2. No water in the fire hydrants;[115]
3. Most materials were reduced to a white/gray ash, with the exception of some blue, green, and red objects that stuck out among areas of gray;

---

113 https://www.bbc.com/news/articles/czddewn1gd1o
114 https://www.vinadelmar2024.sdewes.org/
115 https://www.nytimes.com/video/world/americas/100000009306678/chile-fires-water-access.html

4. Melted materials that would require, traditionally, a fire much hotter than a traditional forest fire;
5. Difficulty in identifying the truth death toll;
6. Little to no warning to the citizens;
7. Scapegoats named.

Below you'll see what we refer to as "leftover colors." The photo shows mostly white ash, but also some shades of red, green and blue. In laser tattoo removal clinics, it's common that after the initial near-infrared invisible laser is used, the colors blue, green and red require a second and third laser to remove.[116]

Removal of red colors requires a 532 nm laser, which is a visible wavelength in the green color of the spectrum. In order to remove blues and greens, wavelengths between 730 and 785 nm are required.

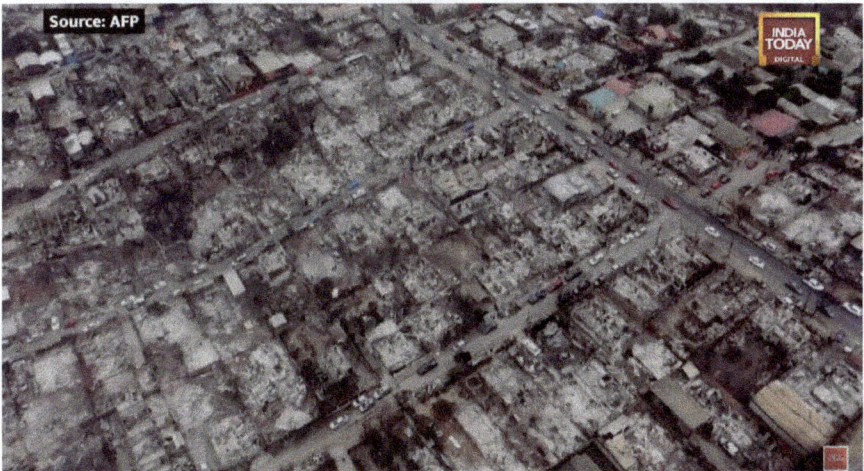

It's commonly known among experienced tattoo removal clinicians that blues and greens are the most difficult to remove, even at the correct wavelength.[117] [118] This is because colors with blue pigments are less interactive with light, which also includes many shades of green. This is especially true for a specific shade of blue called "non-photo blue" (or non-repro blue), which is used by comic book artists and

116 https://youtu.be/D5jpAcNrOMA?si=difzBTJvOW5ITCWZ&t=361
117 https://removery.com/blog/color-tattoo-removal/
118 https://www.youtube.com/watch?v=n_hVWMFiAhI

animators to sketch or write directly on the storyboard or animation frame without having to erase pencil lines, being a particular shade of blue that cannot be detected by graphic arts camera film.[119]

Below, you'll see five images that give a panoramic view from one side of a street to the other. This was taken from a video during which a camera pans from one side of the street to another. The video clearly illustrates that the damage somehow skipped the blue house on the left. The fence between the truck and the blue house is also damaged, with burned debris at the bottom of the fence.[120]

The Chile fires also exhibited strange burn behavior, similar to Maui. For instance, combustible materials only burned within a few feet of metal objects (such as the pallet seen below), and metals such as aluminum were melted into a running liquid, which usually would require temperatures well above 1,220 degrees Fahrenheit.

The most clear "ringer" for directed energy is the fact that even steel was softened and glass was melted. These could indicate the energy equivalent of temperatures around 2,750 degrees Fahrenheit.

The aluminum and glass from the car in the photo below were both melted, and the wooden pallet only burned up to a few feet away from the car, almost as if the car itself was a source of radiative heat. The pallet no more than six feet from the vehicle remains untouched or unaffected, according to what this photo reveals.

Radiative heating follows the "inverse-square law" in physics, which decreases exponentially with distance, unlike convective or

---

119 https://en.wikipedia.org/wiki/Non-photo_blue
120 https://youtu.be/dD0m6XFGjYs?si=1t6KOQs5y0ZFWlq1&t=1060

conductive heating.[121] This might explain why the pallet was only burned in close proximity to the car. It may also explain why there is a clear line where the burn stops between one pallet to the next, despite wood being traditionally and normally very flammable.

F.

In the photo above, also notice that next to the right side of the car is a blue polycarbonate water jug, which would've been within the same radius that "burned" the wood. Nonetheless, the blue plastic appears to be unaffected. It's entirely possible that the container could've been placed there afterward. However, this footage was shared before many could return to their properties, and a curfew was put in place to limit travel and theft that evening.[122]

During the Chilean fires in February of 2024, not only rims, but aluminum engine blocks melted as well, as seen from India Today on February 5th.[123] This would require a much longer or hotter "burn" than would be required to melt rims. The rims would begin to melt around 1220 F, but a fully liquified engine block could indicate an energy equivalent of temperatures up to 1,400 degrees fahrenheit, and for a longer time than most combustibles or accelerants would typically burn.

---

121 https://en.wikipedia.org/wiki/Inverse-square_law#Light_and_other_electromagnetic_radiation

122 https://apnews.com/article/chile-forest-fires-drought-casualties-4f85c0671d70cfcb0a677d410a0b3961

123 https://youtu.be/EFdu2iFhUuA?si=EFu7rWdQzzUZG7cm&t=232

Image from India Today, February 5th 2024 [124]

In the image below from Al Jazeera on February 4, 2024, you will see a vehicle that appears to have lost all of its aluminum, including door handles. The back window has fallen out and draped itself across the trunk. The glass window was only softened and not liquified, which could indicate an energy equivalent of temperatures around 2,750 degrees Fahrenheit.[125]

Image from Al Jazeera, February 4th, 2024

124 https://youtu.be/EFdu2iFhUuA?si=EFu7rWdQzzUZG7cm&t=232
125 https://youtu.be/6pobnGdW78o?si=5Ub6tk4g4jGQ7kCo&t=13

The image below shows the structural steel alloy frame of a building in Chile that has burned and partially collapsed. For a structural steel alloy to soften like this, it could indicate the energetic equivalent of a possible temperature of around 2,500–3,000 degrees Fahrenheit.

Most of the materials that burned in Chile were in close proximity to metals, and the metals themselves didn't appear to fare very well, either, according to images we've seen.

DEADLY WILDFIRES
OVER 100 DEAD AFTER CATASTROPHIC WILDFIRES IN CHILE

Another DEW giveaway is below. The tree at center right seems to be burning a little too evenly along its surface, where it appears to be enveloped by a layer of flame (or possibly plasma) about an inch thick along its entire length. It appears as if the entire length of the tree is equally energized, which would not likely happen if a combustive flame started at one end and worked its way along the length of the tree, regardless of whether it came from the top or bottom.

The next image shows the leaves on that same tree, which are being ignited simultaneously as if they were all being equally energized at the same time, without having been ignited by a combustive flame that would travel from one leaf to the next as it makes its way along the branches.

A couple days after the fire, the current Chilean president, Gabriel Boric, surveyed the damage to Viña del Mar and Valparaiso via helicopter.

A couple days later, the former Chilean president, Sebastian Pinera, died during a helicopter crash while everyone else on board survived.[126]

President Gabriel Boric of Chile, February 2024

Reuters   World ∨   Business ∨   Markets ∨   Sustainability ∨   More ∨   My View ∨   Q

Americas

Chile's former president Sebastian Pinera dies in helicopter crash

By **Natalia A. Ramos Miranda**, **Anthony Esposito** and **Fabian Cambero**

February 6, 2024 9:44 PM CST · Updated 4 months ago

SANTIAGO, Feb 6 (Reuters) - Chilean ex-President Sebastian Pinera died in a helicopter crash on Tuesday, sending the country he led for two terms into mourning and prompting an outpouring of condolences from leaders across Latin America.

The helicopter carrying Pinera, 74, and three others plunged into a lake in southern Chile. The former president was pronounced dead shortly after rescue personnel arrived at the scene. The other three passengers survived.

---

126 https://www.reuters.com/world/americas/chile-ex-president-sebastianpinera-dies-helicopter-crash-local-media-says-2024-02-06/

Why mention this helicopter crash of Chile's former president, Sebastian Pinera?

Pinera wanted to nationalize Chile's lithium industry, which would have seized control of lithium mines from the private businesses that were using Chile's lithium to become the world's largest producers of lithium batteries.

With the globalist's green movement in full swing, lithium is now being pushed as the "new oil".

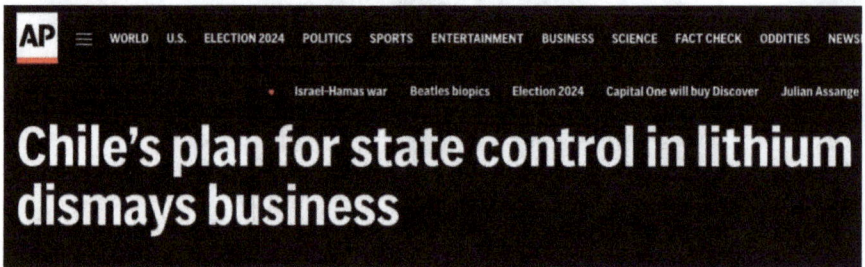

Chile's plan for state control in lithium dismays business

Which companies would have been most affected by Chile's attempts to seize control of their lithium?

According to our research, the leader in the world's lithium production is "Albemarle," a U.S. company that only leads in production because of its access to Chile's lithium mines.

Who owns lithium mines in Chile?

Currently, only two companies mine lithium in Chile: Chilean firm SQM, which is nearly a quarter-owned by a Chinese company, and U.S. firm Albemarle. They are both private and operate in the largest of the country's more than 40 salt flats that are home to lithium reserves. Jun 23, 2023

Without having access to Chile's lithium, Albemarle likely wouldn't be in position to lead the global push to go "all electric" on lithium batteries.

TECH

The rise of Albemarle, the world's largest lithium producer

PUBLISHED SAT, JUN 3 2023·8:00 AM EDT | UPDATED MON, JUN 5 2023·7:28 AM EDT

Shawn Baldwin

SHARE f 𝕏 in ✉

Who is behind Albemarle and their rise in dominance, despite the world's reluctance to go electric? As you can see, by this "Yahoo Finance" search of the ticker symbol ALB for "Albemarle," their major shareholders include "Vanguard Group," "Blackrock Inc," and "State Street," nearly identical to the shareholders of Hawai'ian Electric Company (HECO,) Pacific Gas & Electric Company (PG+E) of California, and virtually every other major energy provider.[127]

yahoo! finance

ALB

Top Institutional Holders

Holder

Vanguard Group Inc

Blackrock Inc.

Capital Research Global Investors

Capital International Investors

State Street Corporation

What your authors find most curious in common with these fires isn't just the Vanguard, Blackrock, and State Street holdings in the utility

---

127 https://youtu.be/QsiGiziM7Vw?si=fFmoYYigrgeHAC0A

and energy companies, but the number of cities that have historic wildfires which also have Smart City development plans on the table.

Valparaiso, Chile has been a hub for Smart City development since at least as early as 2017, with the launch of their "Smart City GO! Campaign. Valparaiso hosted their "Smart City Business Valparaiso 2017" international seminar and expo, with "international experts" trying to sell Smart City tech-apologies to create a new form of techno-fascism through public-private partnerships.[128]

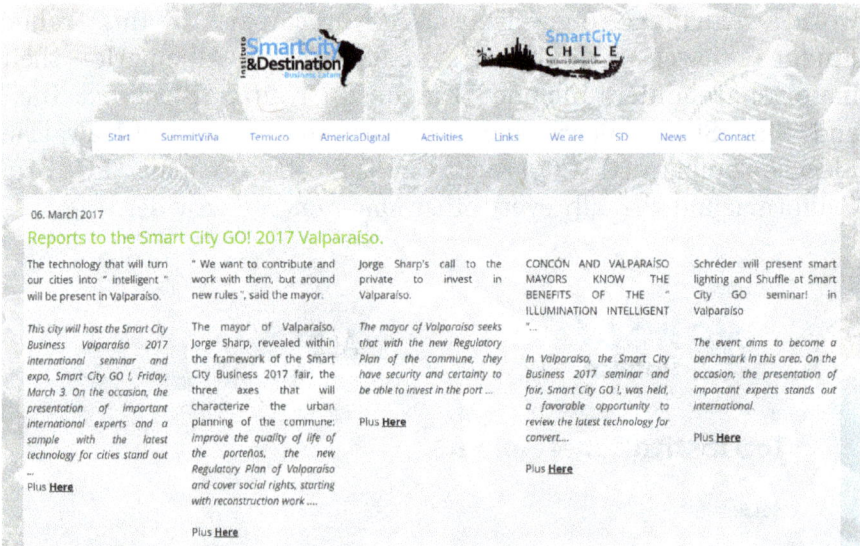

Viña del Mar, in the Valparaiso region, is the headquarters for "Smart City Business Chile".[129] I looked up their address at 230 Calle Seis Oriente, and it conveniently sits just outside of the burn zone, on the Viña del Mar side of Valparaiso.

---

128 https://www.smartcitychile.cl/2017/03/06/reportajes-al-smart-city-go-2017-valpara%C3%ADso/

129 https://www.zoominfo.com/c/smart-city-business-chile/425333445

Z zoominfo

Smart City Business Chile
Business Services · Chile · <25 Employees

View Company Info for Free

About

Headquarters 230 Calle Seis Oriente, Vina del Mar, Valparaiso, 2530769, Chile

Phone Number +56 954418249

Website www.smartcitybusiness.cl

Revenue $6.6 Million

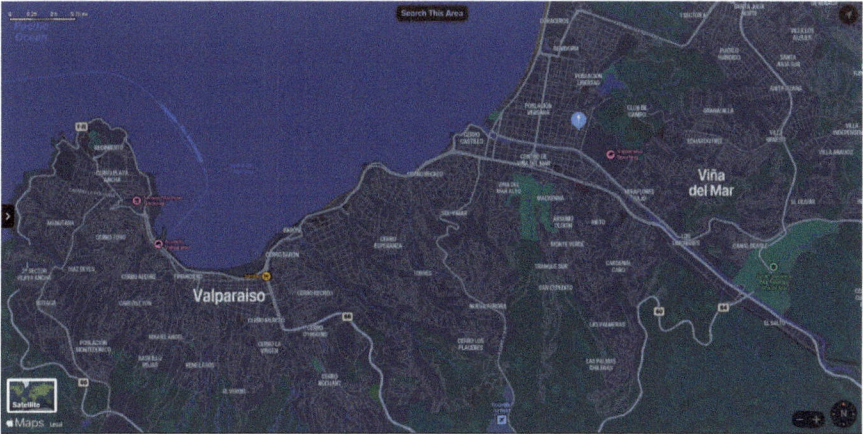

It seems as convenient as it is coincidental that the energy institutions had a "Smart Grid" conference in Vina Del Mar from January 14th to the 17th, just two weeks before the fires![130]

---

130 https://www.vinadelmar2024.sdewes.org/

In fact, Chile leads Latin America in deployment of smart city applications, with Santiago poised as the leader in the race to become the next smart city.[131]

We recommend that you be vigilant about any SEGITTUR "Smart Tourism Destination" requirements, 15-minute city plans, or TOD corridor projects going on in Santiago, or in your own community, for that matter.

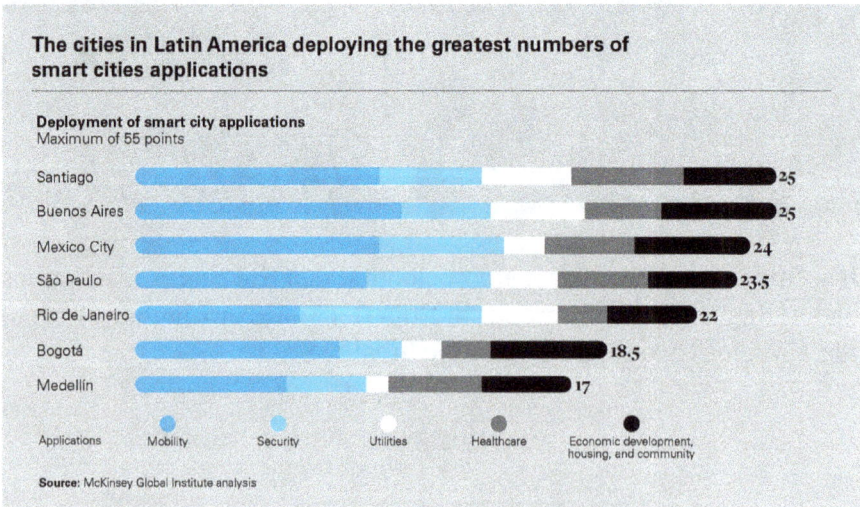

The cities in Latin America deploying the greatest numbers of smart cities applications

Deployment of smart city applications
Maximum of 55 points

Santiago	25
Buenos Aires	25
Mexico City	24
São Paulo	23.5
Rio de Janeiro	22
Bogotá	18.5
Medellín	17

Applications: Mobility • Security • Utilities • Healthcare • Economic development, housing, and community

Source: McKinsey Global Institute analysis

---

131 https://www.jdsupra.com/legalnews/a-bright-future-smart-cities-in-latin-8247484/

The fact is that virtually every major city has plans for public-private partnerships that usher in this sort of techno-fascism through Smart City development. Global corporations are making deals with local politicians that have been either bribed or bamboozled into buying and promoting their propaganda.

Shane has gone into detail on most of the urban planning "transit-oriented development (TOD) plans for the State of Hawaii on Traci's "Brush Junkie" channel. However, covering every major city is an undertaking that's too arduous for even the most dauntless researcher.

If you're interested in finding smart city plans near you, start with their Strategic Plans for "Transit Oriented Development (TOD) Corridors," "Long Range Transit Plans," "Community Corridors," "Commercial Corridors," "Smart Grids," "Wildland Urban Interfaces (WUIs)," "Ecobarrios," "Smart Tourism Destinations," "15-minute cities," and anything labeled "Smart," "sustainable," "carbon neutral," or "zero carbon."

The 2024 Texas Fires

2024 has been a banner year for the largest "forest fires" in a community or country's history.

The Texas Smokehouse Creek Fire began on February 26, 2024 and continued through March 14th, and is the largest fire in Texas history, as well as the largest fire of 2024, similar to Lahaina being the largest fire in Hawai'ian history. This fire devastated the Texas Panhandle, including Amarillo, and parts of Oklahoma, scorching over 1.2 million acres, destroying 500 structures, and leading to 3 deaths, including Zeb Smith, a fire chief who died from a heart attack while he was fighting a structure fire. Smith and his team had been battling the fire for nine days prior to his heart attack.

In Texas, one of the earlier official causes of the fire is from a downed power line due to a broken utility pole combined with strong winds and hotter than normal conditions. This sounds eerily familiar to how the Lahaina fire was rumored to have begun, at least before people started to wake up and observe the obvious holes in that theory.

This single broken utility pole, owned by Xcel Energy, is being used to explain the entire fire, which included other fires that sprung up within twenty-four hours of ignition as strong winds fanned the flames eastward. Xcel Energy is also involved in lawsuits by the victims of the Texas "Wildfire".[132]

According to NBC: "Authorities have not said what ignited the fires, but strong winds, dry grass, and unseasonably warm temperatures fed the blazes.[133]

The narrative of the origins and intensity of the fire and how it was able to spread so quickly is identical to the narrative in Maui.

The area burned is considered the beef capital of the world and home to 85% of the state's cattle. This fire will have devastating effects on the cattle industry for years to come.

As of March 15, 2024, it was estimated that 7,000 cattle died in this fire, but the final number is closer to 10,000, possibly due to the fact that many injured cows have been euthanized due to injuries. Many ranchers have not only lost their homes but their source of income and the prospects of starting over are grim since the grazing land, farm houses, and equipment has also been destroyed.

A common sight during these fires was to see cattle still alive but with eyes burned and hoofs bleeding, which meant the ranchers had to put them down. Looking at the remnants of these homes are very reminiscent of Lahaina and Chile, but there are other anomalies in the Texas fire as well. The mainstream media blamed climate change and higher than normal temperatures as the leading factor to why the fire is the largest fire in Texas history, so let's explore that in detail.

On February 29, 2024, while the fire was still raging through the Texas panhandle, there is evidence that temperatures dropped to 30 degrees fahrenheit and snow was falling.[134] That invalidates the theory that the Texas fires were caused by hotter than normal temperatures.

According to the National Weather Service, Amarillo's average temperature for the month of March is a high of 63 degrees fahrenheit and a low of 33 degrees, making it 30 degrees lower than normal. Many videos and pictures were taken of the snow-covered landscape that blanketed the scorched land, such as the one below.

---

132 https://en.wikipedia.org/wiki/Smokehouse_Creek_Fire#:~:text=The%20Smokehouse%20Creek%20Fire%20was,including%20the%20town%20of%20Canadian

133 https://www.nbcdfw.com/news/local/texas-news/snow-falls-in-texas-panhandle-after-states-largest-wildfire-scorches-more-than-1-million-acres/3475625/

134 https://apnews.com/article/texas-panhandle-fire-evacuations-cbbb6a279bef1bd020722ed48927114a

Eighty-three year-old Joyce Blankenship was unable to escape the fire. Because of a roadblock, her son was unable to rescue her in time. Blankenship was later found deceased in her home. The only other official fatality of this fire as of the time of this writing is Cindy Owen of Amarillo, Texas, who died February 29th in a burn center in Oklahoma City.[135]

After researching Amarillo's City planning website, we find that they stated:

> *City Plan — Vision 2045 (Comprehensive Plan) is a groundbreaking, community-driven initiative, a long-term strategic framework shaped to foster equitable growth, elevate the quality of life, and guide investments in Amarillo over the next two decades.*

This plan comprehensively addresses key facets of city life—businesses, homes, sidewalks, and parks—aligning closely with community values spanning quality of life, economic development, housing, neighborhoods, transportation, health and safety, and growth

---

135 https://abc7amarillo.com/news/local/wife-father-of-woman-killed-in-smokehouse-creek-fire-file-separate-lawsuits-cindy-owen-troy-owen-elaine-denise-sanchez-fm-33-hemphill-county-burn-center-oklahoma-city

management. They are in the planning stages for implementing the redevelopment and have already had many meetings on this.[136]

Below you will see the Amarillo, Texas S.M.A.R.T. City planning map.

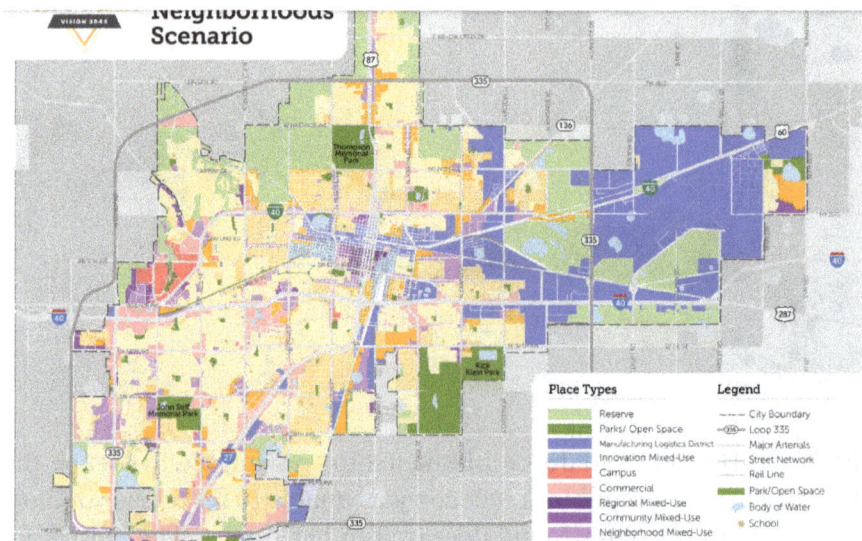

Amarillo is one of the more advanced communities on their way to becoming a SMART City, but was there another motive to start this fire?

The destruction of the Panhandle's cattle industry will have devastating effects on beef availability and prices. If you are one of the many Americans who is a vegetarian, this might not phase you. However, the burning down of America's food supply seems to be a trend with hundreds of food processing plants being burned mysteriously over the past decade or so.

Tyson chicken facilities have experienced a large number of devastating fires since at least 2020 with a fire at the Tyson food facility in Nashville, Arkansas. The Tyson River Valley ingredients plant in Hanceville, Alabama burned on July 30, 2021. Tyson food processing plants have closed in many locations including Van Buren Arkansas,

---

136 https://www.amarillo.gov/our-city/cityplan#:~:text=City%20Plan%20%E2%80%94%20 Vision%202045%20(Comprehensive,over%20the%20next%20two%20decades.

Perry Iowa, Glen Allen Virginia, Dexter Montana, and North Little Rock Arkansas.[137]

These closures cause serious economic burdens on the towns affected, and these Tyson employees are often unable to find work. Will our sources of protein come from bugs and engineered meat as suggested by the Gates Foundation? For a refresher on plans to eat bugs and other horrific plans by globalists, see the "WEF" chapter in Stephanie's *Burn Back Better*.

In an article by the Bill and Melinda Gates Foundation titled "All Things Bugs, LLC," the authors address the proposed development of producing bug protein for human consumption.[138] Gates' projects get downright ridiculous, going so far as to develop a way to stop cows from burping and farting because he seems to think they are a huge source of dangerous methane gas that contributes to climate change.[139]

This announcement was made in January of 2023. Currently, Gates and his investment group have yet to devise a way to stop cows from burping and farting. Perhaps the public sees the absurdity in this theory? And for that matter, will Gates stop at cows or other livestock, or will he one day propose that *you* are fined or prohibited from your own natural bodily functions? If we're going to be ludicrous, why stop at cows, Mr. Gates?

An interesting reaction to the Texas Smokehouse Fire was Governor Greg Abbott's comments about the destruction. On March 1, 2024 at a press briefing, he publicly stated his opinion about the leveling of the structures. He said:

> *I have witnessed and observed some extraordinary damage in our state. It could be caused by a hurricane or tornadoes and frequently when you see that damage there's some semblance of a structure that is still there. When you look at the damages that have occurred here, it's gone, completely gone, nothing left but ashes on the ground.[140]*

We can't say with certainty that Governor Abbott has knowledge about the effects that directed energy weapons have on structures; however,

---

137 https://www.youtube.com/watch?v=-UMaGWjv1j4

138 https://www.gatesfoundation.org/about/committed-grants/2012/05/opp1044748

139 https://www.youtube.com/watch?v=IEy4SDoHWXQ

140 https://www.youtube.com/watch?v=nwEqS6UUWuk

he is an official member of the World Economic Forum where it appears that members are often associated with organizations and philosophies that promote a decrease in population (by what means?).

However, Abbott's reaction appears to illustrate genuine concern as well as confirmation that he witnessed structures reduced to dust like we have seen in Maui. Was Abbott making a stand against the globalist plans to destroy much of his state? Or was he playing his part in the slow introduction of the globalist plans for his state? Below you will see an image of one burned property in the Smokehouse Fire that was reduced to white ash.

Image from David Erickson, Associated Press via "Boston Globe" [141]

On the topic of top politicians making statements that could be referring to advanced technology being used as a weapon, the current U.S. President Joe Biden has publicly stated how the head of FEMA for the Pacific region, Bob Fenton, was on the ground in Hawaii before the fire, referring to his dedication to his role with FEMA. Stephanie details this in her book *Burn Back Better*.

Fenton is, at the time of this book development, the Regional Administrator for FEMA Region 9 which includes California, Nevada, Arizona, Hawaii, and other American territories in the Pacific such as

---

141 https://www.bostonglobe.com/2024/02/29/nation/texas-panhandle-wildfire/

Guam. Fenton was on Oahu for a conference that Herman Andaya and General Hara attended, as well.

We may never know if this was coincidence or part of a plan to keep key players from being properly informed about the fires on Maui. Andaya did not return to Maui until the day after the fire. He claims he did not know there were fatalities until August 9, 2023.

Days after the devastating fires in Texas, Joe Biden made a public speech about the devastation seen there. He now famously stated; "If you fly over these areas that are burned to the ground, you'll see in the midst of twenty homes that are just totally destroyed and one home sitting there because it had the right roof on it."[142] We know that quote was used in Part One, but it's so surprising and curious that we chose to include it in this portion of the book, as well.

The Hurricane Otis Acapulco-lypse

*Image from Rodrigo Oropeza / AFP / Getty Images,
via "The Atlantic," October 30, 2023* [143]

---

142 https://youtu.be/wD6tq8gJm98?si=u_zs9CmsKWqpDTgm&t=50
143 https://www.theatlantic.com/photo/2023/10/photos-acapulco-aftermath-hurricane-otis/675835/

On the morning of October 24, 2023, a tropical depression with 45 mph winds was brewing hundreds of miles offshore from Acapulco. It was originally forecast to only be a tropical storm that would track west, avoiding Mexico altogether. Over the next 12 hours, Hurricane Otis would defy all predictions to become the most rapidly intensifying Category 5 hurricane to ever make landfall in the Pacific, reaching sustained winds of 165 mph and gusts of up to 205 mph. However, once inland, the hurricane quickly weakened before dissipating. Otis had turned north and raced directly toward Acapulco, making landfall at 12:45 a.m. on the mainland, five hours ahead of schedule and with little to no warning.

Acapulco was caught off guard by a "surprise" Category 5 hurricane. There were no warnings sent out in Acapulco, and most victims had already gone to bed on the 24th without even knowing there was a hurricane. Although it was only classified as a hurricane for about 12 hours, Otis is the most damaging hurricane ever to hit Mexico, costing between 12 and 16 billion dollars.[144]

The rapid intensification of Otis was among the most poorly forecast in the modern era. Meteorologists Jeff Masters and Bob Henson at Yale University called the underestimation "one of the biggest and most consequential forecast-model misses of recent years".[145] The rate of Hurricane Otis's intensification was among the fastest observed in the satellite era. In a 21-hour period, the hurricane's maximum sustained winds increased by 105 mph.[146]

Masters and Henson surmised Otis's landfall saw the most people ever impacted by the eyewall of a Category 5 hurricane, with over a million people located in the damaged area.

On October 30th, the National Autonomous University of Mexico tweeted that data from two weather stations in Acapulco Bay were recovered.[147] [148] One station measured peak sustained winds of 113.64 mph with a gust to 204.90 mph at 12:40 a.m. CDT.

In its Advisory, the National Hurricane Center (NHC) and Central Pacific Hurricane Center upgraded Otis to a Category 5 hurricane, just

---

144 https://en.wikipedia.org/wiki/Hurricane_Otis#cite_note-TCR-3
145 https://yaleclimateconnections.org/2023/10/nightmare-scenario-category-5-hurricane-otis-devastates-acapulco/
146 https://www.nhc.noaa.gov/data/tcr/EP182023_Otis.pdf
147 https://x.com/SMareograficoN/status/1719114842525905322
148 https://en.wikipedia.org/wiki/National_Autonomous_University_of_Mexico

three hours and forty-five minutes before landfall. The NHC described the situation as a "nightmare scenario."[149] Once onshore, the hurricane rapidly weakened, and within two hours its eye disappeared from satellite imagery and lightning activity ceased.[150]

NATIONAL HURRICANE CENTER and
CENTRAL PACIFIC HURRICANE CENTER
NATIONAL OCEANIC AND ATMOSPHERIC ADMINISTRATION

ANALYSES & FORECASTS ▾   DATA & TOOLS ▾   EDUCATIONAL RESOURCES ▾   ARCHIVES ▾   ABOUT ▾   SEARCH ▾

Hurricane OTIS

```
ZCZC MIATCDEP3 ALL
TTAA00 KNHC DDHHMM

Hurricane Otis Discussion Number  12
NWS National Hurricane Center Miami FL       EP182023
1000 PM CDT Tue Oct 24 2023

A nightmare scenario is unfolding for southern Mexico this evening
with rapidly intensifying Otis approaching the coastline. Satellite
images show that Otis has continued to intensify, with Dvorak
Data-T estimates between 130-145 kt during the past few hours.  The
initial wind speed is set to 140 kt as a blend of these values,
making Otis a Category 5 hurricane.  Otis has explosively
intensified 95 kt during the past 24 hours, a mark only exceeded in
modern times by Patricia in 2015.
```

Across Guerrero, Mexico, thirty-seven transmission lines, twenty-six electrical substations, a power generation plant, and 10,000 light poles were downed,[151] resulting in more than 500,000 households losing power.[152] [153]

Throughout Acapulco, 51,864 houses were destroyed, while 79,510 others suffered severe damage and 80,823 other homes suffered minor or moderate damage.[154] About 80% of all hotels in Acapulco sustained damage, which fared better than most homes.[155] The federal

---

149 https://www.nhc.noaa.gov/archive/2023/ep18/ep182023.discus.012.shtml
150 https://cimss.ssec.wisc.edu/satellite-blog/archives/55347
151 https://www.jornada.com.mx/noticia/2023/10/28/politica/suman-220-mil-35-viviendas-afectadas-en-acapulco-evaluacion-continua-9939
152 https://www.cnn.com/2023/10/24/weather/hurricane-otis-acapulco-mexico/index.html
153 https://www.theguardian.com/world/2023/oct/29/hurricane-otis-death-toll-mexico-coast-acapulco
154 https://www.jornada.com.mx/noticia/2023/11/01/mundo/2018otis2019-destruyo-51-mil-viviendas-por-completo-y-dejo-80-mil-con-danos-graves-3437
155 https://www.cnn.com/2023/10/26/weather/hurricane-otis-acapulco-mexico-impact-thursday/index.html

civil defense agency tallied 220,000 homes that were damaged by the storm.[156] The city also lost access to drinking water.[157]

Image from Oscar Guerrero Ramirez/Getty Images, via Axios.com [158]

Communication during the storm was heavily cut off, initially leaving information about the hurricane's impact largely unknown. Eighteen radio stations in Acapulco were down, and all communication was cut off in the city.[159] The president of Mexico, López Obrador, had called on the armed forces to set up checkpoints in the city to deter looting and robbery. The government presence found in the touristic center was not made available to residential neighborhoods, which had no signal, no water, and no food. This created conditions where aid was slow to arrive. The Category 5 storm's destruction cut off the city of nearly 1 million people for the first day, and it had intensified so quickly that little to nothing had been staged in advance.

156 https://apnews.com/article/otis-mexico-acapulco-government-response-survivors-storm-4c33ae4a3ebcf272eb05b89ae898bb28

157 https://apnews.com/article/mexico-hurricane-otis-acapulco-17b4b34147a2fe5acbe980a0b5b06aa7

158 https://www.axios.com/2023/10/27/acapulco-hurricane-otis-aftermath

159 https://web.archive.org/web/20231025090122/https://www.nytimes.com/live/2023/10/25/world/hurricane-otis-acapulco

Soldiers oversaw the distribution of gasoline, presumably to avoid the uncontrolled ransacking of stores that happened across the city in recent days. The federal government rejected calls from the Chamber of Deputies to use oil surpluses, estimated to total up to 80 billion pesos, to fund additional recovery efforts.[160] A sit-in outside the National Palace was organized to protest the lack of government assistance.[161]

By November 1st, the government had only delivered 63,000 food packages to the 1 million+ victims, and about 1,600,000 liters of water.[162] That only amounts to about 1 food package for every 16 people, and just over 1 liter of water per person, if it was even possible to distribute them all equally. By November 5th, they delivered 204,092 meals, which is only enough to feed a single meal to one out of every five people, after twelve days without.[163] By November 7th, 8,602 kilograms (18,964 lb) of cargo had been airlifted, which is only about a dozen pallets worth and could fit in a single box truck.[164]

The government of Guerrero mobilized thousands of military members, seemingly to prevent recovery efforts by blocking the roads and turning back supplies. Thousands of recovery items had to be smuggled to those affected. Acapulco resident and responder, Jeff Berwick, was interviewed by Jean Nolan on the INSPIRED YouTube channel about the Acapulco attack, and his quotes speak for themselves as a first-hand testimony to the tragedy:

> There's a military base in Acapulco. They usually drive around with all their guns and stuff all the time because they're bored. After this happened they took off, they're gone. There's no government presence whatsoever, they're gone. The president said he was gonna try to come, but his jeep got stuck in the mud so he didn't come. None of our cars have gotten stuck in the mud."[165] "They're not allowing

160 https://www.jornada.com.mx/noticia/2023/11/06/politica/rechaza-amlo-creacion-de-fondo-para-acapulco-con-excedentes-petroleros-6852

161 https://www.jornada.com.mx/noticia/2023/11/06/politica/caravana-201cacuerdate-de-acapulco201d-instala-planton-frente-a-palacio-nacional-3019

162 https://www.jornada.com.mx/noticia/2023/11/01/politica/se-localizo-a-394-personas-con-vida-en-guerrero-informa-salgado-2505

163 https://www.jornada.com.mx/noticia/2023/11/05/politica/se-entregaron-mas-de-20-mil-despensas-en-el-primer-dia-8096

164 https://www.jornada.com.mx/noticia/2023/11/07/economia/continua-puente-aereo-gratuito-del-aicm-a-acapulco-hasta-nuevo-aviso-9350

165 https://www.youtube.com/live/zak6AeqOUpg?si=B57YqQjiqXr4tgXq&t=1162

any media into Acapulco by the way. There's been hardly any media coverage of Acapulco this entire week, we're the only ones doing this. We're the only ones trying to get supplies in. They're trying to stop us. I can't give you exact details how we're getting around them, but I'll tell you we're using every single resource we can to get around these roadblocks and get these supplies in.[166] "The only people there are the military stopping aid from coming into Acapulco. This is all planned, this is all by design, this is what they want to happen, and we need to expose them. This is sort of what we heard out of Maui as well, right? The police were trying to get people into the area where they would be burned alive and keep them there. This is the exact same sort of situation."[167]

Berwick also said, "There was no rain with this hurricane."[168] This bizarre weather occurrence is similar to what happened on Maui on August 8, 2023.

Jeff Berwick was interviewed by Jean Nolan for the "Inspired" YouTube Channel

Now that we've seen an Acapulco resident say how their weather event was similar to Maui, we'll also look at how a Maui resident says their own weather event was just like Acapulco. Maui resident and long time

166 https://www.youtube.com/live/zak6AeqOUpg?si=5QPXD_qRt6XPtfkb&t=1285
167 https://www.youtube.com/live/zak6AeqOUpg?si=bo37AaGev6qM14yV&t=1772
168 https://www.youtube.com/live/zak6AeqOUpg?si=6p6ZWrpGa_GxG1WB&t=809

weather tracker, Bruce Douglas, was interviewed on the Blossom Inner Wellness YouTube channel, where he covered the similarities between the Maui and Acapulco weather attacks.

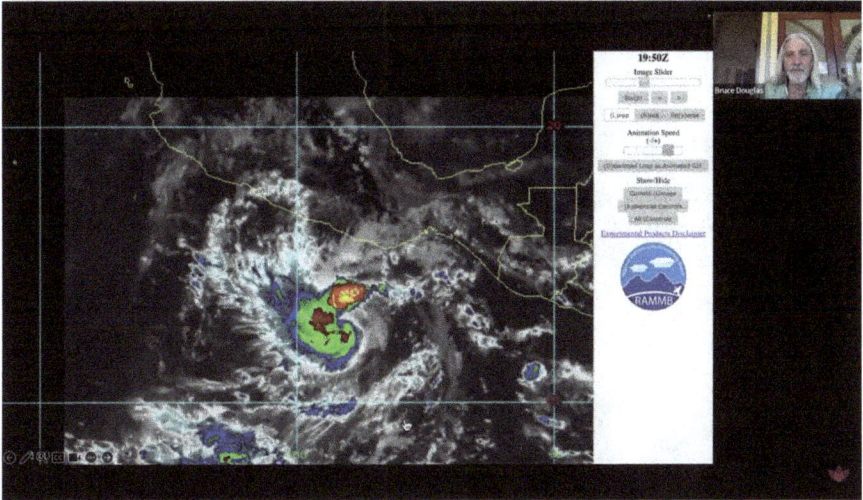

Photo courtesy of a screen capture of Blossom Inner Wellness YouTube Channel

In the above image, Bruce explains how aerosol "clouds" are injected from the surface, which convect into the rotating air above it, causing the entire air column to begin rotating. Bruce stated:

> *What I'm proposing here is, that what's happening is there are boats out in the ocean that have aerosol generators on them and are able to create clouds which basically use these nanoparticles to sequester the moisture".[169] (Bruce assumes the use of coal fly ash, which could also be used in conjunction with wet surface air coolers, land-based versions of which have already been implicated in artificial cloud creation, as seen in the next image.)[170]*

---

169 https://youtu.be/78Det47pZq0?si=Wm4m2HrXeEsWaSxB&t=269
170 https://youtu.be/78Det47pZq0?si=_6AeTI_8gBhXIBHt&t=1129

Bruce goes on to reveal more images that show what appears to be surface-based aerosol injections that strengthen the storm. After a particularly large injection is seen convecting into the storm, the next five hours of satellite images are missing from the data. After they resume, Otis is now a clearly organized storm headed straight for Acapulco.

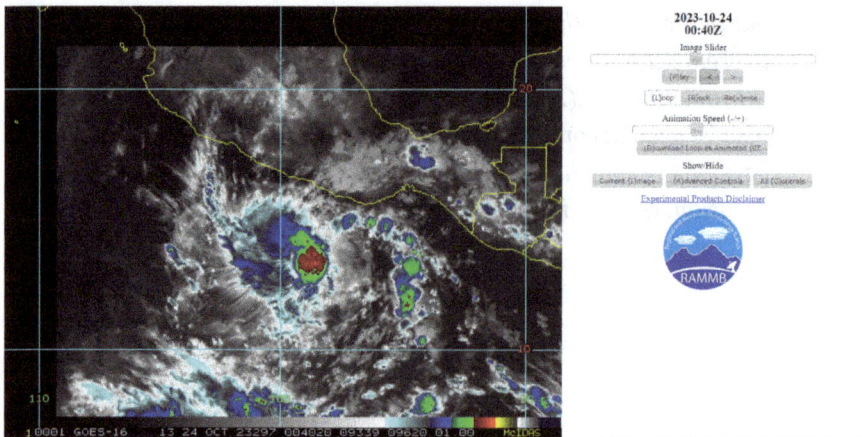

We can see this for ourselves on the Regional and Mesoscale Meteorology Branch (RAMMB) site at Colorado State University, where they have archives of the remaining images that haven't been deleted.[171] Clicking through the image loop in the archives, you can see that the images update every ten minutes, but on October 24th, it goes from 00:40 (12:40 a.m.) to 05:50 (5:50 a.m.) in a single image, which indicates that five hours and ten minutes are missing from the satellite data. This just so happens to be the period of rapid intensification the likes of which we have never seen, and still can't actually "see" because the data is missing.

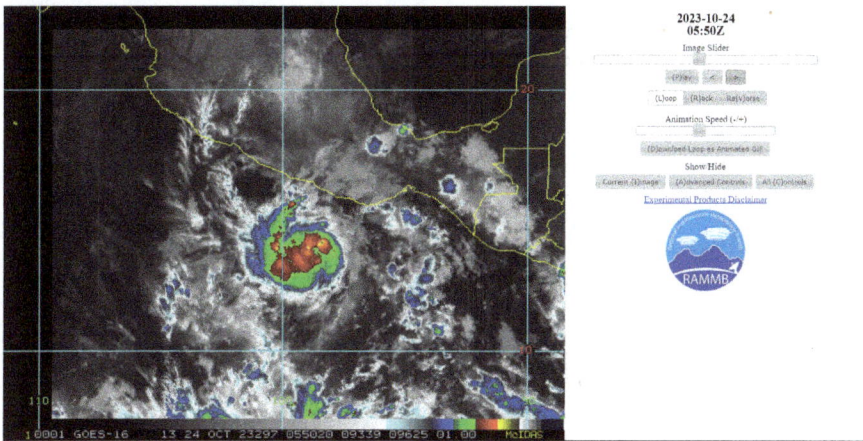

As of December 21, 2023, the official figures stand at fifty-two people killed and thirty-two missing.[172]

Early media reports of an additional sixteen fatalities following a power outage at a Mexican Social Security Institute hospital were denied by the government.[173] Many people also rode out on boats in what had started as a tropical storm, and in just twelve hours it had powered up into a catastrophic Category 5 hurricane. Local officials told The Washington Post that they had counted 120 dead or missing, including twenty bodies that washed up onto Acapulco beach or by

---

171 https://rammb-data.cira.colostate.edu/tc_realtime/storm.asp?storm_identifier=ep182023
172 https://mexiconewsdaily.com/news/officials-update-hurricane-otis-death-toll-to-52-with-32-people-missing/
173 https://www.eluniversal.com.mx/nacion/amlo-senala-a-loret-por-informar-sobre-otis-el-periodista-responde-a-las-calumnias-y-obsesion-con-el/

the docks, ten bodies that were found floating in the ocean sixteen kilometers (10 miles) west of Acapulco, two people who were missing from a vessel of three, and three people who died at sea on a four-person boat.[174]

As she prepared to lay her relatives to rest, Katy Barrera, who had hardly even had a chance to search for her own mother and brother, expressed desperation and frustration at the aid and personnel she had begun seeing in tourist areas of the city, but not in their neighborhood high on a mountainside. "There are many, many people here at the (morgue) that are entire families, families of six, families of four, even eight people," she said. "I want to ask authorities not to lie ... there are a lot of people who are arriving dead."[175]

Locals have criticized the official death toll as an underestimate,[176] to which President Andrés Manuel López Obrador responded by accusing his opponents of making the death toll a political issue, and that his opponents are trying to inflate the toll to damage him politically. On November 12, 2023, a report emerged indicating that Acapulco's funeral homes had calculated a total of at least 350 deaths.[177] [178]

How could there have been over 350 funerals if only 52 people died?

174 https://www.washingtonpost.com/world/2023/11/01/acapulco-hurricane-otis-missing-search/

175 https://apnews.com/article/mexico-hurricane-otis-acapulco-50eb6a8fe677455428cbacf d3966e72c

176 https://apnews.com/article/mexico-hurricane-otis-acapulco-50eb6a8fe677455428cbacf d3966e72c

177 https://mexiconewsdaily.com/news/news-outlet-in-acapulco-says-real-hurricane-death-toll-is-over-350/

178 https://euro.eseuro.com/local/1434943.html

PART TWO:

Government Funny Business

CHAPTER NINE:
Legislative Moves Toward
A *Land Grab*

Twenty-two days before the August 8th fires on Maui, Governor Josh Green made an unprecedented move, declaring an emergency, and signing an "Emergency Proclamation Relating to Affordable Housing," This Emergency Proclamation is thoroughly detailed in Stephanie's book *Burn Back Better*. It is noteworthy to mention that Emergency Proclamations are usually written after a natural disaster, but in this case it was written 3 weeks before the disaster.

Candace Cheung of Courthouse News wrote in September 2023:

> *A lawsuit filed Thursday charges that Green's July 17 Emergency Proclamation allows the government and housing developers to skirt laws that protect the environment, Native Hawai'ian burials, and historic properties. The ACLU and the Sierra Club joined Nā 'Ohana O Lele Housing Committee, E Ola Kākou Hawaii, Hawaii Advocates for Truly Affordable Housing, and Native Hawai'ian cultural practitioner Kū'ikeokalani Kamakea-'Ōhelo as plaintiffs.*

> *Green issued the Emergency Proclamation in response to the extremely high cost of living in Hawaii, often attributed to expensive housing. The proclamation makes it easier to develop new housing and established the Build Beyond Barriers Working Group, also named as a defendant in the suit, along with Nani Medieros, the group's state lead housing officer.*

> *The groups write that Green's proclamation "attempts to circumvent the constitutionally mandated legislative process for addressing public policy issues like housing" under the guise of an emergency.*

A move like this is necessary for the government to make because in the case of Lahaina, there are many structures and properties that are deemed historically significant and are protected by a historic preservation easement which can provide significant protection from future development. With the rich history of Lahaina as the ancient capital, it is home to a number of ancient Hawai'ian burial grounds which are protected by state law by the State Department of Land and Natural Resources (DLNR).[179]

It seems that a goal of this proclamation is to streamline the redevelopment of West Maui and remove cultural "roadblocks" that will get in the way of redevelopment. When visiting West Maui, you can still visit old burial grounds that often occupy valuable beach side real estate that have been untouched by the disaster. This will be important when considering the goals of Senate Bill 3381, which we will discuss in the next chapter.

Senate Bill 3381 and the "Lele" board

Senate Bill 3381 would put Lahaina's redevelopment into the hands of the Hawaii Community Development Authority, which is best known for building Kaka'ako into a posh seaside community of luxury condos. The bill, which would create a new nine-member Lele Community District, is co-sponsored by Senator Angus McKelvey, who represents Lahaina, and Senate Ways and Means Chairman Donovan Dela Cruz, a long-time supporter of expanding HCDA's powers. In the first draft of the bill, the 9 members would be appointed by the governor.

On January 24, 2024, the first draft of Senate Bill SB3381 was introduced by Representatives Donovan Dela Cruz and Angus McKelvey to the Hawai'ian State Senate. There will be 3 more versions of the bill written in the following months. Senator Dela Cruz is already infamous in Hawaii as the representative who has received more than

---

179 https://dlnr.hawaii.gov/shpd/about/branches/ibc/hawaiian-burials/

$57M for land acquisition in his district in just the past ten years, with over $150M more proposed in just two other bills.

About the Bill, the Civil Beat.org reported:

> *The Lele Development District board would have unusually expansive powers, with the authority to impose rent control, for instance, and to take property from one person through eminent domain and transfer it to another.*
>
> *The board would oversee development of a new Lahaina. The bill envisions shoreline setbacks and underground utilities to mitigate risks of climate change impacts. Networks of pathways, bikeways, and public transportation would reduce dependence on private vehicles.*
>
> *The initial board would be appointed by the governor, subject to the Senate's "advice and consent," and replaced by a board elected in the 2026 general election.*

This statement indicates that West Maui would no longer be governed by Maui County; instead a completely separate governing board will oversee West Maui. That board would have nine appointed officials advising them.[180] In the above-referenced interview with Roseanne Barr and Representative Elle Cochran, Representative Cochran referenced this "Lele Community Board" with great concern, aghast that the State of Hawaii would propose removing power from the community and local representatives like her into the hands of a board "elected" from a curated group by outsiders, not the local heroes like Elle who are working for the people, elected by the people, sacrificing their personal income and retirement plans to serve the people, and living among the people.

Here are some highlights from the original writing of SB3381 suggesting an attempt to acquire the properties in West Maui:

---

180 https://www.capitol.hawaii.gov/sessions/session2024/bills/SB3381_SD2_.PDF

- The board shall have sole jurisdiction over the district. The authority shall not have jurisdiction over the district except to the extent that the board is administratively placed under the authority and as set forth in this section.
- Exercise the power of eminent domain to acquire necessary property interests; provided that the exercise of eminent domain shall only be undertaken to achieve the community master plan; and (15) Take any and all actions necessary to carry out its purposes and exercise the powers given and granted pursuant to this part. §206E- Assessment for operating costs.

What is blatantly clear from the map of the "Lele" district is that the board would have sole jurisdiction over the entire West Coast of Maui, as you'll see below. However, it was not the entire West Maui area that was destroyed. However, and most frighteningly, the Lele district proposal would include a much larger area than what was destroyed in the fire; in fact, it goes as far West as Ka'anapali down to the border of Ma'alaea.

What's more, "the authority" would have jurisdiction if the board was "administratively" under it; this means that two groups, one called the "board" and the other called the "authority," would be working together to essentially overtake jurisdiction of the entire habitable West Maui area, far exceeding that which was destroyed in the fire.

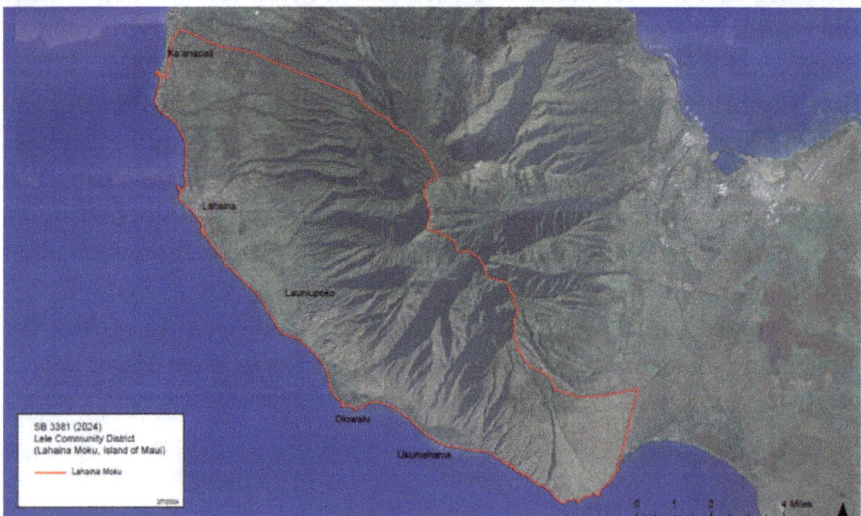

A surprising detail of the bill comes from Page 10, line 13, of SB3381 which reads: "Contract for and accept gifts or grants in any form from any public agency or from any other source." In other words, this is permission to accept bribes.

```
13      (11)  Contract for and accept gifts or grants in any form

14            from any public agency or from any other source;
```

Page 6, lines 1 through 3 (below) reads: "Encourages a thriving, sustainable business sector that includes tourism, and restores community assets, including schools."

The term "sustainability" is being used as a guise for making these changes to our society and this movement has been well underway for many years and lends a hand in furthering the United Nations agenda. The bill was deferred on the house floor on March 7, 2024 and there has been no recent updates as to whether this bill will be further considered. [181]

```
1       (C)   Encourages a thriving, sustainable business

2             sector that includes tourism; and

3       (D)   Restores community assets, including schools,
```

Some weeks after the bill's proposal came State Senator Kurt Fevella from "Ewa Beach," a town that used to be a large plantation farm on Oahu. Fevella, pictured below, got involved with the details of SB3381 and requested reasonable amendments to the bill. One key amendment made was to require the nine Lele board members to be elected officials instead of appointed, and limited to only $100 dollars in campaign money. They also proposed that eminent domain could only be used to achieve greater community purposes and the Lele community plans.

Senator Fevella threw a wrench into the bill by taking control away from the governor and giving it to the people; we applaud his effort. By requesting amendments to the bill at the Ways and Means committee

---

181 https://www.capitol.hawaii.gov/session/measure_indiv.aspx?billtype=SB&billnumber=
3381&year=2024

meeting, it allowed for more time to get the word out on the details of this bill which was then re-written three times at the time of this writing. On March 1, 2024, Senator Fevella thanked the members and chair for working hard on these amendments and so it was passed during the reading at the "Ways and Means Committee."

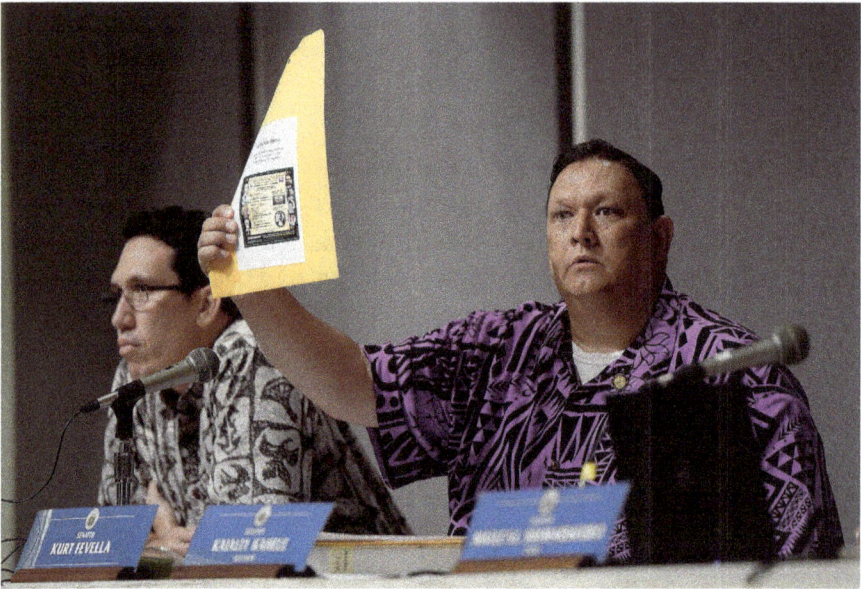

Senator Kurt Fevella from Ewa Beach, Oahu

What happened in the winter of 2024 is not the first and only time Senator Fevella has been instrumental in changing the planning and redevelopment of Lahaina. On September 8, 2024, he made a public statement on a number of local news channels demanding that the planning meetings for Lahaina were moved to Maui and to include members of the community. He made it very clear that his vision for the redevelopment is to return the town to its former glory as the ancient Hawai'ian capital full of historical and culturally significant spaces. This early move on his part eventually led to the halt (very temporarily) on putting Governor Green and his appointees in charge of redeveloping Lahaina.

In response to Fevella's request to move meetings and decisions on redeveloping Lahaina to Maui instead of Honolulu and include members of the community, Mayor Bissen appointed five members to a panel. These included business owners and residents of Lahaina, including community leader Archie Kalepa who is a 9th generation Lahainaian and expert waterman credited with using jet skis in water rescue for lifeguards and helping develop the sport of paddling. Kalepa is the most recognizable member of the panel put together by Bissen of community members in charge of decisions regarding the redevelopment of Lahaina. About a month after assembling this group, Archie made a public statement to the camera about his stance on his vision for the new Lahaina. During his statements, he was reading off a script full of globalist talking points and there was an evident shift in his attitudes about how the aftermath of the fires are being handled by federal agencies. The interview is on Brush Junkie's YouTube video linked below.[182]

It has been stated by multiple sources that Archie is a passionate ambassador of climate change, stating that climate change is to blame for the fire in Lahaina.

Until this day, it is unclear how instrumental this panel is in making decisions on plans for Lahaina, but during events honoring Governor Green and Mayor Bissen, Archie is usually in attendance showing his support for the officials who are responsible for the death and destruction of his ancestral town of Lahaina.

Land-Grabbing in SB3381

Continuing with our investigation of SB3381, page 7, line 4 (below) reads: "Rebuilding in the district shall be compatible with county plans and zoning, as reflected in any relevant county plan and Lahaina historic district, as amended."

This appears to be an intentionally misleading word choice. The bill was going to amend county plans and zoning under the county plan, with no homeowner input. The next part reads: "Building in residential areas shall cater... to the needs of residents,"[183] as seen below.

---

182 https://youtu.be/Dk91sUsgAHU?si=KhVDpnuAyKoJ_usy
183 https://www.capitol.hawaii.gov/sessions/session2024/bills/SB3381_SD1_.PDF

```
4      (7)   Rebuilding in the district shall be compatible with

5            county plans and zoning, as reflected in any relevant

6            county plan and Lahaina historic district, as amended;

7      (8)   Building in residential areas shall cater to the needs

8            of residents, especially those who lost their homes in

9            the fire, in terms of location, type of housing, and

10           cost;
```

Throughout the bill, there are many vague and ambiguous statements that are hard to decipher. The ideal situation for the representatives who wrote this bill would be for it to pass quickly without anyone noticing; similar to many bills; however many people noticed and spoke out against this bill and it was re-written three times.

Both pages 8 and 9 of SB3381 (below) talk about The Lele Board's powers. The bill states, "the board may acquire, reacquire, or contract to acquire or reacquire, by grant or purchase, real, personal, or mixed property of any interest therein, and own, hold, clear, improve, rehabilitate, sell, assign, exchange, transfer, convey, lease, or otherwise dispose of or encumber the same."

It is our interpretation that this is clearly a reference to robbing people of their private property. The next two parts have similar statements, both beginning with, "acquiring or reacquiring," and, "real, personal, or mixed property."

7   **§206E-**   **Board; powers.** Except as otherwise limited by

8 this part, with respect to the district, the board may:

9   (1) Establish and administer programs for purposes of this

10   part;

11   (2) Make and execute contracts and all other instruments

12   necessary or convenient for the exercise of its powers

13   and functions under this part;

14   (3) Prepare or cause to be prepared a community plan for

15   the district;

16   (4) Acquire, reacquire, or contract to acquire or

17   reacquire, by grant or purchase, real, personal, or

18   mixed property, or any interest therein, and own,

19   hold, clear, improve, rehabilitate, sell, assign,

20   exchange, transfer, convey, lease, or otherwise

21   dispose of or encumber the same;

There are many contract opportunities in the aftermath of the Lahaina fire from which disaster capitalists, as well as the State, may benefit, which we'll discuss in the following chapter. In fact, Page 9 of SB3381 (below) reads:

> *"...Arrange or contract for the planning, replanning, opening, grading, or closing of streets, roads, roadways, alleys, or other places, or the furnishing of facilities, or for the acquisition of property or property rights, or for the furnishing of property or services in connection with any project."*

11   (7)   Arrange or contract for the planning, replanning,

12   opening, grading, or closing of streets, roads,

13   roadways, alleys, or other places, or the furnishing

14   of facilities, or for the acquisition of property or

15   property rights, or for the furnishing of property or

16   services in connection with any project;

You read that correctly: the board would have the power to assess all land users (homeowners, farmers, etc.) and require them to help pay for operating the district. The bill appears to state that the board would assess any fees for land owned by the federal government; they would be excluded. However, the board would have been able to charge interest and other fees if private property owners' assessments were not paid on time and "withhold services or approval of governmental permits for land users delinquent in payments."

Another shocking revelation we've had about this bill is that the Lele Board would receive hundreds of millions of dollars from many different places, on top of the sizable donations from any government, profit, or nonprofit agency that the bill permits.

Eminent Domain

There seems to be a trend among areas with plans for redevelopment for a SMART City and fires; including and adjacent to the theme of "eminent domain." Eminent domain is typically used as a way for governments to purchase or acquire private property for the sake of public works projects. Nowadays, this excuse to acquire land seems to be used for more than simply public works projects. In the case of West Maui, this is the avenue that the state was to use to acquire the land that Governor Green has been so vocal about doing. He has said it on camera twice and has come up with some creative ways to use eminent domain to take over private property. One example is his plan to build the "Venice of the Pacific" water project.

As reported by "Civil Beat" in April of 2024, Governor Josh Green plans to take "unilateral action"[184] to allegedly restore a significant historic location in Lahaina. Sadly, he has made it clear that he will use eminent domain to take action, whether Hawai'ians vote it in or not.

In August of 2023, the fire incinerated a park along Front Street that was home to a sandbar island known as Moku'ula and a fishpond, Mokuhinia. Moku'ula in Hawai'ian means "island in the middle of pond" and Mokuhinia means "fish pond." Both sites had been buried for decades under a ballfield. However, they were once the home and burial place of nobility and the location where the 1840 Hawai'ian Constitution was signed.

Some criticize Green, saying that he intends to create a tourist water feature atop a sacred Hawai'ian site. The project name isn't helping locals take him seriously, as it's been referred to as the "Venice of the Pacific."

Your authors aren't visualizing Venice, Italy, but Venice... Las Vegas. Currently there are some locals in support of this project and we will have to see how it honors this historical site.

Remember, fresh water is scarce in West Maui, and there was no water available to put out the fire on August 8th. Whether this plan goes through remains to be seen, but this move being called "unilateral action" suggests that there will be no vote or legislation.

It has been said that two of West Maui's most highly revered community leaders support this project: Archie Kalepa and Ke'aumaku Kapu, locally referred to as "Maku."

What concerns us most about the project is that it will allow the government to inconspicuously acquire land for a public works project; but the adjacent property owners have shown little to no support for the project. While some have stated that due to structures that once diverted water melting in the fire, there is now more water naturally flowing into the area of the "fish pond," others see this as a waste of resources and yet another way to divert Lahaina's water for a tourist attraction. At the time of this writing, it is alleged that 75% of water resources on Maui are diverted for corporate purposes.

---

184 https://youtu.be/KPU2ftbm8uk?si=bGFtPB4XW_K2saAO

Power To The People

Have you ever had attendance required at a meeting that you weren't wanted at? For instance, Stephanie had to conduct veritable scavenger hunts in the Aspen, Colorado area, where she lives, in order to figure out when school board meetings and working sessions were being conducted... because they didn't want her or any other concerned parent there when they were assertively pushing through a pornographic health curriculum for children as young as kindergarten. Meetings would be announced in hidden places within hours of the event, and when arriving at the event there were instances where the doors to the Civic Center were locked or a sign posted on the door read that the meeting had been postponed or rescheduled to an unspecified later date or time.

The same kind of thing happened on Maui. The first hearing for SB3381 was scheduled for February 14, 2024 at 1:00 p.m. in Honolulu, with an initial vote that was deferred until March 1, 2024. However, these dates were difficult to find on the State Capitol website. It was clear that dates and details were being purposefully obfuscated from the public.

What's more, the hearings for SB3381 were held in Honolulu, which made it difficult for Maui residents to attend. In fact, a friend of the authors named Stacy Sills flew all the way to Honolulu from Maui on the 21st after learning about SB3381. She sat through a hearing about amounts that would be paid to victims of the Lahaina fires, but nothing was said about 3381. She asked Representative Donovan Dela Cruz if they would be discussing SB3381, but he told her that it had been pushed back... but the date was still unknown.

At this time, your authors felt confident that the people of Maui would be playing a game of "hide and seek" if they wanted to be a part of these hearings. Thanks to YouTube channels such as "Brush Junkie," and "Hawaii Real Estate," some citizens were aware of the details of these bills. The government, however, was anything *but* transparent.

CHAPTER TEN:
Disaster Capitalism

Disaster Capitalism

It is important for the readers to understand that Hawaii is an occupied territory taken over by the United States but was never fully annexed as a state. This is roughly detailed in Stephanie's *Burn Back Better*, in Chapter Five, entitled, "Stealing The Heart Chakra of The Planet;" but this book will dive further into the ramifications of this "stolen state" throughout the manuscript.

The process of milking a disaster for profit is commonly referred to as "disaster capitalism." It is the opinion of your authors that the Lahaina fires are among the strongest examples in history of such a thing.

Lima Charlie, Inc

Among the many clear pieces of evidence of disaster capitalism include the use of property management companies to assist victims and FEMA workers' housing on Maui. Instead of hiring a local property management company to handle the housing crisis, an outside company from the mainland, based in California, called "Lima Charlie, Inc.," has been retained—a decision from the Department of Homeland Security—"to find housing for FEMA employees and victims of the fire who lost their homes."

It seems reasonable that a well-established company would be brought in to handle 12,000 displaced residents. However, there is a more sinister reason for why this particular company was chosen.

Like so many of the roads we'll travel in this book, the path leads to money—not for the people. For instance, the Lima Charlie management company can potentially earn over 100% in management fees for the properties they are leasing out to victims and FEMA workers.

As of April 25, 2024, here are the statistics for amounts awarded so far:

> - *Current number of leases: 539 and growing*
> - *Median award for 1 lease: $241,000 per year, $20,083 per month*
> - *Monthly lease amounts approved and announced by Governor Green in December 2023 during a news briefing:*
> > - *Studio, 1 bed: $60,000 per year, $5,000 per month*
> > - *2 Bed: $84,000 per year, $7,000 per month*
> > - *3+ bed: $132,000 per year, $11,000 per month*

According to USAspending.gov, Lima Charlie, Inc. manages 539 rental units on Maui, with a total of $125,901,638.14 obligated from FEMA.

From $125,901,638.14 in annual rent income, the median total lease amount for the year is $241,000 per unit. Divided by twelve months in a year, this means that Lima Charlie, Inc. collects a median of $20,000 per unit, per month from FEMA.

Even with the very high rents being allotted by the government, the majority of that goes to Lima Charlie. Here are 2 likely examples based on the median lease amount and the rent prices set by Governor Green (source below):[185]

> *Example 1:*
> *Rental price: $11,000 per month x 12 months = $132,000 per year.*
> *$241,000 - $132,000 = $109,000 or $9,083 per month in property management fees*

> *Example 2:*
> *Rental price: $7,000 per month x 12 months = $84,000*
> *$241,000 - $84,000 = $157,000 or $13,083 per month in property management fees*

---

185 https://youtu.be/PVvfSpUKDNA?si=ckgPBLK4PlNmA8-N&t=1498

(The leases are all public information at USASpending.gov.)

This is federal taxpayer money being frivolously spent on an outside agency instead of going toward victims or property owners. That amount would help a family of four live comfortably and even save for the future. Let's not forget that the federal government gave each household a humiliating and offensive mere $700 after the disaster, and nothing more was given afterward. Again, this crisis is a ladder for those willing to climb it.

Typical property management fees go up to 10% of the lease amount; in this case, $1,100 per month or $13,200 per year. This makes the property management fees that Lima Charlie receives extremely high. Remember, each household got $700 as a one-time award from the government. Imagine if the victims got the fees that Lima Charlie is collecting. It would pay for their monthly expenses and allow them to save for the future.

Coincidentally, the highest yearly amount awarded to a property was $420,737/year or $35,061 per month.

Rentals

Nearly nine months after the fire, many of those affected are still living in tents, on beaches, or in cramped quarters that aren't merely uncomfortable but also unsafe for children. Eight months after the fire, approximately 3,000 people still lived in hotels. FEMA has assertively asked people to leave the island for Oahu or even for the Continental U.S. By all appearances, it seems, according to Maui resident testimonies gathered by Stephanie during her last visit to the island, that FEMA is aggressively interested in breaking apart the Maui community and moving former Lahaina residents away from their homelands. As you read this book, tie a string around that fact, as you'll continue to learn why government entities want to rid Maui of Hawai'ians altogether.

Our understanding is that Governor Green has proposed a handful of options for these tenants, including the use of short-term rental properties as long-term rentals. Green has allotted a generous subsidy for land owners who use their properties to house affected people. According to Governor Josh Green, here are the rates being offered:

- $5000 for a one-bedroom
- $7000 for a two-bedroom
- Up to $11,000 for a 4-bedroom[186]

Other incentives given to property owners included tax breaks and waived capital gains tax if an owner sells their property (assuming to the state). Governor Green also threatened to ban short-term rentals altogether, but he backed off when people stood up for their rights, as is evidenced from a March 27, 2024, news briefing. Green was asked why he did not ban short-term rentals, and he said flatly, "people have stepped up."[187]

Cleanup

For over six months, the "burn zone" in Lahaina remained relatively untouched with regards to cleanup, save the application of Soiltac®, a "water based glue" that was supposedly biodegradable and non-toxic, designed to keep ashes from the fire from spreading. In various places throughout the burn zone, Stephanie saw signs like the following, which stated: "This property's hazardous material removal is deferred. Ash and other materials remain a hazard," which means that as of January 2024, Soiltac® doesn't appear to have gotten very far.

After the fire on August 16th, (eight days after the fire), The Hawaii Department of Transportation (HDOT) started installing a dust screen that was nearly 30,000 feet long. They stated it was to protect highway users on Honoapi'ilani Highway. It stretches more than five miles. Three million dollars in quick-release Emergency Relief (ER) funding was approved for this project and others like it on August 21st (13 days after the fire) from the Federal Highway Administration (FHWA). Building and installing the screen is estimated to cost $2.4 million dollars.

---

186 https://youtu.be/PVvfSpUKDNA?si=ckgPBLK4PlNmA8-N&t=1498
187 https://www.youtube.com/live/8cdOtGV4gdc?t=1656s

From the time of the fires, there was a concern that the ash and hazardous toxic waste from the fires would affect the community, as well as the wildlife, both on and off the land in Maui. Engineer Bruce Douglas, and co-founder of Maui Community Investigation, had the soil tested and found traces of lead, arsenic, and more.

According to Sam Eaton, a veteran firefighter who works to raise awareness about the high cancer risk for firefighters and has helped with the cleanup after a myriad of other major fires that will be discussed later in this book, the toxic ash and miniscule, undetectable toxic particulates emitted by a burn zone like Lahaina's can travel 55 kilometers. With that math, we understand that the entire island of Maui is being affected by the toxic dust from the fires. These particles enter the body's lower lung and are associated with many of the diseases we saw first responders and residents around the World Trade Center suffer from, including cancers like leukemia. In fact, leukemia is the 10th most common cancer in the U.S., accounting for 3.2% of all new cancer cases.

It is our sacred responsibility to point the reader toward www.Deconpac.com if they live on Maui or have been in proximity to the fires. According to Eaton, due to the proliferation of synthetic materials since 9/11, the materials that burned during the Maui fires are potentially much more lethal than even those in the Trade Towers during 9/11. You can review this and more information about detoxification and hazardous materials in Chapter 16.

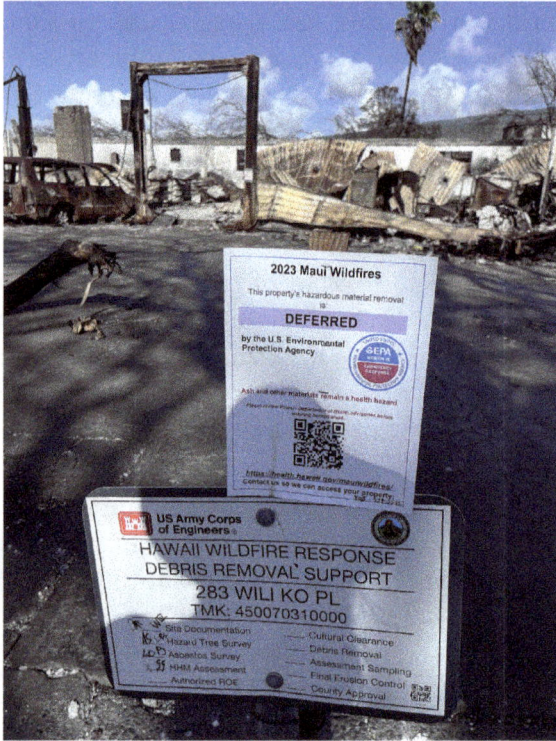

Photo from January of 2024 courtesy of Stephanie Pierucci

That said, what is Maui County doing about the waste? There were over 400,000 tons of it after the fires, and as of mid-January when Stephanie visited the burn zone, there had been a range of little to nothing done. Residents were allowed to enter the burn zone and retrieve things that had been recovered from their homes or places of work, but aside from that, the burn zone was a veritable ghost town. For miles, she drove through the burn zone and would see nothing but checkpoint agents (the burn zone was not open to the public, but only to people who lost homes or businesses, and not to insurance adjusters—which we mentioned in Chapter One) and some police officers. Of course, if you stopped to take the random picture of a blue umbrella, you might see a mysterious black Escalade that served as a warning that your time in the burn zone had come to an end...

Naturally, the community was eager for some closure on the burn zone and the 400,000 tons of waste therein. But the decision, as most things involving the Hawai'ian government, was not being made without a division in the community. That division amounted, essentially, to the debate over the Olowalu dump site.

In December of 2023, the Maui County Council was set on using an area in Olowalu to house the waste from the fire. Olowalu is a community of about 20 homes closest to the point where East and West Maui meet. While Stephanie was on island in January, she witnessed dozens of signs that were "anti-Olowalu-dump-site" and learned that hundreds of people protested the proposed site for toxic fire debris, with nearly 9,000 people signing a petition expressing their adamant opposition to the Olowalu dump site, citing fears of risk to the air, water, soil, and people in Olowalu where native Hawai'ian families still reside.

On January 12, 2024, from "Hawaii News NOW," Maui County Council member Tom Cook, before helping approve the Olowalu toxic landfill location, stated, "the public needs to understand they're in the driver's seat for when we have a final repository for this. The public will decide if this is one year, two years, ten years, or 50 years."

The Council ignored five hours of the public opposing this site. Are people supposed to believe the County Council would honor their vote on the permanent site in the future?

On January 13, 2024, an article on the MauiNOW.com website reads: "all agreed the decision was a difficult one, with one member calling the choice a "lose-lose situation." Another criticized the administration, saying the council was left out of the site selection process and now felt pressure to approve or lose funding.

To approve something against the will of the people because you'll lose funding is fraud; it's also considered bribery. The administration doesn't state who would be providing the funding, but a good bet would be the federal government. Another concern is that the area experiences extreme wind, which makes not only transporting but also storing the waste a dangerous task. On their Instagram page, @ olowaluhui posted a video of 45 mph winds ripping through the area where workers delivered "burritos" of toxic waste—units of waste wrapped up in black material—that were falling apart in the wind while the workers continued to deliver them from Lahaina to the dump site.

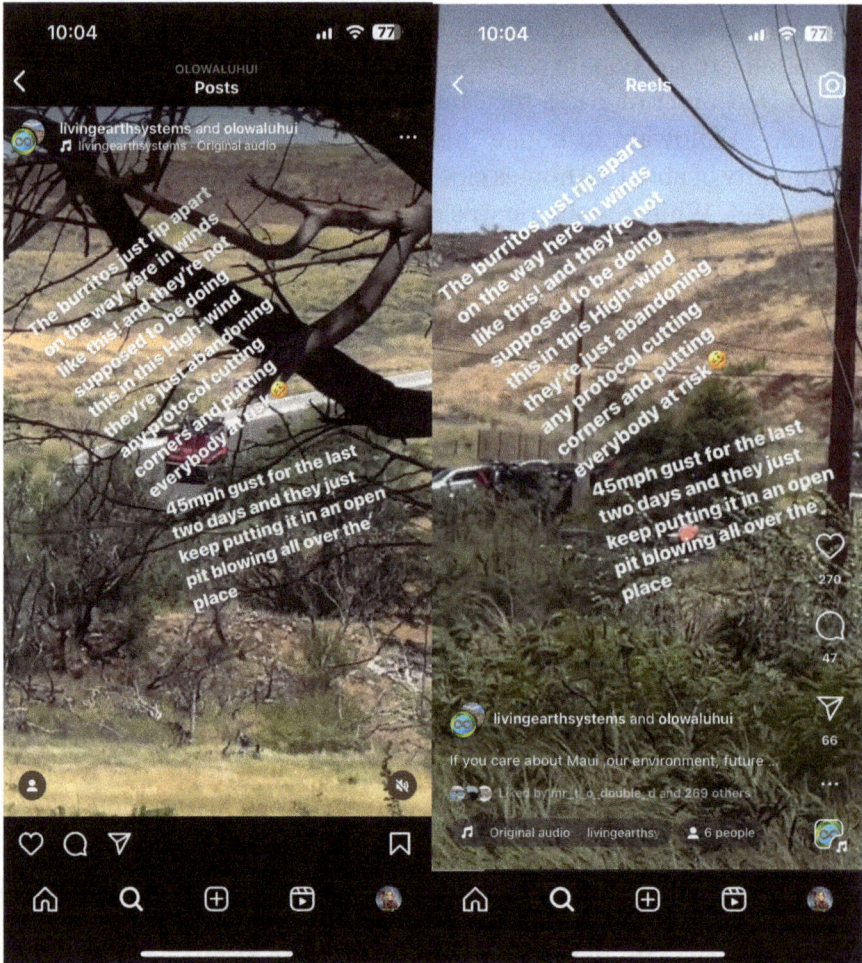

Instagram screen captures from account @olawaluhui

Although Maui County eventually determined that the Olowalu dump site would be temporary, opponents fear that the temporary location will eventually become permanent. As of the time of this writing in July of 2024, officials are already starting to question the viability of moving the toxic waste out of Olowalu, which was the fear of many residents.

"There are other solutions that have been put forward. We need to exhaust every possible solution. We need to not rush into it. We need a geological survey here. We need an archaeological survey here," Eddy Garcia, Regenerative Education Centers Executive Director, told Hawaii News Now (HNN).

"If we look at where they chose to put the waste, it's on a slope in very, very viscous material. Very easily, the toxic waste will go through that land and go right into the ocean here. It's only 700 yards away," said Lukas Nelson according to HNN.

Supporters of the site point out that the debris in the burn zone would get washed away by rains if not mitigated soon. They argued that it would take billions of dollars to move it off the island and several years, which would prohibit rebuilding. Interestingly, some supporters also indicated that residents wanted the debris to remain on the island since it contained human remains.

Any way you cut it, the removal of debris from the burn zone has been a hotly contested issue. Traci Derwin was instrumental in not only acquiring signatures on the Change.org petition but also encouraging the public to testify against the plan. Maui City Council, nevertheless, voted on the Olowalu site, calling it "temporary" in order to appease opposition. It was later stated by Council member Johnson:

> Our backs are against the wall, and I think it's due a lot because the administration has had time to do things that they could have done, and they haven't included us in this discussion. Now, it's just, 'do this, or we lose all this money.'

This signals another potential form of bribery and fraud on the people. Within five years, the county will need to find a permanent site for the 400,000 tons of toxic debris.

Enter Komar Investments, LLC. The Central Maui Landfill is the spot designated for the permanent resting place for the 400,000 tons of debris from the Lahaina fires, the land adjacent to which is owned by Komar Investments, LLC. According to a report on Hawaii News Now, Mayor Bissen has offered $830,000 for the entire twenty acres owned by Komar Investments, LLC. Although Andy Naden, Vice President at Komar, has stated that five acres will be enough to house the debris. Komar has even offered to donate that land to Maui County, which would allow them to build their landfill with the remaining fifteen acres.

According to an HNN report from April 9, 2024, Maui County announced in February that the land next to the Central Maui Landfill would be the "Permanent Disposal Site" for the debris. The Maui City

Council summarily voted to acquire the land from Komar Investments, LLC. by eminent domain.

"Not everyone realizes this, but under our constitution and laws, the government can actually take your private property, so long as first, they can show that it's for a legitimate public use, and then second, if they do something like that, they have to compensate you justly for that," said former Attorney General and Legal Expert Doug Chin.

The county doesn't want the five acres required for the debris' Permanent Disposal Site, but they stated that their long-term plan requires 20 acres.

"With all due respect to Mayor Bissen and to Director Agawa, we believe they are overreaching in terms of how much property they need, and they are undervaluing in terms of what the property is worth. That, my friend, is a problem. That's when the government needs to be put in check," said Naden.

The web becomes stickier. In 2005, Komar was alerted that the land was for sale but was then prevented from developing it for ten years. In 2017, former Mayor Arakawa stated in a signed letter that the County had no intention of condemning Komar's land. Shayne Agawa stated that the county now needs twenty acres and more to "provide for the health and safety of our residents."

Naden pointed out that the county receives $46 million in tipping fees, at $116 a ton, from the federal government for moving the ash to this site. However, the county has rejected Komar's offer and is determined to acquire the entire twenty acres for $830,000 because they're receiving the $46 million "tip."

On July 17, 2024, a federal judge ruled against the County of Maui in favor of Komar Maui Properties and the Central Maui Landfill will remain privately owned, for now.[188]

More evidence that this land will not stay with their property owners can be seen in the strict rules regarding the clean up and removal of toxins from the burnt-down properties. The majority of property owners who plan to rebuild have been pressured into handing the detoxification of the land over to the Army Corps of Engineers (a federal agency). The Maui County Council voted unanimously on Bill

---

188 https://www.civilbeat.org/2024/07/federal-judge-rules-against-maui-county-quickly-taking-private-land-for-lahaina-fire-debris/

86, stating that the initial cost of this clean up will be covered by FEMA, but afterwards, any insurance money will have to pay this expense back. Most residents of Lahaina do not know of this detail, and because this process costs approximately $70,000, most home owners cannot afford to pay this.

Time and time again, county members vote against the residents' interests, and our understanding is that the affected citizens are not aware of this. This is a task that Traci has been very diligent in reporting on her YouTube Channel "Brush Junkie." Issues such as the dump site in Olowalu to the rules and regulations relating to the rebuilding of Lahaina are being decided on by the nine members of the Maui County Council, who appear to be controlled by forces above them.

During the final vote for the decision of where to put the toxic waste produced by the fire, council member Tamra Paltin admitted that they were pressured into voting for the Olowalu site or their budget would be taken away. There was a huge public outcry to find a more suitable site for this waste, but it seemed like this decision had already been made, and no matter how many objections were made, the site was not going to change. The council received over four hundred testimonies objecting to this ruling, but it seemed like the members had already decided.

Reasons for not wanting Olowalu as the dump site were obvious. First of all, the site was only 2,000 yards from the ocean, where the "mother reef" is located. This reef is home to precious sea life and coral reefs that are responsible for the preservation of the ecosystem, which is a huge value to Maui for many reasons; one being that this area is a huge tourist destination filled with snorkeling, paddleboarding, fishing, and surfing. Allowing for these toxins to be so close to this precious natural resource is a risk to all organisms, including humans and the vast number of people consuming fish from these waters.

Another risk is the proximity to housing, since these toxins can be very harmful when released into the air and breathed in by residents and tourists. Often, these risks are not seen for many years, but children are extremely susceptible to these contaminants, and these are associated with cancers and other health problems. There is also concern that these toxins will leach into the groundwater, despite there being a barrier under the toxic material.

The Red Cross Regional CEO
Who Was Fired for Supporting Maui Survivors

After the dark and devastating news of this chapter, we would like to recognize the story of former Hawaii Red Cross CEO Diane Peters-Nguyen. Peters-Nguyen tried to push for reform but was fired in early May of 2024 after she urged the Red Cross to stop prodigy Maui fire victims to move off island. Peters-Nguyen filed a complaint against the Red Cross with the Hawaii Civil Rights Commission and Equal Employment Opportunity Commission on April 9th, 2024. The complaint alleged that the Red Cross retaliated against their CEO for complaining in defense of Maui families.

According to her attorney, on April 16th Peters-Nguyen was placed on administrative leave and fired on May 3, 2024. According to "Civil Beat," Peters-Nguyen "...was shocked and pretty devastated because she contributed a lot to the organization and was very loyal and proud of a lot of the things she accomplished while she was there."Peters-Nguyen's attorney Bridget Morgan-Bickerton stated, "she was just very disappointed that the national Red Cross kind of failed to give Hawaii a voice in how to handle the aftermath of the Hawaii fires," indicating that her client raised concerns about volunteers pushing disaster victims to leave the island of Maui.[189]

One of our key sources on Maui for information from the "inside" stated that he, too, was encouraged to go to the mainland, but by FEMA. They offered him $1,600 a month toward rent, which he refused. A lifelong resident of Hawaii who grew up on the Big Island, this citizen journalist and disaster victim couldn't deal with losing his homeland on top of his business and home, as well as his dog and best friend.

Happily, holding out was a good choice as FEMA eventually found this man a condo in Lahaina where he now lives and has one year of rent covered by the organization.

We pray that every victim of the fire who wants to stay in Lahaina or on Maui will find a way to stay in their homeland, even if their homes have been lost and may never be rebuilt.

---

189 https://www.instagram.com/p/C7mxf1nB3QD/?igsh=cjBhbHZ5ZTYzbnRo

CHAPTER ELEVEN:
The True Number of Deceased?

A huge question that has been difficult to accurately answer is: *"how many people were lost in this tragedy?"*

Over the months following the fire, the number of missing and deceased went down significantly. It was difficult to keep up with the drastic changes. In this chapter we will look at various statements and figures that have been released to various news outlets as well as in interviews and written testimony with the authors of this book.

If you find the numbers difficult to follow; you are not alone. The figures provided regarding the number of deceased and missing have changed dramatically with time. With so much deception going on it's expected that officials will have a hard time keeping their story straight, which is where the "truthers" in our audience pick up the slack to expose the darkness.

Happily, the truth stays the same and lies are not consistent. Documented statements and witness testimony will be listed in this chapter which shows the lack of transparency in the official numbers.

Initial Figures

A couple weeks after the fire, Governor Josh Green gave a news report about the unaccounted for at 1,050 and that the search is far from over. In an interview on August 21, 2023 with CBS "Face the Nation", Green stated, "there are 1,050 still unaccounted for. We have extreme concerns because, due to the temperature of the fire, the remains of those that have died may be impossible to recover, meaning there are going to be people that are lost forever."

Governor Green did not state a death count number. The reporter then asked, "a local Maui official said a large number of the dead may actually be children because they were left home that day due to schools being closed. Many of them were alone or with their grandparents. Is that the case, Governor?"

Green replied, "That's possible. That's what we're sharing here internally. It's possible there will be many children. This is the largest catastrophe that has ever hit Maui—probably that has ever hit Hawaii, outside of war time."[190]

As you will see, the comments from officials regarding the number of deceased and missing have come to a halt. Therefore, we refer to the reports that were made in the few weeks following the fire.

In the month of August, a number of individuals spoke publicly about the people they rescued or recovered, but as time progressed, there are very few individuals willing to go on the record about the recovery. It is our understanding that Coast Guard or watermen who were tasked with retrieving bodies from the water signed NDAs, as did, surprisingly, a woman rumored to have been hired to clean in the King Kamehameha III elementary school; but those are unfounded rumors we gathered from citizen journalists on the island who would prefer not to be named.

To our understanding, the only politician publicly speaking on this issue is State Representative Elle Cochran who covers West Maui and has been a resident of the area her entire life, living with her husband near the high school where the big "L" is on the hill above Lahaina.

On September 19, 2023, Elle Cochran went on the record with "Fox 11 News" stating that the number of missing and deceased is minimizing and that she does not understand how these numbers can decline. When asked what she thinks the real number is she states, "thousand plus".[191]

The official count ended with three children having perished in the Lahaina fire. Their ages were 7, 11, and 14, which remains constant at the time of this writing. The number of deceased ticked up to 101 with

---

190 https://www.youtube.com/watch?v=UijEBIHvMlQ
191 https://youtu.be/cWiBKayCWv0?si=TeskkbkCiyqGT_iU

the report of Lahaina's beloved artist, craftsman, and wood carver Paul Kasprzycki, 76, who was mentioned in Stephanie's book *Burn Back Better* as the man whom Spice Prince went after when he returned to the fires to find and assist his friend who allegedly wanted to "stay with his cats." Just after first penning this paragraph, we learned that the official number crept up after the "discovery" of Kasprzycki to 102 deceased.

August 8th was the largest fire in Maui's history, with no warning sirens, and it spread extremely fast. Children were not in school; the elementary school was canceled for the day allegedly due to "high winds," and the middle schools and high school were not yet in session. These children often had no other place to go outside of the home; more than likely they were in Lahaina either with a parent or guardian, or alone.

Obviously, those who are most vulnerable to perishing in a fire are very young children, the disabled, and the elderly. If an individual is unable to drive, move independently, and or find their way to safety; they are at a higher risk of not surviving. This basic fact makes the number of minors lost very unreliable. A citizen journalist on the island recently (spring of 2024) attended an event with a man who stated that he still didn't know what happened to his fourteen-year-old boy. However, this is a rumor without the names or specifics attached to it.

On August 29, 2023, "ABC News" report stated:

> *So far, 115 people have been declared dead in connection with the fire... 388 individuals are unaccounted for which is a large reduction from the 1,000-1,100 reported missing on the 23rd. The FBI-validated list is in addition to lists compiled by other organizations, which counted the missing at more than 1,000. The FBI list only includes people for whom authorities have a first and last name and contact information for the person who reported the missing persons case.[192]*

In order to be considered missing, a report needs to be given to the Maui Police Department, and for many residents this requires a ride

---

192 https://abcnews.go.com/US/maui-officials-search-wildfire-victims-ocean-land-search/story?id=102648231#:~:text=There%20were%2012%2C000%20people%20living,long%2Dterm%20solutions%20for%20housing

to the police station. Another point to consider is that there may not be a relative or friend to make a "missing persons report" for some of the missing or deceased due to the fact that this was such a large tragedy.

Lahaina is home to a large number of homeless individuals, and even those who know of a missing person often do not go through the process to report it. What's more, many migrants lived in Lahaina working in tourism, which to our knowledge is now losing $14,000,000 daily for the county.

While Traci was in Lahaina, she met a number of survivors who can't find friends but have not made an official report. Some survivors have a hard time even thinking about it, and much of that seems to be the trauma from hearing of the many gruesome ways people died or were found dead. For instance, bodies were allegedly found en masse on a back road where smoke blocked the driver's view that were, apparently, "smashed" into the road. Another report widely circulating among locals is of multiple bodies that were visible but, when touched, turned to ash.

On September 15, 2023, Chief Pelletier held a press conference with an explanation of why the numbers of deceased and missing have changed so much.[193] In the end he states that ninety-seven was the number they are going with. As of the time of this writing (7/1/2024) there are officially 102 deceased.

Questions About The Coroner

A detail that needs to be addressed is that the Police of Chief has also served as the coroner for as long as this position has existed. According to Clyde Holokai (retired assistant police chief) who served twenty-eight years with the Maui Police Department, this is how it has always been; it's not a conspiracy or position adopted just for (or after) the fires.

The coroner mainly signs the death certificates, but the medical examiner determines the cause of death and the other details required for an official death to be recorded. Therefore, despite internet chatter,

---

193 https://www.youtube.com/watch?v=taw8GKg1X1A&t=0s

there was no conspiracy to assign the police chief as the coroner for the sake of this event or ones like it. This is protocol that just happens to give the chief more control outside of his main duties.

Hawaii House Bill 869, "RELATING TO CORONERS'," was introduced to legislation December 11, 2023. The Bill will separate the positions of Police Chief and coroner separate from one another

> *The legislature finds that coroners should be separate from law enforcement and free to make independent judgments when investigating deaths. Under current state law, the chief of police for a county serves as the coroner if the county does not have a medical examiner. Making coroners independent from law enforcement will promote transparency, avoid conflicts of interest, and encourage more confidence in coroners' rulings.*

On page 2, line 10, this bill reads as follows: "the [chief of police or his authorized subordinate of the counties of Hawai'i, Maui~ - and Kaua'i, and the] medical examiner of [the city and county of Honolulu] each county shall, ex officio, be the coroner for [his] that respective county."

On the Lahaina bypass road, white crosses are posted for those who died in the fire and yellow ribbons for those still missing. Lahaina resident Ann Williams counted them on April 7, 2024, and found 142 crosses and 19 yellow ribbons. This is not an "official" count, and there have been many who have left the island. However, it does show the local count does not match the official count. Again this suggests that the number of deceased is higher.

Solid evidence that there were probably more than just 102 deceased can be found looking at the number of refrigerated shipping containers that body bags were being placed in. There are nine shipping containers seen below, suggesting if each container can fit 50 bodies, at least 450 deceased have been discovered, and that does not take into account the existing morgues on Maui that were full to capacity. A video can be viewed in a "Daily Mail" article of body bags being transferred into these shipping containers so we know that these containers were there to store the deceased.[194]

---

194 https://www.dailymail.co.uk/news/article-12420893/Maui-wildfires-death-toll-update.html

We would like to close out this chapter with a detailed message that was sent to one of the authors, with additional facts that suggest the official death toll is much higher than 102.

What you are about to read is two parts from an email sent to Stephanie after she wrote *Burn Back Better*. First, you will read a short summary of the death toll "oddities" with additional details about the inconsistent reports by officials on Maui. We the authors have performed some light spell-checking that doesn't take away from the original email but makes it a bit more readable, according to the authors and with the approval of the original authors of the email, who are residents of Hawaii. More information about "missing children" will be covered in Chapter 13.

Oddities Summary
1. *Pelletier's police report indicating "four dead on Front Street."*
2. *Governor Green saying, "most bodies found on street by the sea."*
3. *Three children died but three different last names were found in homes, even though at least two additional children died in*

cars. The children found in the same home would presumably have had the same last names if they lived in the same home.

4. *Kekoa Lanceford pulled many more bodies out of the water.*

5. *Noah Thompkinson was in the water at 5:38 p.m. but the fire chief said people jumped in at 9 p.m. In his escape video, Noah Thompkinson shares in a timestamped phone record that there were more than just a few people in the water.*

Competing Reports

1. ***Pelletier: Four dead on Front Street.***
   Read the article from Honolulu Civil Beat dated 2/5/2024 written by Cammy Clark titled: "Maui Police Report Reveals Locations of Lahaina Fire Victims And Lessons Learned." The article clearly states: "...and only four of the dead were found on Front Street. One of those was in a structure, two were found over a seawall and one person died near a car that was not theirs." (This is found in paragraph 6.) Pelletier's report is included in this article. Both the article and his report need to be reviewed with a fine toothed comb... [195]

2. ***GoverNUT Green addressing bodies by the sea.***
   View a video dated August 16th from "Good Morning America" which can be viewed on YouTube. It is titled: "Hawaii Governor Details Recovery Efforts In Maui Fire." At the beginning of his interview, he literally said, "Many of the fatalities were on the road down by the sea." (Is he referring to Front Street? Because Pelletier's later report, which I mentioned above, indicated that there were only four... What does Josh Green quantify as "many?" Is the road down by the sea Front Street?) [196]

3. ***Three children died but Governor Josh Green said a family of four died with 2 children in the back seat of the car.***
   This video is titled: "Children Among Lahaina Fire Victims Found During Search and Recover Operations." It was featured on August

195 https://www.civilbeat.org/2024/02/maui-police-report-reveals-locations-of-lahaina-fire-victims-and-lessons-learned/

196 https://www.youtube.com/watch?v=WYfyqai4hFs

15th via "Hawaii News Now." Those two children would or should have the same surname. Only three youths have been identified: Tony Takafua, Keyiro Fuentes, and Justin Recolizado. If my memory serves me correctly, the last two were in residences...[197]

4. **View the video "Lahaina Man Recounts Rescuing Multiple Burn Victims From Lahaina," dated August 16th from Hawaii News Now.198**

   During this segment, the man mentioned that he saw children... but how many did he see?! He never mentioned a specific number...

   Also read the article from August 11th from "The Daily Mail" titled: "Bodies of Hawaii Victims Are Pulled Out of the Sea." [199] It says, "We still have dead bodies floating in the water." The man literally rescued people on August 8th. He has claimed that he retrieved the deceased from the water the following day. My guess is that he did so as a caring citizen. His accounts would then not match that of Pelletier's later report...

   Editor's Note: from "The Daily Mail Article:"[200]

   > *A Hawaii resident in the middle of the state's apocalyptic wildfires has revealed the charred remains of numerous victims have been washing up amid the crisis.*

   > *Kekoa Lansford said his town of Lahaina, the epicenter of the blazes on the island of Maui, is going to take 'years to fix' after the dust settles on the natural disaster.*

---

197 https://youtu.be/BExcOE3fmUc?si=cc4AQan2AAu8VWoD&t=161
198 https://www.hawaiinewsnow.com/video/2023/08/17/lahaina-man-recounts-rescuing-multiple-burn-victims-lahaina/
199 https://www.dailymail.co.uk/news/article-12395835/Bodies-Hawaii-fire-victims-pulled-sea-14-500-people-evacuated-2-000-left-without-place-sleep-dead-bodies-floating-water.html
200 https://www.dailymail.co.uk/news/article-12395835/Bodies-Hawaii-fire-victims-pulled-sea-14-500-people-evacuated-2-000-left-without-place-sleep-dead-bodies-floating-water.html

'This is not even the worst of it," he told the BBC as he pointed to the leveled town. "(We) still get dead bodies in the water floating, and on the seawall."

Speaking before President Biden promised unending federal aid on Thursday, Lansford slammed the response from officials as he said: "I feel like we're not getting the help we need."

His remarks came a day before Hawaii Governor Josh Green announced the death toll had risen to 53, a number which was expected to rise 'significantly' in the coming days.

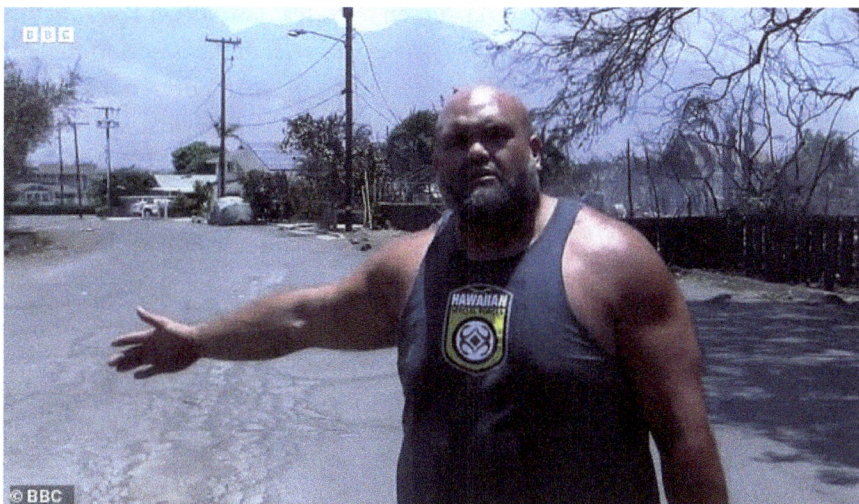

Kekoa Lansford said his town of Lahaina, the epicenter of the blazes on the island of Maui , is going to take 'years to fix.' Photo courtesy of the "BBC."

5. **Noah Tompkinson/Fire Chief... Noah's video shows that he entered the waters at 5:33 p.m.201**

The fire chief of Maui indicated that individuals entered the waters much later. View the video "Maui Fire Chief Brad Ventura discusses

---

201 https://youtu.be/Yp34Ttnv3uQ?si=hQalKCE3GacJcQHV&t=168

*the August 8 Lahaina Wildfire" dated August 20th on "Maui Now."
It is still available on YouTube [at the time of this email]. Right
around the 3-minute mark he states that individuals entered the
water around 9 p.m...*[202]

*As per the fire chief, why is he stating a three and a half hour time
difference? I could understand 10 or 15 minutes, maybe even 20
minutes or half an hour maximum at the time of commotion, but a
three hour time difference?*

*Another video that needs to be viewed is: "Local Woman Escapes
Lahaina Fire by Jumping Into Ocean." It was featured by "Rebel
News" on August 23rd. It's fifteen minutes. It's still on YouTube [at
the time of this email]. Her name is featured in the description. Her
account does not match that I described in bullet point number one.
She literally said that her family members from Molokai delivering
supplies from that island were retrieving the deceased in the water
two days later! The details of the instances I provided are not
correlating with later reports.*[203]

*My hope is that my email response will provide detailed assistance
because my observation is that these few instances do not reflect
what was officially reported later. I did hear the following but I can't
remember where although it was independently filmed. Apparently,
there were a number of residents on Maui that addressed their
concerns and were vocal about August 8th. But, those same
individuals never really spoke much about it later due to "county
interests"..... My guess was the typical county job...*

---

202 https://www.facebook.com/reel/1358227075107017
203 https://www.youtube.com/watch?v=_4hnr5QbH8g

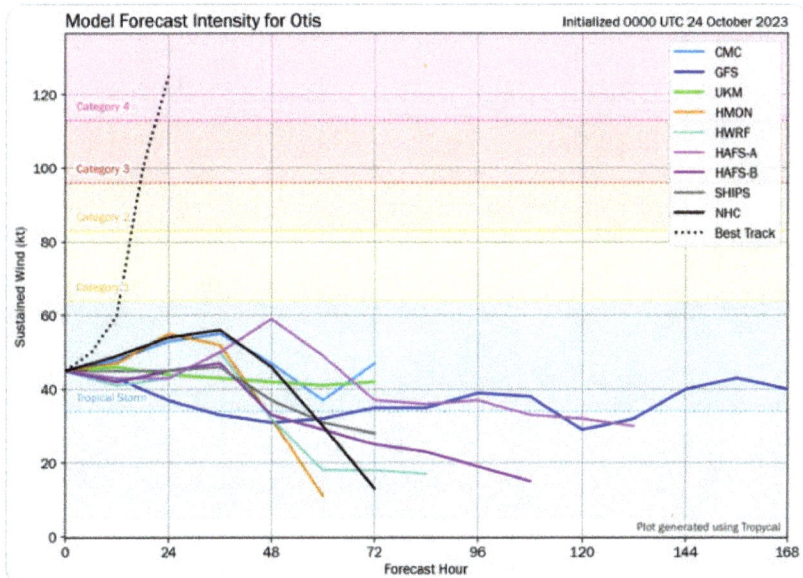

Tomer Burg
@burgwx · Follow

X

Just to emphasize how poorly hurricane & global models performed for Hurricane Otis... here's the intensity forecasts initialized 24 hours ago, with the dotted black line showing verification:

Model Forecast Intensity for Otis   Initialized 0000 UTC 24 October 2023

CMC
GFS
UKM
HMON
HWRF
HAFS-A
HAFS-B
SHIPS
NHC
Best Track

7:19 PM · Oct 24, 2023

CHAPTER TWELVE:
Whodunit?
A Deep Dive Into the Maui
Police Department

Maui's Police Chief John Pelletier is an intriguing character who's been pinned all over internet memes as a curious potential "culprit" in the Maui fire of August 8th. However, after a thorough investigation, you will be shocked to learn that your authors don't see him as a direct participant of the fires, but potentially installed for a very different game altogether. Keep reading this chapter to see how we fit dozens of puzzle pieces together to come to a conclusion that is unlike anything you've read about Chief John Pelletier.

There are a myriad of confounding facts surrounding Pelletier before and after the fires. First of all, Pelletier is the first non-native of Hawaii to hold this position. He's the highest-ranking police officer, yet he is not a local. The rules in the "Hawaii Revised Statute" for employment in that position state that you must be a Maui resident for at least a year.

Hawaii has a truly unique culture not found anywhere else in the world. It's a melting pot of many cultures who have immigrated to this land for over one hundred years. The rule regarding a police chief being required to live for at least one year on Maui was waived for Chief Pelletier, which is starting to become a trend among the police chiefs in Hawaii (more on that later).

Pelletier came from Las Vegas but started his career with the FBI where he got his initial training before joining the Las Vegas Police Department for twenty-three years. The biggest incident Pelletier claimed to oversee was the Mandalay Bay shooting in Las Vegas, which killed 58 people, making it the largest mass shooting in U.S. history.

Initially, Pelletier claimed he was the Incident Commander for the mass shooting, but upon further investigation, it turns out he was not. The real Incident Commander was Lieutenant Ray Spencer. We have proof of this from a number of sources, including William Hankins, who is a retired lieutenant with the "Maui Police Department." Three articles and a documentary film have been made naming Spencer as Incident Commander.[204] [205]

We also have documented proof that Pelletier lied on his resume and application for the chief position, which is grounds for termination if the Police Commission ever finds out and isn't already corrupt itself.[206] It is listed as his "number one" accomplishment.

It is the belief of your authors that Pelletier claimed to have this experience because he knew it would help him get the position of Police Chief. He lied about it to get the job, from what we can see in our research. Below you will see John Pelletier's resume, where he indicates that he was the "incident commander for the "One October" mass casualty incident in Las Vegas."

John Pelletier

███ ███████ ██████ ██ ██ ██████ █████ ███████████

ACCOMPLISHMENTS

- Incident commander for the One October mass casualty incident in Las Vegas. Created and set up a uniform command and mitigated the threat. Established various divisions and branches during the incident to handle the event until the safe conclusion. Subsequently, have traveled presenting lessons learned and identified how to maximize event response.

- Reduced violent crime for three consecutive years within in the Las Vegas strip corridor, one of the largest tourist destinations in the Nation.

- Created and facilitated the Hero's United project as the Administrative Lieutenant at the North West Area Command. The project resulted in the most violent neighborhood decreasing violent crimes exponentially. Coordinated a collaborative effort between police, business partners, community partners, faith based partners and non-profits in an innovative approach to policing which ultimately resulted in substantial quality of life increase for families and children in the affected area.

- Awarded the Medal of Honor for pulling a citizen out of a motor vehicle that was on fire.

---

204 https://www.knpr.org/magazine-desert-companion/2022-09-30/ray-spencer

205 https://www.police1.com/active-shooter/articles/5-officers-5-years-later-reflections-on-the-anniversary-of-the-las-vegas-shooting-N1VeyQIwx6J6tbaw/

206 https://drive.google.com/file/d/1zMmmi7JFl7CtxFvvN_q8SgkNC3DG8DN-/view?usp=sharing

Something else to highlight about Chief Pelletier is that his acquisition of the position of Chief of Police of Maui was a significant jump in rank for him. He went from Captain with "Las Vegas Metro" to Chief of Police of Maui, bypassing the ranks of Assistant Police Chief, Senior Assistant Chief, and Deputy Chief. His starting salary of $158,000 may be a lot to some, but it was still below some of the lower ranking officers who had many more years with the Maui Police Department.[207] [208] Chief Pelletier used this as justification to get a $46,000 raise during the salary meeting.[209]

Chief Pelletier also enjoyed the benefit of having all moving costs covered by Maui County, totaling approximately $15,000 (a cost that could have been avoided by hiring a local officer).[210] Currently, he is involved with numerous complaints, along with court cases which could result in multi-million-dollar payouts, resulting in Maui taxpayers a lot of unnecessary costs and hardships.[211]

The position for Police Chief opened up after former Maui Police Chief Tivoli Fa'aumu was forced to retire early. Fa'aumu was a Tongan Police Chief, having served the Maui Police Department for nearly 36 years. He was loved by many and known to be a very kind man. On May 10, 2021, "Maui News Now" printed the following: "He's (Fa'aumu) fulfilled everything we asked him to do, plus much more," said Roger Dixon, who was Chairman of the Maui Police Commission who voted unanimously to select Fa'aumu as Police Chief in September 2014.[212]

A very strange hit-and-run incident that took place in a parking garage preceded Fa'aumu's early retirement. The alleged hit-and-run was in an underground mall parking lot in Kahului Maui. The surveillance videos show Chief Fa'aumu backing up into a motorcycle while exiting his parking stall. You see the truck back up toward a

207 https://www.mauicounty.gov/DocumentCenter/View/131312/Presentation_Department-of-Police_Salary-Commission-Meeting_2021_v3

208 https://www.mauicounty.gov/ArchiveCenter/ViewFile/Item/28992

209 https://www.mauicounty.gov/DocumentCenter/View/131719/Written-Testimony_from-Deyna-Puckett_for-Salary-Commission-Meeting-on-2112022_Regarding-the-pay-raise-for-Chief-of-Police-John-Pelletier

210 https://drive.google.com/file/d/1LWIrCU_VSgFMHsGMCVzSTT35uyrW5gQp/view?usp=sharing

211 https://mauinow.com/2022/08/18/maui-police-commission-reviews-complaints-against-chief-and-executive-staff/

212 https://www.mauinews.com/news/local-news/2021/05/tivoli-faaumu-first-tongan-police-chief-in-state-retires/

parked motorcycle. When the truck is about two to three feet from the motorcycle, there is a glitch in the video. It literally stops, and when the video starts again, the truck is seen hitting the parked motorcycle and then driving away. Neither the Chief nor his passenger have any kind of reaction in the truck. The motorcycle is seen still standing, and you can't see any damage or debris on the ground. The owner of the motorcycle did not file a police report for a "Major Motor Vehicle Accident" (MVA) or a claim with their insurance company; so it's unclear if there were any damages whatsoever, and there was obviously no injury. Accidents are considered minor if there was less than $3,000 or less worth of damage and there are no injuries or deaths involved.[213]

The Maui Police Department had two officers write up a report, considering it a minor traffic or vehicle accident. However, the officers felt it was a conflict of interest to investigate their own police chief, so they escalated this hit and run to the Honolulu Police department. After that, there was a 158-page report written up on this alleged hit and run, and they changed it to a major traffic incident.[214] From there, it went all over the news, and Fa'aumu was being blamed for this horrible hit-and-run. A few months later, in April of 2021, he retired of his own accord.

Following the bizarre hit-and-run, the evidence of corruption and collusion was fueled at the Police Commission with a man named Mark Redeker. Redeker is no longer in the Commission, but he had an official complaint of an ethics violation because he was caught making a trip to Vegas to meet with the potential Police Chief (Pelletier) and was accused of giving him sensitive information before his testing and interview.

First off, it's against the law for a police commissioner to give any information or to meet with candidates before their interview and testing. Pelletier was up against three local officers: Vic Ramos, John D. Jakubczak, and Everett Ferrera. It was well known that the police commissioner had an adversarial relationship with all of the local candidates, as well as the previous chief, Tivoli Fa'aumu. When Pelletier went in for his testing and interview, he basically aced every question;

213 https://www.civilbeat.org/2021/05/the-investigation-into-the-ex-maui-police-chiefs-hit-and-run-is-in/

214 https://s3.documentcloud.org/documents/20787997/may-agenda-item-11-c-chief-faaumus-incident-11-7-2020-review-ofinvestigation-report-part-iii.pdf

he had the best answers according to reports. An insider who was in that meeting said that when Pelletier came up to answer questions, all of the commissioners perked up and listened very carefully. He then shared insights into the Hawaii way of life that were hard to believe someone from Vegas would have known. He even used a local word, "pono," which means to make right. It was almost like they were expecting to pick Pelletier as the next police chief, and the vote for Pelletier was unanimous among all 9 members of the Police Commission.[215] After being hired, Pelletier again waived the residency requirement and brought along his deputy, Charles Hank, who is also from Vegas.[216]

A secret recording was made of the new police chief's first meeting with his officers that gives us a peek into his management style. From the recording, with Pelletier speaking:

"The administration is me. The administration is me, and we all march to the same drum, and if I have somebody that's gonna go against the administration, that's not gonna go very well for them." Charles Hank ("The Shank") stated: "his [Pelletier's] desire is to make this the model agency, not just for the islands, but for the whole country."

Clyde Holokai states:

> *I know who you guys have been talking to, people. This is me; you work and I'll be your best friend. You don't work or you're a crooked cop, I'm gonna be your worst enemy. You look at my record; it speaks for itself. We've gone after... When I was a cop in the city, we put away plenty of cops who were dirty, and I hated it, and I'll do it again.*[217]

Those were just some excerpts from the meeting. Clyde Holokai, who at the time was Assistant Police Chief, had retired shortly after Pelletier became the Police Chief. During this time, Chief John Pelletier had accrued eight official complaints from the department, mainly about creating a hostile work environment, which caused a lot of people to leave the department or retire early.

215 https://mauinow.com/2021/10/05/breaking-john-pelletier-selected-as-final-candidate-for-maui-police-chief/

216 https://www.mauicounty.gov/DocumentCenter/View/131160/JAN-12_Item-No-A4d_Complant-No-21-09_Unethical-Behavior-Police-Commissioner

217 https://youtu.be/DrXmM6Szrkk?si=Ca7OaaFGIF4lcXJp&t=309

There is a theme that comes out with Pelletier and his Deputy Hank: they're looking to make the Maui Police Department the model agency for the State and a best practice for the rest of the country (this was on his application). The new police chief and his deputy actively tried to get certain officers to quit or retire while demanding blind loyalty from the other officers. These recordings are recorded in the first commanders' meeting. You'll hear the same theme in that first commanders' meeting about Pelletier hustling to try to become the model agency for the State and for the country.

It looks like Chief Pelletier has a bigger responsibility than what happened in Lahaina. Is he trying to overhaul the agency and make it into something that someone else is telling him to make it into? This becomes even more evident during the first commanders meeting. These meetings happened shortly after he became the police chief.

Secret recording of commanders meeting with Pelletier speaking:

> Prior to that, I had the strip for three years. I was either the Incident Commander or the Commander of three actual active shooters that were active shooters. One would be one October; everybody knows that year; One would be the CiCi/Walmart incident where we lost Alyn and Igor, Alyn Beck and Igor Soldo, in a CiCi's pizza on June 8th 2014. And then, on my first day as a Captain on the strip, there was an active shooter on a bus in front of the Cosmo. He shot three people, killing one, and the FBI deemed that as an active shooter. So, I tell you that and the dates so that you understand I'm not saying something I don't mean. If I say it, then it's real.

Notice how Chief Pelletier glazed over the largest shooting in U.S. history that he claimed to be Incident Commander of, even though we now know this was a lie, after our investigation.

Things get more odd and hostile from here. Chief Pelletier continues in the same recording to make a threat to the commanders. He says what will happen to the first person that does not support his agenda. During this secret meeting recording, Pelletier says:

> I'm the administration. We know this. Okay? You all are the administration, through me. You're the administration. Everybody in this room is given a lawful order. You have to

support the administration; you have to. Okay? I will not tolerate insubordination. I understand where it falls in codes of conduct, and I understand how severe it can be, and anybody that is grossly insubordinate will not leave in good standing. I will not have it; I just won't. I will not have individuals or groups undermining the administration. That's all I'm gonna say on it. I think everybody knows exactly what I'm saying, but please do not be the one I make the example out of first, because I will FILET the first one, and then everybody will understand very quickly what I mean."[218]

Effective immediately, Alana (Pico) is going to be assigned directly to the Deputy Chief as the Information Specialist. Because we will control the message. Everyone. This is one team. One voice. Things will not leave here. I will not have 3 different people speaking on a crime scene, giving a different message. God forbid there's a critical incident. It's gotta be one message. Gotta be controlled.

Pelletier mentions that he wants everyone to be on the same page, not telling their own version of the story, which comes into play later on August 8th. He continues to state, "I made it very clear in my speech the other day; I said my goal is to make this a model agency for the state and a best practice for the nation."[219]

What's interesting regarding one man, Captain Ricky Uedoi, is that he was reassigned to Molokai; a role reserved for rookies. That is a huge demotion. He had been with the Maui Police for almost twenty-three years and was by no means a rookie. By putting him in Molokai (another island off Maui), it appears as though the administration was intent on getting Uedoi out of the way, and out of his role as "Head of Internal Affairs." Shortly after his reassignment, he retired early. He presumably felt that the demotion was a big slap in the face.

There is a rule that officers are not supposed to perform more than two tours on Molokai because it is so hard on an officer's personal life; they are required to travel often. Ricky had an especially difficult time during his two tours in Molokai because he was far away from his family. (source: Clyde)

218 https://youtu.be/c5aDs7p9M1I?si=yp_wYH9efVLV1Mlu
219 https://youtu.be/c5aDs7p9M1I?si=yp_wYH9efVLV1Mlu

Melissa Magonigle, who was in charge of human resources and finance and her husband were also fired, which was in retaliation for them speaking out against the Chief.[220] "Maui News Now" reported on February 8th, 2023:

> *Alleging gender discrimination and retaliation from the Maui Police Department chief and his former deputy, three female employees — two officers and one police department administrator — recently filed separate lawsuits in 2nd Circuit Court against the department.*

> *Lt. Audra Sellers, Sgt. Ka Lae O Ka Ena Brown and Melissa Magonigle, who is in charge of human resources and budget and finance for MPD, are also alleging violation of the whistleblower's protection act, saying there was retaliation for reporting illegal practices at MPD.*

> *The women, in their separate lawsuits filed on Jan. 30, detailed the treatment they've received in various incidents under Police Chief John Pelletier and former Deputy Chief Charles Hank III. Hank retired late last year.[221]*

In her own investigation, Traci Derwin heard from people in the Maui Police Department that after Pelletier fired the high ranking female officer, he made it very clear to the entire department that she was fired, apparently with the goal of making her an example of what can happen if you speak up against the Chief. He was not idly claiming that he was going to make an example of the first person who spoke out against him: he followed through.

In the case of Melissa Magonigle and her husband, there is an active case against the Chief, and it has been found to be substantiated. It is predicted that she will eventually win in court. Many Maui officers allegedly hope that Pelletier may finally be held accountable, but it has yet to be seen at the time of this writing.

---

220   https://www.mauinews.com/news/local-news/2023/02/lawsuits-against-mpd-claim-gender-discrimination-retaliation/

221   https://www.mauinews.com/news/local-news/2023/02/lawsuits-against-mpd-claim-gender-discrimination-retaliation/

Some people have wondered why more Maui officers are not speaking out. Like many of us, they have jobs and families to support. They have pensions that they're hoping to receive in order to retire. Furthermore, it is against Department policy to speak out publicly. If they speak out, Pelletier has allegedly said that he will sabotage their retirement, and he has the power to do so. If someone retires, Chief Pelletier can manipulate the paperwork to appear as though they are not retiring in good standing, which circumvents their ability to receive the full benefits that they have earned.

Another controversial incident happened just fifty days after Pelletier became the Chief of Police. He requested a pay raise, and a pretty significant one, shortly after taking this position. He initially requested a $40,000 pay raise, then the commission offered $46,000. This is much higher than the maximum pay increase set forth by the police union. Now, we don't have confirmation that his salary did go up to that because we receive conflicting information in our investigation. Some say his salary didn't increase, but others say it did.

It would go against the Union laws to provide Chief Pelletier such a significant pay raise, however we have acquired an official complaint from Deyna Puckett asking the Commission to wait six months before they consider this pay raise. At that time, Pelletier had only been in this position for fifty days, and we learned that morale was low. The complaint indicates that officers with fifteen to twenty years of service to the Department were going to quit, and they were willing to sacrifice their pensions. That doesn't just exhibit low morale, but absolute desperation. These officers allegedly felt that if Pelletier had gotten this pay raise, it would have made things worse. Since then, many good cops and senior officers have left the department, which is sad for all of Maui. Clyde detailed a time when an officer cried at their retirement party because they were not ready to leave. A moment that should have been commemorated with joy was overshadowed with sadness.

Another incident that happened after John Pelletier became the Chief happened on February 24, 2022. Terry Jones, who was Chief Pelletier's personal secretary, died in a car crash.[222] The official story is that at 4:40 in the morning, she was taking a nap in her car. She was

---

222 https://www.mauinews.com/news/local-news/2022/02/police-chiefs-secretary-killed-in-crash-while-pursuing-thief/

supposed to be delivering newspapers for her daughter, who stayed at home. During her nap, two men, Robert Nelson and Jesselee Decoite, stole her purse and sped away in a car. Jones woke up during the theft and pursued the purse thieves. She was going too fast around a curve and hit a tree. When the ambulance came, they did not rush her to the hospital or attempt to resuscitate her; instead, she was declared dead at the scene. This was a very suspicious time for the Chief to lose his personal secretary in such a tragic and violent way and under unusual circumstances. William Hankins, who was in charge of the investigation, did want to go on the record and say that she was on the phone with dispatch during the car chase. He does acknowledge that the timing was very unusual but that their findings are just what we heard; it was a tragic car accident that led to her demise (William Hankins). In her coverage in "*Burn Back Better*," Stephanie did not uncover any more information than what is stated here, but you can read another detailed account in that book, which serves as the "prequel" to this continued investigation.

The death of Terry Jones was a very traumatic thing for the entire Department because Jones was with the Department for thirty years. She was the matriarch to the department, and the epitome of a true Hawai'ian auntie. She had a pidgin accent and cheerful demeanor. She was always eager to help. Many have given insight that she was poorly treated by the new administration. Clyde Holokai said that he saw her in tears in her car in the parking lot, crying because of the treatment she was getting from Pelletier and the Deputy. That was a point of contention because, during her eulogy, Chief Pelletier spoke of her very highly, as if she meant so much to him, and that he was so devastated for her loss. In reality, our understanding is that he did not treat her well at all.

Holokai and Hankins were not allowed to attend the eulogy that the Chief held in front of cameras. That didn't settle well with the other officers who loved and cared about her. What's odd is that Pelletier and Hank wanted to classify this accident as a murder since her purse had been stolen and this is what led to the accident. Legally, they cannot categorize this as a homicide because she was the one pursuing the thieves.

Fast forward a week after the accident when William Hankins, Ricky Uedoi, and Clyde Holokai retired early. These men had many years with the department. William Hankins was the Traffic Commander, Ricky Uedoi was Commander of Internal Affairs, and Clyde Holokai was the Assistant Chief.[223] Together, they stated they were no longer going to put up with the treatment they had received. The death of Jones may have been the "straw" that broke the camel's back, so to speak. Both Holokai and Hankins were written up for "reluctant compliance" (following orders with reluctance). Clyde believes he was targeted so that he would leave the department. It seems like all three of these officers were forced out of the Maui Police Department. Some say that Pelletier wanted to get the good cops out of the way and put in other officers to take their place.[224] Other reports say that the Department was riddled with corruption, and that they were happy to see some of the bad cops go. Overwhelmingly, we have heard good things about the three men who retired.

One news report from "KITV" details just how bad the work environment was for these men. The article stated:

> *Some say the climate is pushing many officers to consider leaving the force. A'ali'i Dukelow has new details about the ongoing strike at MPD. Maui Police Chief John Pelletier was on the job for about 7 months and racked up 7 official work environment complaints. The employees who filed the grievances didn't want to speak out because of fear of retaliation, but former ranking officers, speaking on their behalf, have said one involves a woman who was cursed at during a meeting, and that working under Pelletier had led her and several others to seek help from psychiatrists and anxiety medication. It was a dictatorship. Former Maui Police Department Lieutenant William Hankins had more than 30 years of service under his belt. Hankins worked under 5 different chiefs but says he retired early because of Pelletier. He alleged the recently installed head created what he called a "hostile and toxic work environment from the very first meeting. When the Commander and Chief says, 'If you don't agree with him and support him, he's going to filet you,' people walk on eggshells. Nobody wants to say anything." Then, after 28 years on the force, former Assistant Chief Clyde Holokai*

223 https://youtu.be/KOe--xOqy7w?si=g2Ipnsc46MSWTsR1
224 https://www.youtube.com/watch?v=mj6bHfbeCUQ

retired early because of Pelletier's management. The internal friction
at MPD was unprecedented for Holokai. He believes the stress of
working under Pelletier even took a physical toll on him. "In about
2 months, I lost about 15 to 20 pounds," says Holokai. The Police
Union surveyed 60% of its personnel back in April. The results were
quite alarming. A third of those surveyed reported they are thinking
of leaving within the next 2 years, many citing morale as a top
reason for considering a departure. The Maui Police Department is
already a hundred officers short. Workers surveyed gave Pelletier
poor scores in 12 out of 13 categories. One question asked whether
the Chief fostered strong morale. Most responded not very well or
not well at all. The Police Union is waiting on the final findings of the
complaints to determine the next steps to be made. The complaints
will be discussed at the next Maui Police Commission meeting.[225]

After these complaints were made public, there was a discussion with
the Police Commission, and the question was asked, "what is going to
happen to Chief Pelletier?" The only solution offered was to hire a coach
to help the Chief with his management skills, which is very unusual. In
an interview with Traci, even Clyde said that if someone needs a coach
to help with officer relations, it is a sign that a person is not ready to
be Police Chief. He also said that the Department has a "no-tolerance"
policy. Therefore, once the first complaint comes in, normally, one
is taken out of that position. The person is either demoted, fired, or
suspended. However, Pelletier racked up eight complaints with very
little done to him. That, to your authors, is a huge red flag.

On the day of the Maui fire, Chief Pelletier went against the General
Orders of the "All Hazard Plan" by not being at the "Emergency
Operations Center" (EOC). Chief Pelletier was one of the most
important people that needed to be present at the EOC because of his
rank. He was of the rank to give orders across different departments at
the EOC in order to coordinate rescues and collaborate with agencies
such as "HECO," "Roberts Bus Company," "Maui Fire," and other
emergency agencies; yet he was not there. In fact, Chief Pelletier was
never there. He even admits on camera that he sent an Assistant Chief

---

225 https://www.kitv.com/news/it-was-a-dictatorship-former-maui-police-officers-shine-light-on-complaints-against-department-chief/article_0ea3830e-0fa0-11ed-a1b1-ebfecbec9097.html

in his place who turned out to be Greg Okamoto. Okamoto signed into the EOC at 17:20 or 5:20 p.m., after much of the town of Lahaina had already burned.

The authors and anyone we've interviewed finds that the delayed sign-in of Okamoto was inappropriate because the Assistant Chief can't do the job of the Chief. After all, he doesn't get paid the big bucks that Pelletier does, right? But on a serious note, instead of going to the EOC, Chief Pelletier set up his own "Department Operation Center" at Maui Police Headquarters, where he stayed with several members of his command staff including his deputy. Holokai says:

> *The department is typically taken care of by an Assistant Chief. So the Chief and other members of the Chief's office are available to work directly with the county and leaders of other emergency response agencies at the main EOC. Having the right people collaborating together in the same room is crucial. If you're not used to that type of situation at the very least, it's gonna be very inefficient. If you're not of a higher rank, then you cannot command another officer across a different bureau to take action immediately. Pelletier not being at the EOC caused problems.[226]*

One of the most shocking parts of the August 8th disaster were the at least nine roadblocks that were erected in Lahaina, as shown in the map below. In this image, the blue stars mark locations of police roadblocks, and the lightning bolt symbols are where HECO, or "Hawaii Electric Company," blocked the roads. At first, Pelletier said that he did not set up any roadblocks. When he was confronted by Jeremy Lee (reporter from KITV) at a press conference and asked if he had blocked traffic, he denied it. He was asked point blank if he blocked roads going out of Keawe Street, which would allow the traffic to leave the area. Pelletier very emphatically stated, "they were not directed towards the danger."[227]

226 https://youtu.be/fCQ3hTcuvm0?si=NF3325IRaqPVg2nU
227 https://www.youtube.com/watch?v=v7-scIQVTiU

The yellow area was
trapped, but safe

Fire jumped the
bypass and spread to
the red areas

All of the areas in red were
trapped, and also burned.

However, evidence proves otherwise. In one case, the public was
diverted into a parking lot where there was no other exit. They were
corralled, and because of this, many people died in their cars or were
forced to go into the water.

Image courtesy of cell phone video footage from Noah Thompkinson, Maui resident

When many eyewitnesses came forward with videos and pictures evidencing these roadblocks, Chief Pelletier had to backtrack and use the excuse: "well, yes, there were roadblocks, but that was because of the downed power lines that were energized".

That statement was either an excuse or a lie, because there were seventeen calls recorded between the Maui Police Department and Hawai'ian Electric in which one can hear "Hawai'ian Electric" saying that the power lines were not energized.[228]

We know now that power was turned off from around 4:00 a.m. until 6:30 a.m. on the morning of August 8th, which is why school was canceled and so many people unable to work indicate that during the fire they were napping in their homes. Power came back on for a little while and then it was announced at 6:40 a.m. that HECO turned the power off again because of the early morning Lahaina fire. Power lines were not energized. There was no danger for traffic leaving, yet they were blocked anyway by the police. It should be noted that Chief Pelletier was now in the EOC or "Emergency Operations Center" like he was supposed to be. If he was, he would have been in the same room as representatives from HECO, as well as other companies that are instrumental in an emergency, and there would have been

---

228 https://youtu.be/loOFNII38Z4?si=scw3b7R0k87e0Sx9&t=33

clearer communications between agencies. We believe that with clearer communications that many lives could have been spared.[229]

Here is what Anne Williams, a resident of Lahaina, has to share about her experience:

> *I ran down the hill, and at the bottom of the hill is where I saw my daughter, already stopped by the police. She was on the highway, trying to go north. She was in her truck, so I jumped in. We sat there, being blocked by a police officer right there at Lahainaluna Road. Nobody could get on the highway going north, which is the way we wanted to go. I knew we couldn't just sit there. The fire was coming down. It was coming down quickly, and I knew this police officer would be running for his life any minute, so we just took off not obeying the traffic cop. We had to go down towards Front Street and then make our way through the streets in town going north. We eventually did get out of town by going out the Fleming's Road exit near the old Chart House restaurant; it was still open at that time. We were able to turn onto the highway going north. It was free and clear; no poles or anything down. No electric lines were down. It was a safe exit. Cars could get out. It was the only exit to the highway at that point. I did notice that later after I left, that exit was blocked by 2 police cars not allowing anybody else to go out of that route.[230]*

Heroic citizen journalist Eric West recorded a now infamous video with a homeless man known by locals as "Fish." The entire interview is transcribed in Stephanie's book *"Burn Back Better"* and, because it was the interview that "woke up" so many hundreds of people with whom we've spoken, it is worth reading the book just to read Fish's harrowing account. By God's grace, the original interview with Fish will still be available on YouTube as you're reading this book if you visit the astounding investigative work on Eric West's channel. [231] [232] The original interview with Fish was one of the most miraculous events that became a world-famous event. Eric calls Fish one of the wisest

---

229 https://youtu.be/st8t7bg0Sc8?si=mmY30uIVsCjq_Iqc&t=562
230 https://www.youtube.com/shorts/_qOhjsznrMA
231 https://www.youtube.com/watch?v=easMHBYdpJo
232 https://www.youtube.com/watch?v=6jVDTfp7gFc

people that he knows. When he sees Fish, West was filming another interview for his channel.

When Fish walks up to Eric, you can see and feel the joy and elation with Eric seeing that this precious Lahaina resident was alive and walking right up to his friend Eric. The videos at https://www.youtube.com/@hawaiirealestateorg are now an American treasure and Eric deserves a Nobel Prize for his brave citizen journalism and dedication to providing information about Lahaina that would never have been reported on were it not for his huge heart for Maui, love for the community, and dedication to the truth, even when fellow neighbors and residents of Lahaina trolled and mocked him, even threatening his life.

Fish provided what was, for many, the wakeup call that something "fishy," pun intended, happened in Lahaina with the roadblocks. Fish illustrated that those who survived were those who "disobeyed" the police orders. You see, Fish saw the roadblocks and asked the officer why he was doing that. The police officer responded that they were "just following orders." Later the next day, Fish came back and said he saw many cars completely burnt.[233]

After the fire, on August 16th, Pelletier was in a press conference and said:

> We're doing data scrubs... We want to get people out, and so let me answer it like this; there is going to be a very detailed long after-action that might be the longest after-action that's ever been. Every data point is going to be scrubbed, looked at, and meticulously gone through. We have detectives. It's not just MPD; it's also the FBI. It's also Honolulu PD. We've got folks from the Big Island that are assisting at the perimeter...
>
> We're doing data scrubs, and so I guess we're drilling down. If I say scrub, I don't want you to think we're washing something away. We're drilling down."[234]

It does look like there was a very big effort to scrub the data. For instance, police body cam footage came out and was very limited. A

---

233 https://youtu.be/easMHBYdpJo?si=5lv0UsjFTtM_S9Us
234 https://www.bitchute.com/video/k4ADPrDw1D5v/

FOIA request for the "Emergency Operation Center's" sign-in and sign-out form took months to receive. The emails were scrubbed from Herman Andya, who resigned from the Maui emergency management team and was held responsible for not sounding the world's best emergency system alarms on the island. Most of the communication that we were looking for was not included in those emails. Pelletier was instrumental regarding this incident and the cover-up. Was it part of his duty to cover it up?

At this time, we request that if you have any ability to obtain dispatch reports that you contact www. MauiCommunityInvestigation.com where the team is working on island to obtain information the public deserves to have in a fair, unbiased, and transparent public investigation.

A preliminary after-action report was released on February 5, 2024, and it was a fairly lengthy one. It says, regarding the large number of missing children, that the investigators had contacted the "Department of Education" and verified there were no missing children, and that the Department was able to contact every student, including those that left the island or state.[235]

This is a contradiction because there have been several reports from officials admitting that minors were lost during this fire.[236] Many witnesses say they know families that were completely wiped-out: children, parents, and grandparents. It's simply not possible that every single child was accounted for. However, that is what was alleged in the after-action report. The report says that there are "Lone Wolf actors" and sometimes foreign governments spreading misinformation.[237] The report didn't name exactly who, but the Governor, early on, accused Russia and China of providing misinformation about this tragedy. It might be malinformation because the government doesn't want it out, but that doesn't make it false. It is true information that goes against the mainstream narrative, or any statements that question authority, similar to communist countries where they do not have free speech rights. If you go against the government and say something that they

---

235   http://www.mauipolice.com/uploads/1/3/1/2/131209824/pre_aar_master_copy_final_draft_1.23.24.pdf

236   https://youtu.be/UijEBIHvMlQ?si=hlB0awwoaVTlWm1Z

237   https://youtu.be/tVBmPbikiE0?si=2HzFy9BV2WG8Qors

don't want you to say, they consider it malinformation and discredit that information. They're trying to discredit those with an outside narrative to the mainstream media. Malinformation is a fairly new term and many times considered an act of terrorism. The report is supposed to help aid in future tragedies. While recommendations are made in the report, there are many items that are unsubstantiated, with evidence and hints to a cover-up. Pelletier was in charge of the Lahaina after-action report, as well as the after-action report of the Mandalay Bay shooting in Las Vegas.

After researching the department and the Chief over the past months, it looks like his position was not given simply for this incident. From speaking to people in the department, he may have a lot more to accomplish. He could very well be part of helping usher in the new SMART City, or modernized version of Lahaina, that began with "JUMPSmart Maui." [238] [239]

Also curiously, Craig Nakamoto from the "Hawaii Community Development Authority," (HCDA) is trying to bring gambling and more tourism into this area, just like he did to Kaka'ako. [240] [241] In fact, legislation just legalized the first Casino on Oahu, and they have recently legalized online betting and football-like fantasy football betting. Not that long ago, all forms of gambling in Hawaii were illegal. They wanted to keep the islands free from those types of things. Traditionally, people go to Vegas to gamble. Is a Vegas strip coming to Hawaii? Bringing in people such as Pelletier would help do that. Is it a coincidence that the Police Chief of Kaua'i is also from Vegas, along with his Deputy? It looks like it's part of a bigger plan and just the beginning of this new change that they're bringing to the Hawai'ian Islands. Pelletier is still working at the department and carrying out his expected duties. It doesn't look like he's going to resign or get fired at the time of this writing. With plans potentially on the table to turn Lahaina into an even more robust tourist destination, potentially with gambling involved, why would they turn their backs on a Police Chief from Las Vegas?

238 https://www.nedo.go.jp/content/100864936.pdf
239 https://youtu.be/2ZIAyFWTSv0?si=1cVjw6nA_wVWicuG&t=608
240 https://www.civilbeat.org/2024/03/this-state-agency-transformed-kakaako-should-it-do-the-same-for-lahaina/
241 https://dbedt.hawaii.gov/hcda/kakaako-plan-and-rules/

Some news about Kaua'i's Police Chief Todd Raybuck, who is a retired Police Captain from Las Vegas, has surfaced about a complaint filed against him because he misplaced his firearm in the restroom at the station. He left it in one of the stalls between the handicap rail and the wall. After this incident, it was reported that this was not the first time Raybuck misplaced his firearm, which was fully loaded with a round in the chamber. A spokesman for the Chief stated that the restroom where the gun was left in is for employees of the police department, but that turns out to be false. This restroom is often used by witnesses, suspects, and other guests of the office. This is a very serious infraction at the Kaua'i Police Department, and at the time of this writing, no disciplinary action has been taken.[242]

A representative from the police union made a public statement saying that this restroom is not an "employee-only" restroom but is used by guests, potential suspects, and visitors to the station.

This was not the first complaint filed against Raybuck as Police Chief. In March 2021, he made a public apology for discriminatory comments made to an officer during a meeting. He made disparaging comments about Japanese people while squinting his eyes. The commission suspended him without pay for five days after a court decided Raybuck had mocked people of Asian descent. Given the serious nature of this finding and the cost of the settlement of the case ($350,000) plus legal fees, it is unusual that the punishment is very minimal. This settlement, along with other cases against a county official, comes out of the county budget, and this usually puts pressure on the commission to replace this person.[243] In due time, we will see how much money Maui County is willing to pay out to keep Chief Pelletier in office. It is predicted that his settlements could be in the multi-millions of dollars.

At this time your authors are actively collecting evidence for a potential third book as well as the motion picture documentary, Sound The Alarm.

---

242 https://www.hawaiinewsnow.com/2024/04/12/law-enforcement-union-accuses-embattled-kpd-chief-downplaying-lost-gun-incident/

243 https://www.hawaiinewsnow.com/2024/04/06/kauai-police-chief-pay-350000-settle-alleged-racial-discrimination-suit-former-captain/

CHAPTER THIRTEEN:
Ominous Questions We're All Asking...

In an article on the "DailyMail.com" published on August 17th, 2023, entitled, "Maui boy, 7, is found burned to death in car, as local lawmaker says she fears HUNDREDS of children may be dead after power cut kept them home from school on day of inferno," one may read:

> *Lawmaker Elle Cochran, who is in the Hawaii House of Representatives, said it could grow to hundreds as search operations continue. Cochran fears many of the dead could be children because many schools in Lahaina were closed on the day of the fires due to power outages. A lot of children stayed at home while their parents were at work and might have been trapped and perished. Jessica Sill, who teaches at King Kamehameha III Elementary School, said: 'Without school, there was nowhere for [kids] to go that day.'*[244]

In her book, *Burn Back Better*, Stephanie Pierucci largely dispelled any theories of missing children. However, the question is worth revisiting. Below you'll find detailed tracking of the now infamous eleven school buses, two tour buses, and entourage.

There has been much controversy about whether children were abducted from Lahaina during the tragedy on August 8th. As of the time of this writing, only three minors have been reported as deceased.

---

244 https://www.dailymail.co.uk/news/article-12416967/Maui-boy-7-burned-death-car-local-lawmaker-says-fears-HUNDREDS-children-dead-power-cut-kept-home-school-day-inferno.html

One point to consider is that there are videos that were filmed of eleven unmarked and darkly tinted school buses in the motorcade (above) going towards Lahaina, passing by Ma'alea.[245] This likely occurred on August 8th, indicated by the traffic jam congestion, wind noise, and police presence blocking the road. These buses are brand new, late-model Bluebird Vision school buses, which appear to match the ones seen parked on Lahainaluna road behind Pioneer Mill. They even have no letters or numbers on them as well.

---

245 https://youtu.be/aBB-6DXvFt0?si=u44GAaLceS5IKkXQ&t=398

There was also a Roberts Hawaii bus motorcade (pictured above) going towards Lahaina, passing by Launiupoko, but we can't verify whether it was on the 8th or another date.[246] Traci Derwin has asked many residents and survivors if they saw children being taken or seen on any of these school buses, but she has not been able to verify this. It's been reported that most schools in Lahaina were not in session on the 8th except for freshman and new student orientation, although Kihei already started on the 7th. However, the educators have been silent on this topic.

Later, aerial images revealed that school buses were parked at the Kapalua Airport, which has recently closed its commercial operations although it did provide bus services for displaced Lahainaluna students when the new high school re-opened in Kihei about a month later, after another fire on August 9th, which was right behind the school in Kihei![247] [248]

Another group of forty plus school buses (far right, below) are seen in satellite photos near a motocross dirt bike and race track in Pulehunui, behind the "National Guard Armory" off Veterans Highway.

246 https://youtu.be/aBB-6DXvFt0?si=4xu6z02oA14rgcMT&t=465
247 https://www.mauinews.com/news/local-news/2023/09/bus-service-for-impacted-lahaina-students-begins-today/
248 https://www.civilbeat.org/beat/bus-services-commence-for-lahaina-students/

Adjacent to the warehouse and parking lot full of buses is "Aloha Waste Systems" and "Valley Isle Pumping," which may still have a freight elevator to an underground tunnel that goes three hundred feet below the surface. Video of this tunnel was taken in the 1990s by motocross racers who had wandered inside after a few drinks one night, but it's unclear what it's being used for. It contains massive machinery and tunnels that appear to be some sort of waterworks from the 1930s, which were still being maintained in the video from the 1990s.

The video shows a group of young men going into this underground entrance through an old-fashioned freight elevator.[249] It's easy to see why there is speculation that children were abducted, but as of now, there has been no solid evidence that there were any abductions that took place. We are currently looking for someone on Maui who can further investigate these buses and tunnels in person to verify what they're being used for.

At the time of this writing most respected citizen journalists and Maui residents scoff at the notion that children are missing, stating that in a community that small they would "know" if any children were taken. What's more, even the residents we interviewed who claim that the death toll is above 1,000 or even closer to 2,000 don't believe that a significant portion of those deaths were children. Although we are quite certain that more children perished that is officially reported, it

---

249 https://www.youtube.com/watch?v=96gB5V4TTD4

does not appear at this time that "scores" or even "dozens" of children are missing. When questioning parents on the island, few if any know of a single child who is missing from their child's classroom, which is encouraging to the authors. Nevertheless, the buses and tunnels are curious details that we will continue to investigate.

Our online investigation found that the property with the buses was the first one to be built within the new "Pulehunui Industrial Park," as older satellite photos have shown.[250] This property was lot #13 at Nopu St and was first purchased for $3.7 million on July 16, 2018, and which is pictured below.[251]

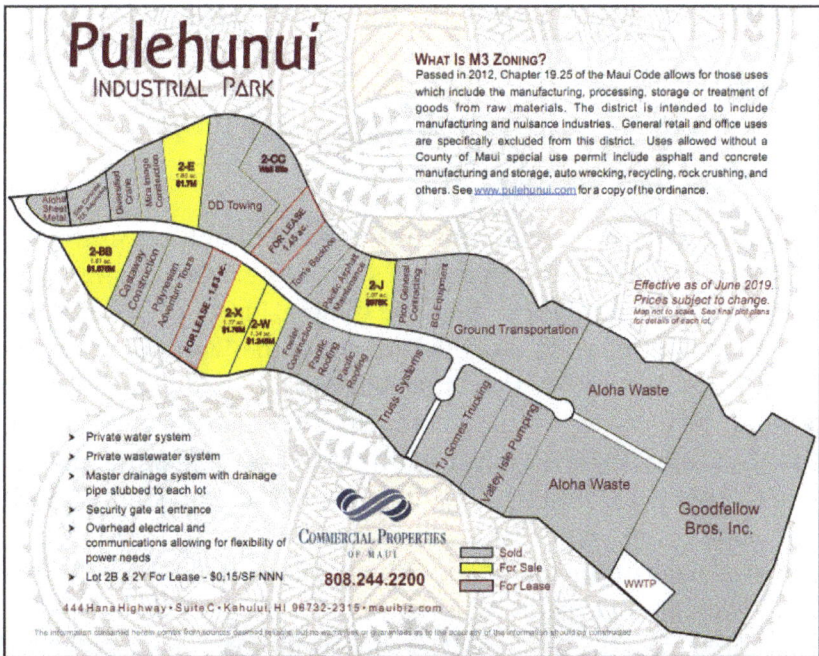

The August 8th Lahaina fire "After-Action Report" says that all of the children have been contacted by the Department of Education. However, as stated in an earlier chapter, that would be impossible, because there were minors who perished in the fire. There are many red flags surrounding this topic, including the Mayor shutting down

250 https://www.mauibiz.com/docs/flyers/pulehunui_industrial_park.pdf
251 https://www.vyllahome.com/commercial-for-sale/0-Nopu-St-Lot-2-M-Kahului-HI-96732-192980337

a press conference because a reporter asked how many children are missing, as well as pressing the Mayor for an approximate number, but he could only answer this question with: "I don't know how many children are missing."

Another topic that has been ignored is what happened to the children in daycare and preschool. No reports of what happened to those children have been discussed. There are also children who were homeschooled, and no word about those students have been made either. These young children are some of the most vulnerable, being that they cannot fend for themselves, and their parents may not have survived. What happened to these very young residents, and why has this issue not been addressed? The silence is deafening.

The role of the Military Industrial Complex and Military Operations

In this section we will detail what we know about military exercises in the weeks prior, and craft that were seen flying over Lahaina during the fire. Major General Hara, Adjutant General for the "State of Hawai'i Department of Defense," and the Director of the "Hawai'i Emergency Management Agency," claimed that helicopters couldn't fly because of the wind.[252] However, we have obtained a video that shows the "U.S. Coast Guard" MH-65 Dolphin that rescued seventeen people after being dispatched from the "U.S. Coast Guard" cutter Kimball during eighty mph winds, which contradicts Hara's claim.[253]

A brief background on Major General Hara brings some clarity on his role during this event. As of November 2024, General Hara will have retired from the military after serving for forty years, and he will also be relinquishing his position as the head of the "Hawaii Emergency Management Agency (HEIMA)." [254] Yes, he held these two positions simultaneously, which is a conflict of interest, to our understanding.

According to policy, HIEMA needs a declared state of emergency in order to request military support. This request is then given to the military who then orders support; in this case General Hara would be

---

252 https://youtu.be/CRXiX1HmXjY?si=eyzoS7tj3N5zeDId&t=264
253 https://youtu.be/CRXiX1HmXjY?si=RYcAQIuw_v0_Zh9p&t=42
254 https://youtu.be/02RZFX3OxF4?si=qS6__31rdKhjPT2r

responsible for taking this request and making arrangements to send aircraft, and Navy vehicles to the affected areas.

As stated by a number of witnesses, the morning of August 9th, the day after the fire; the streets were empty and there was no military presence trying to rescue them from land and sea. Videos we have obtained of people walking the streets on the morning of August 9th, including the YouTube video we cited in an earlier chapter by "Haiku," show that the streets were a veritable ghost town.

General Hara's retirement is part of a worldwide trend of high-ranking military officials deciding to retire at this time. In fact, there are so many military officials retiring that the "U.S. Air Force" has opened a program for retirees to come back to active duty as reported by the Air Force Times on February 7, 2024.[255]

Another chopper also appeared in the referenced video, which was found to be a "U.S. Navy Seahawk" from the "Easyriders" of "Helicopter Maritime Strike Squadron 37" (HSM-37) and is one of two Seahawks that were dispatched from the "USS Wayne E. Meyer" to Lahaina, Maui on August 8th.[256] In the above photo, this Seahawk is clearly missing it's ID number. This was reported by Air Force Brigadier General Pat Ryder at a Pentagon press briefing on August 10th, in addition to several other helicopters that he also confirmed were present that day. [257]

This Seahawk is equipped with a side-mounted fuel tank for extended range, and a standard issue nose-mounted "Raytheon Multi-Spectral Electro-Optical Targeting System" (EOTS) for targeting

255 https://www.airforcetimes.com/news/your-air-force/2024/02/07/air-force-seeks-retirees-to-come-back-to-active-duty/

256 https://youtu.be/CRXiX1HmXjY?si=ByEB3vU7RYbD_fMh&t=504

257 https://youtu.be/YPGlciWyLaE?si=0aqbzc6UW0cgwxGJ&t=36

and imaging.[258] The multi-spectral targeting system is essentially an electronic eye that can see in multiple spectrums at once, such as the visible spectrum as well as infrared, or "heat vision."

In this Navy photo of Easyrider #41, it still has the standard nose-mounted Raytheon Multi-Spectral Electro-Optical Targeting System (EOTS) for targeting and imaging, but it's shown here without the extra fuel tank for extended range. This is the same exact helicopter that was missing it's ID#, and we'll show how we know this to be the case.

Seahawk detachments typically perform anti-submarine and anti-mine operations, which often utilize a laser module about the same size and shape as the extra fuel tank (and in the same position) so it's easy to confuse the two, especially when the identifying number had been removed or covered as it was over Maui. Seahawks can also perform search and rescue operations, but the only helicopters that rescued anyone were a "Navy CH-47 Chinook" that rescued 14 people[259] and a Coast Guard MH-65 Dolphin that rescued 17.[260] [261]

The crew of this particular Seahawk posted about their mission on Facebook, where they claimed to have "searched the coastline for survivors who escaped the wildfires in Lahaina and helped coordinate firefighting efforts by identifying hotspots from the air."[262] Based on the configuration of the chopper, this does appear to be what they were actually equipped to do, so why cover or remove the numbers?

258 https://www.militaryaerospace.com/communications/article/16718620/raytheon-wins-another-contract-for-multispectral-targeting-systems-for-navy-helicopters

259 https://youtu.be/YPGlciWyLaE?si=S7ynIzyAzVpUmK8C

260 https://www.youtube.com/watch?v=YPGlciWyLaE

261 https://www.facebook.com/USCGCKimball/posts/pfbid0Gomrf5HVF5MMd6ma7J5hJfwiJadavDjGsaJt85ndhCLCfJFb39D9rCrTtvDLxYial

262 https://www.facebook.com/HSM37EasyriderOhana/posts/pfbid02iea6VZT1EfwFJ2xSc2Vos5idc1sWSR2wCDvWZfL2zrWtxyVPa4GqMS6bgsgrH97Rl

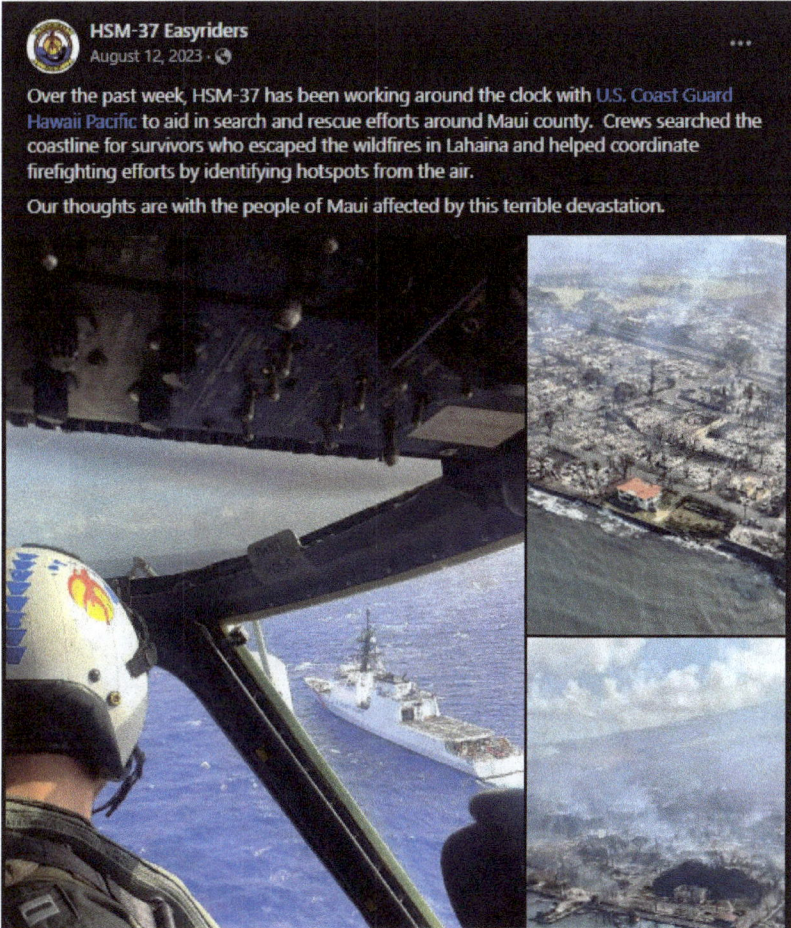

Seahawk detachments routinely participate in Fleet and Theater exercises[263] (RIMPAC,[264] Foal Eagle,[265] Cobra Gold,[266] CARAT,[267] C/JLOTS,[268] and TALISMAN SABRE[269]) and also provide a wide variety of support services at NAB, Coronado, California.[270] [271] [272]

263 https://en.wikipedia.org/wiki/Naval_Beach_Group_One
264 https://en.wikipedia.org/wiki/RIMPAC
265 https://en.wikipedia.org/wiki/Foal_Eagle
266 https://en.wikipedia.org/wiki/Cobra_Gold
267 https://en.wikipedia.org/wiki/Cooperation_Afloat_Readiness_and_Training
268 https://en.wikipedia.org/w/index.php?title=C/JLOTS&action=edit&redlink=1
269 https://en.wikipedia.org/wiki/Exercise_Talisman_Saber
270 https://en.wikipedia.org/wiki/Naval_Beach_Group_One
271 https://en.wikipedia.org/wiki/Exercise_Talisman_Saber
272 https://en.wikipedia.org/wiki/Naval_Beach_Group_One

Exercise Talisman Sabre (which claims to be "not just an exercise" on its own site) took place from July 22nd to August 4th, hosted by the "USS Ronald Reagan Carrier Strike Group" (CSG-5) in the waters northeast of Australia, with the participation of thirteen nations and over 30,000 personnel.[273]

Easyriders #31 and #41 from "Detachment One" were previously in Japan, and the "USS Ronald Reagan Carrier Strike Group" (CSG-5) was allegedly en route from Australia to Japan when they received the HIEMA request for Defense Support of Civil Authorities (DSCA) on August 8th, which activated the entire Indo-Pacific Command.

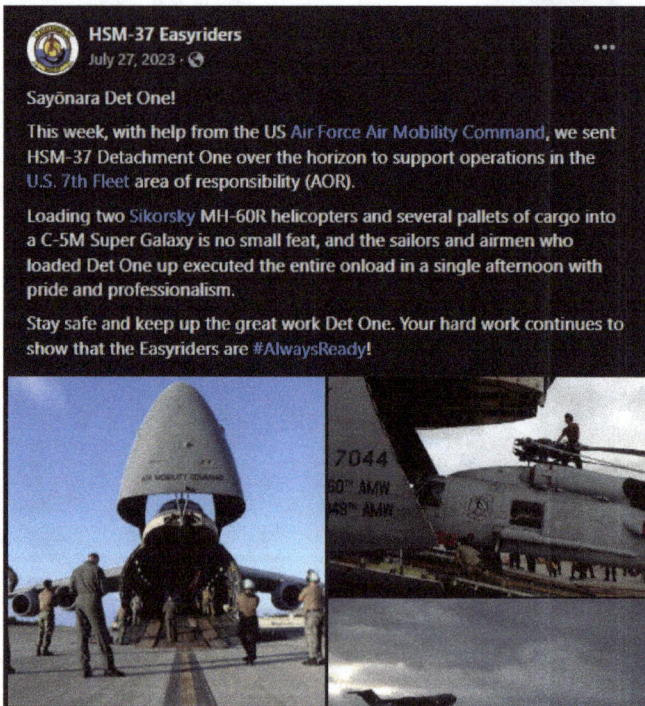

Besides the missing number on the chopper, another oddity is found in their Facebook posts from the days prior to the fire,[274] when they packed up before the end of Exercise Talisman Sabre[275] and shipped out

---

273 https://www.defense.gov/Multimedia/Experience/Exercise-Talisman-Sabre/

274 https://www.facebook.com/HSM37EasyriderOhana/posts/pfbid0LetXRRHkP6ZvhHj48c7W1X9aezabCnbDKhEPb8nXi2FoN8St7aJNvrDMjsCubrk4l

275 https://www.defense.gov/Multimedia/Experience/Exercise-Talisman-Sabre/

to rendezvous with the USS Wayne E. Meyer[276] stationed out of Pearl Harbor, just in time to respond as part of the Defense Support of Civil Authorities (DSCA).[277] [278] This was requested by General Hara, director of HIEMA and Adjutant General to the Department of Defense, in the hours after 3:21 p.m. on August 8th, when acting Governor Sylvia Luke declared a state of emergency in Governor Green's absence, who was conveniently on the mainland at the time.

Another Easyriders Facebook post shows a reel taken from aboard the C-5M Super Galaxy cargo plane that transported them to Pearl Harbor-Hickam. In this reel, Easyrider #31 can be seen with its ID# clearly displayed, which was also still present in a subsequent video taken over Lahaina that was posted on the YouTube channel "MrHipnautical."[279] [280]

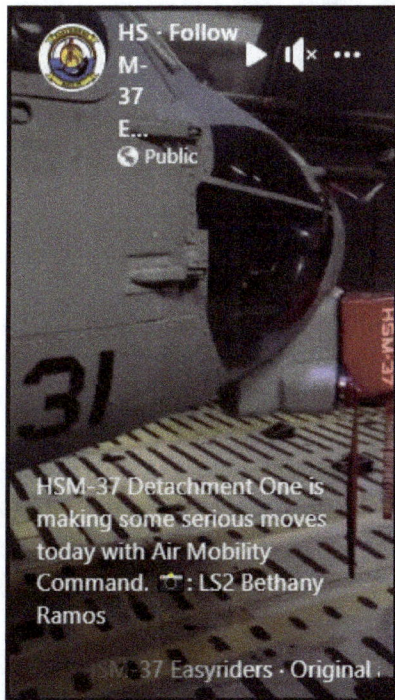

276 https://en.wikipedia.org/wiki/USS_Wayne_E._Meyer
277 https://www.facebook.com/HSM37EasyriderOhana/posts/pfbid0LetXRRHkP6ZvhHj48
     c7W1X9aezabCnbDKhEPb8nXi2FoN8St7aJNvrDMjsCubrk4l
278 https://en.wikipedia.org/wiki/USS_Wayne_E._Meyer
279 https://www.facebook.com/reel/1672737933176841
280 https://youtu.be/5PXHaQpH0_Q?si=x2H_SH3f14uK_xYI

Another Facebook photo (above) shows Easyrider #41 (according to its red exhaust covers) aboard the plane to Pearl Harbor, which may not have its ID# displayed. Since Brigadier General Pat Ryder reported that only 2 Seahawks were sent to Maui, and the other one clearly has its number showing, then #41 must be the helicopter that was seen over Maui without an ID#.[281]

In the hours after Hawaii's acting Lieutenant Governor, Sylvia Luke, declared the emergency at 3:21 p.m., HIEMA requested Defense Support of Civil Authorities (DSCA) from the Joint Task Force Civil Support (JTF-CS).[282] The DOD dispatched the US Northern Command[283] (US NORTHCOM), and the US Indo-Pacific Command[284] (US INDOPACOM), which just finished hosting the war games Exercise Talisman Sabre (NOT JUST AN EXERCISE) aboard the USS Ronald Reagan[285] (which is ironically called upon for help).[286]

---

281 https://www.facebook.com/photo.php?fbid=611590104435253&set= pb.100067528056461.-2207520000&type=3
282 https://www.jtfcs.northcom.mil/About/Factsheets/Article/1199952/joint-task-force-civil-support-fact-sheet/
283 https://sgp.fas.org/eprint/northcom-opplans.html
284 https://www.ndia.org/events/2021/3/8/1540---post-2021
285 https://youtu.be/AjMz2Ufi_E0
286 https://youtu.be/AjMz2Ufi_E0

The following diagram shows the authority of the Governor over the different mobilization orders for the National Guard during DSCA. Title 32 of the United States Code outlines the role of the United States National Guard in the United States Code. It is one of two ways the National Guard can be activated by the U.S. Federal Government. Under Title 32, the National Guard remains under control of the state. Mobilization orders may come with different duties. Normally, Title 32 orders are for natural disasters, while Title 10 orders are for national defense. However, this isn't always the case. Guard members may also be ordered to active duty solely by command of their state's governor. This is known as "State Active Duty" or "State Call Up" and generally is in response to state-level disasters. When ordered to State Active Duty or Title 32 orders, Guard members may be granted the ability to act in a law enforcement capacity (as they were on Maui); this is prohibited when they are activated under Title 10 unless authorized by Congress. A Title 32 Mobilization order in response to a state disaster would be under the authority of the Governor, but subject to the direction of the President, if applicable.[287]

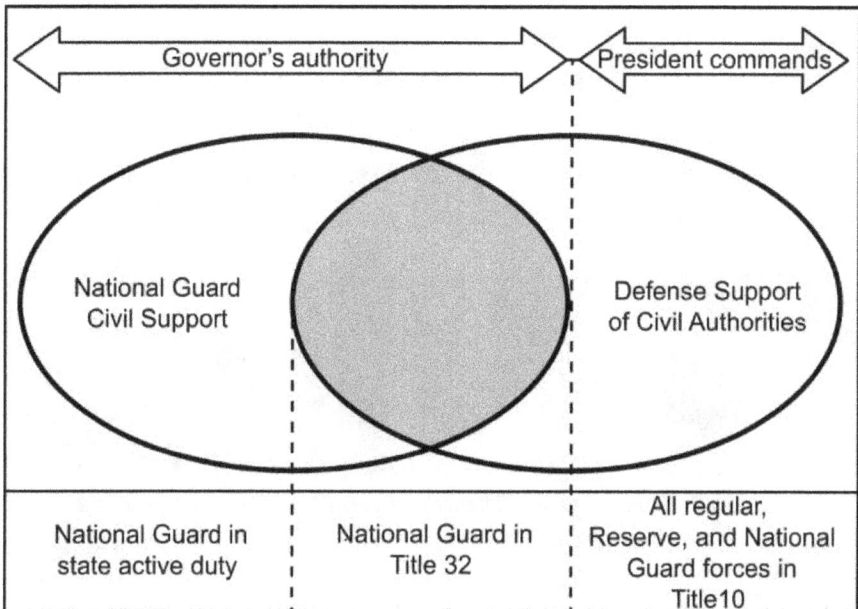

Governor's authority		President commands
National Guard Civil Support		Defense Support of Civil Authorities
National Guard in state active duty	National Guard in Title 32	All regular, Reserve, and National Guard forces in Title 10

287 https://www.military.com/benefits/reserve-and-guard-benefits/whats-difference-between-title-10-and-title-32-mobilization-orders.html

Various other craft were also seen flying over Maui on August 8th in the video from MrHipnautical's sailboat anchored offshore from Mala Wharf in Lahaina.[288] These crafts are pictured below.

The Coast Guard MH-65 Dolphin that rescued 17 people, which was even seen in another video flying out of the smoke during the early evening of August 8th, when it was claimed that helicopters couldn't fly.[289]

The Maui Fire Department's small helicopter (MFD Air 1) at the time of the fire, a Eurocopter BK117-850G2 aircraft named "Iolani" (royal hawk in Hawai'ian).[290]

---

288 https://youtu.be/5PXHaQpH0_Q?si=li8wabi_ncJdy1VO
289 https://www.youtube.com/watch?v=CRXiX1HmXjY&t=42s
290 https://mauinow.com/2022/05/20/new-air-1-helicopter-expands-capabilities-for-rescue-and-firefighting-operations-on-maui/

The other Seahawk (with a much clearer insignia) was also dispatched from the USS Wayne E Meyer.

In the coming months and years we hope to have more clarity about what aircrafts were flying over Lahaina, who flew them, and what their intentions were.

CHAPTER FOURTEEN:
The Strong Movement's Dark History

When one hears about a "strong" movement in a community, they often subconsciously associate this with a legitimized grassroots movement created to advocate for the victims of a given tragedy. It's reasonable for devastated communities to use a phrase that symbolizes strength. You might have also noticed that these "Strong"-themed movements seem to gain the most instant and lasting support, as well as connections and political influence. When you dig into some of these movements, you'll see that they might not be as altruistic as they appear.

For starters, there have been many Strong movements associated with the globalist UN agenda. For example, after the devastating fire in Paradise, California, there was a "Paradise Strong" movement that gained exceptional attention, including a "Paradise Strong" baseball game at the San Francisco Giants Stadium, complete with its very own "Paradise Strong" commemorative T-shirt for the event.[291]

---

291 https://sfgiants.mlblogs.com/sfgiants-to-host-paradise-high-school-baseball-game-at-oracle-park-c3160fb1b870

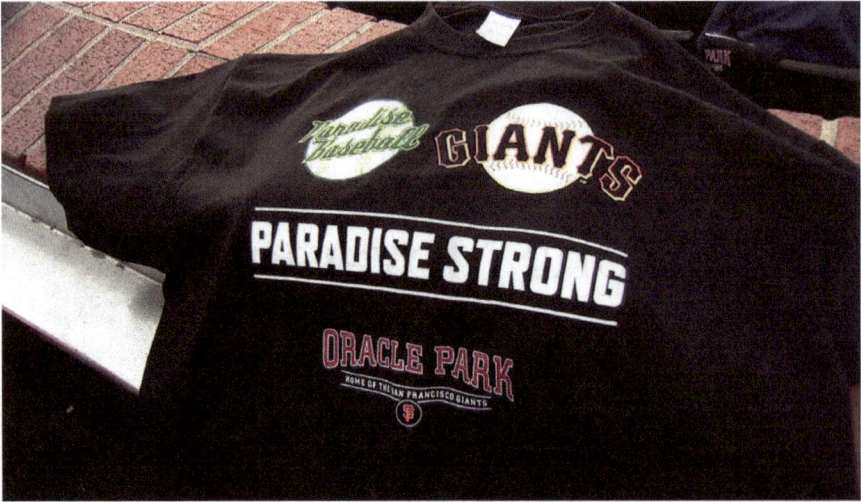

The Mars rover Perseverance also had a tribute to Paradise, with the words "Paradise Strong" engraved upon it. This spacecraft is embedded with two chips engraved with the words 'Town of Paradise, California" and "Paradise Strong," along with the names of the eighty-five people killed in the fire.[292]

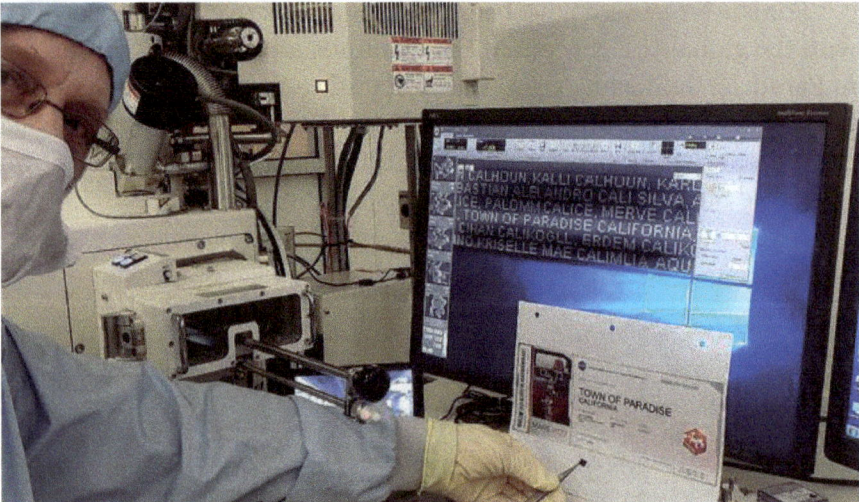

---

292 https://krcrtv.com/news/local/paradise-strong-emblazoned-on-mars-rover-perseverance-as-it-reaches-the-red-planet

We'll look more into the similarities between certain "Strong" movements (with t-shirts, pre-disaster funding before the event, the eventual shift in perspective of the movements, and the resulting political influences). But first, we must introduce the "godfather of climate change," the late Maurice Strong.[293]

Maurice Strong is the man who inspired early versions of "Strong-"related movements. He had globalist values and was instrumental in the environmentalist movement that caught the attention of the world by preaching sustainability, preserving the environment, and coming off a dependency on oil.

Born on April 28, 1929, Maurice Strong grew up in Manitoba, Canada. Mr. Strong went on to hold top positions in some of North America's largest energy corporations and environmental entities.

So, what does Maurice Strong have to do with Maui? It's a long story that's worthy of an entire chapter to explain.

Maurice Strong originally laid out the strategy for multiplying and amplifying small niche voices such as his own, as well as those of the UN and WEF, through various NGOs, relief organizations, activist groups, and others. He sought to leverage these strategic partnerships to get a foot in the door of local political processes and influence public and political opinion. That's what his original strategy had intended, and the UN has continued to do this as a tribute to the "Strong" legacy.

Strong, whom we refer to as a "United Nations Eco-terrorist," wrote a perfect description about the kind of brinkmanship the world is facing today.[294]

"Brinkmanship" is the practice of trying to achieve an advantageous outcome by pushing dangerous events to the brink of active conflict. The maneuver of pushing a situation with the opponent to the brink succeeds by forcing the opponent to back down and make concessions rather than risk engaging in a conflict that would no longer be beneficial to either side. That might be achieved through diplomatic maneuvers, by creating the impression that one is willing to use extreme methods rather than concede. The tactic occurs in international politics, foreign policy, labor relations, contemporary military strategy (by involving the threat of nuclear weapons), terrorism, high-stakes litigation, and now

293 https://expose-news.com/2022/08/28/maurice-strong-invented-climate-change/
294 https://canadafreepress.com/article/covid-19-the-answer-to-maurice-strongs-autobiographical-question-where-on-e

environmental terrorism via weather warfare, also known as "climate change."

Strong believed that by conspiring against humanity by hammering the message of manmade climate change that he could bring civilization to collapse. When asked during an interview about a book he'd like to write, Strong stated:

> *What if a small group of world leaders were to conclude that the principal risk to the Earth comes from the actions of the rich countries?... In order to save the planet, the group decides: Isn't the only hope for the planet that the industrialized civilizations collapse? Isn't it our responsibility to bring about that?*[295]

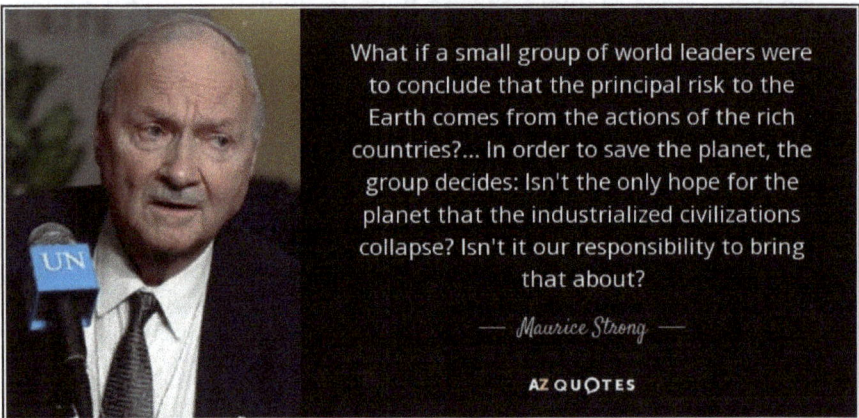

> What if a small group of world leaders were to conclude that the principal risk to the Earth comes from the actions of the rich countries?... In order to save the planet, the group decides: Isn't the only hope for the planet that the industrialized civilizations collapse? Isn't it our responsibility to bring that about?
>
> — *Maurice Strong* —
>
> AZ QUOTES

Sometimes truth is stranger than fiction. In the next few paragraphs you'll learn that Maurice didn't merely have masochistic dreams about the collapse of civilization and dismantling wealthy, stable countries, but he was diplomatically and professionally devoted to the cause through association and leadership in some of the most nefarious organizations ever conceived. You can download "Limits To Growth" for free by visiting the Dartmouth University website at the link in our resources.[296]

---

295 https://timesofindia.indiatimes.com/blogs/toi-edit-page/looking-behind-the-scenes-of-the-well-orchestrated-climate-hysteria/

296 https://collections.dartmouth.edu/teitexts/meadows/diplomatic/meadows_ltg-diplomatic.html

In 1947, Strong took his first job as a clerk at the United Nations in New York. There, he befriended David Rockefeller, who helped to advance Strong and provided him with a network of influential contacts.

In 1966, Strong became head of the "Canadian International Development Agency" (CIDA). Six years later, UN Secretary General U. Thant asked Strong to organize the 1972 "Stockholm Conference on the Human Environment," which became the first Earth Summit.

Under Strong's guidance, the "Canadian Club of Rome" was founded in 1970 with the leadership of a misanthropic array of Privy Council technocrats, including Pierre Trudeau, which provided taxpayer funding for the infamous MIT study, which was published in 1972 in the form of "Limits to Growth," a study conducted and reported using the most sophisticated computers at the time that predicted that the economic growth the world had enjoyed up until that time would not last past the first few decades of the twentieth century.[297] The graph from this study is featured below.

The "Club of Rome" and subsequent "Canadian Club of Rome" were think tanks that were informally assembled and largely concerned with climate change; bent on blaming modern industrialization for the imminent collapse of civilization. By selling people on the idea of manmade climate change, climate and energy policies may be adopted that will, in essence, materialize the collapse of these communities, industries and nations. The Club of Rome founders would stand to make a hefty payday if they sold this lie of manmade climate change.

For instance, by convincing the public to adopt the theory of manmade climate change, fossil fuels will be taxed or limited, energy costs will skyrocket, and the use of modern conveniences will slowly be eradicated in favor of returning to a more primitive time. Climate change is being weaponized both as a psychological and political tool to bring down nations and facilitate societal collapse, which is detailed at length in Frank Lasee's book Climate and Energy Lies. In the end, the result will be the siphoning of power and money away from the little guy to the rulers at the top, who dream of keeping helpless citizens trapped in "sustainable development" communities that will eventually resemble prison camps... because that's what they will be.

---

297 https://a.co/d/0fk5qB53

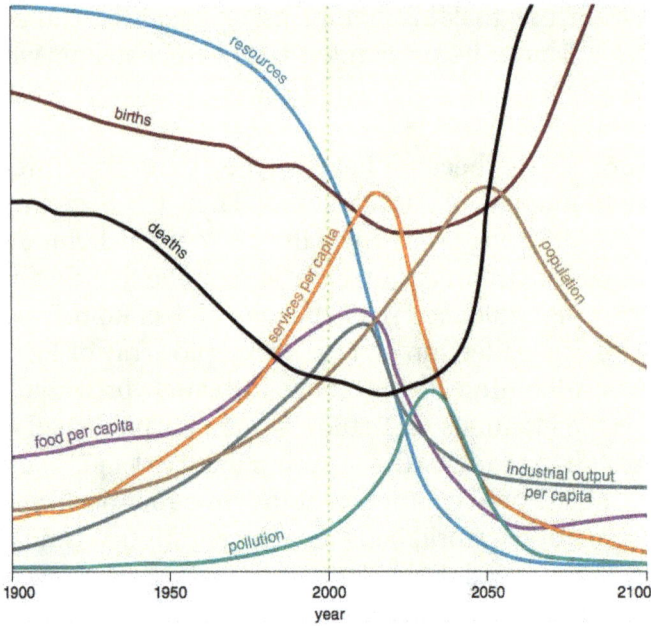

The leading point man of the Club of Rome, Sir Alexander King, later described the group's accomplishments in 1990, saying:

> In searching for a new enemy to unite us, we came up with the idea that pollution, the threat of global warming, water shortages, famine, and the like would fit the bill... All these dangers are caused by human intervention, and it is only through changed attitudes and behavior that they can be overcome. The real enemy then, is humanity itself.[298]

In 1971, while still heading up the Canadian International Development Agency, Strong became a founding member of the "1001 Nature Trust," which was an international organization created by Prince Bernhard of the Netherlands and Prince Philip Mountbatten. The 1001 Trust worked in tandem with Prince Bernhard's other secretive club, known as the "Bilderberg Group," which he founded in 1954, and was designed to fund the emerging new ecology movement (all 1001 members paying

---

298 https://canadianpatriot.org/2020/11/25/maurice-strong-and-the-roots-of-the-great-reset-agenda/

$10,000 for their membership, which was pooled to fund the World Wildlife Fund and other green organizations).[299]

In December 1972, the UN General Assembly elected Strong as the first Executive Director of the new UN Environment Program (UNEP), which was an outgrowth of the Stockholm Conference. During his three-year tenure with UNEP, Strong worked to establish the agency's Earthwatch network and its foundational programs: the Global Environment Monitoring System (GEMS), the Global Resource Information Database (GRID), the International Environmental Information System (INFOTERRA), and the International Register for Potentially Toxic Chemicals (IRPTC).

In its 1976 report from the first World Conference on Human Settlements, UNEP articulated a strongly anti-capitalist, pro-socialist position: "Private land ownership is a principal instrument of accumulating wealth and therefore contributes to social injustice. Public control of land use is therefore indispensable." "Accordingly," added UNEP, "Public ownership of land is justified in favor of the common good rather than to protect the interests of the already privileged." In 1976, Strong described himself as "a socialist in ideology, a capitalist in methodology." He also advocated a "collectivist global government."[300]

Big government, the eradication of private land, and pro-socialist, anti-capitalist positions? Sounds like the birth of modern slavery to us. What about you?

The story gets even seedier.

In his role as President of Petro Canada (1976–78), Strong endorsed the national call to create a nuclear moratorium for Canada, which had been carried out by the Canadian Coalition for Nuclear Responsibility in 1977. This document not only demanded an immediate halt to the continuation of all reactors then under construction but also made the sophistical argument that more jobs could be created if "ecologically friendly" energy sources and conservation methods were developed instead of nuclear and fossil fuels. Strange desires coming from an oil executive, but not so strange considering Strong's 1978–1981 role as Vice-President of the World Wildlife Fund (WWF), an organization

---

299 https://www.newins.ru/en/articles/west/maurice_strong-_the_godfather_of_-climate_change

300 https://www.discoverthenetworks.org/individuals/maurice-strong/

founded by the British and Dutch monarchies as a Royal Dutch Shell initiative in 1963. Strong was Vice President during the same interval that WWF co-founder Prince Philip was its President.[301]

Contributing to green movements and the WWF sound like noble enough pursuits, but don't let Strong's PR prowess fool you into thinking his love for the planet was innocent.

For instance, Strong was the most active and influential member of the "Brundtland Commission," a panel which the UN General Assembly established in 1983 to promote "sustainable development." He helped produce the Commission's 1987 report, "Our Common Future," which, as a result of Strong's influence, placed a heavy emphasis on the dangers of anthropogenic climate change and the virtues of socialist redistributionism. In layman's terms, social redistributionism in this context means stealing from the poor to give to the rich.

In 1988, Strong persuaded UNEP and the World Meteorological Organization (WMO) to co-found an Intergovernmental Panel on Climate Change (IPCC) to monitor manmade global warming and recommend measures, most notably wealth transfers from affluent to impoverished nations, by which the UN and Western governments could address that problem.[302]

In July 1989, the Sierra Club held its Third International Assembly at the University of Michigan Ann Arbor. The most important events of the meeting were held in the university's Plenary Hall, a large Federalist-style building. In the lobby, Sierra Club personnel had set up booths to sell T-shirts, hats, posters, and jewelry to benefit the cause of the Brazilian rainforest. At their press conference, a journalist who was invited to the event asked how environment groups could stop deforestation in Brazil without appearing to meddle. The answer was to encourage them to work through local organizations in Brazil. It was stressed that the "peoples of the rainforest" could do a better job of defending the forest than people on the outside.[303]

In 1989, Strong was appointed Secretary-General of the upcoming 1992 Earth Summit. Maurice Strong had been assigned to head the

---

301 https://canadianpatriot.org/2020/11/25/maurice-strong-and-the-roots-of-the-great-reset-agenda/

302 https://expose-news.com/2022/08/28/maurice-strong-invented-climate-change/

303 https://books.google.ca/books?id=ui2OTJqsqI8C&pg=PR1&source=gbs_selected_pages&cad=1#v=onepage&q&f=true

second Earth Summit (the first having been the 1972 Stockholm Conference on the Human Environment, also chaired by Strong). Also in 1992, Strong founded the Earth Council Alliance (ECA) and became its chairman for many years. Through ECA, he worked with Mikhail Gorbachev (acting as chairman of the Green Cross International) to create the "Earth Charter," which called for a "sustainable global society founded on the principles of respect for the Earth and life in all its diversity, economic, and social justice, and a culture of peace and non-violence."

Likening environmentalism to a religious faith, Strong declared that "the real goal of the Earth Charter is that it will in fact become like the Ten Commandments." He and Gorbachev urged the UN to adopt the Charter, which they called a "citizen-based initiative." They pointed out, however, that if the Charter were to be implemented, it would not "be subservient to the rules of state sovereignty, demands of the free market, or individual rights." Strong himself had long supported global governance at the expense of national sovereignty.[304]

The Earth Charter itself rests in the "Ark of Hope," a literal ark that was constructed specifically to house the original document in an obvious reference to the Ark of the Covenant. The ark was unveiled on September 9, 2001, and then carried 350 miles to the United Nations in the wake of 9/11. The Earth Charter Commission member who presided over the unveiling just happened to be none other than Steven C. Rockefeller.[305]

Claiming that the creation of a One World Government would help to promote security for all the earth's people in a 1992 essay entitled "Stockholm to Rio, A Journey Down A Generation,"[306] Strong wrote:

> *The concept of national sovereignty has been an immutable, indeed sacred, principle of international relations. It is a principle which will yield only slowly and reluctantly to the new imperatives of global environmental co-operation. It is simply not feasible for sovereignty to be exercised unilaterally by individual nation states,*

---

304 https://www.discoverthenetworks.org/individuals/maurice-strong/

305 https://corbettreport.com/meet-maurice-strong-globalist-oiligarch-environmentalist/

306 https://quotepark.com/quotes/1876039-maurice-strong-it-is-simply-not-feasible-for-sovereignty-to-be-ex/

*however powerful. The global community must be assured of global
environmental security.*

In the early 1990s, Strong founded "Agenda 21," a program run by
the United Nations to promote sustainable development, curb global
warming, and minimize the ways in which humans negatively impact
the environment. From its inception in 1992 at the United Nation's
Earth Summit, 50,000 delegates, heads of state, diplomats, and
non-governmental organizations (NGOs) hailed Agenda 21 as the
"comprehensive blueprint for the reorganization of human society."
The 350-page, 40-chapter Agenda 21 document was quite detailed
and explicit in its purpose and goals. They warned readers that the
reorganization would be dictated through all-encompassing policies
affecting every aspect of their lives, using environmental protection
simply as the excuse to pull at our emotions and get us to voluntarily
surrender our liberties.[307]

To introduce the plan, the Earth Summit Chairman, Maurice
Strong, boldly proclaimed: "current lifestyles and consumption
patterns of the affluent middle class—involving meat intake, use of
fossil fuels, appliances, air-conditioning, and suburban housing—are
not sustainable."

Of course, according to the plan, if it's not "sustainable," it must
be stopped. The "American Policy Centre" also noted that Agenda 21
was summed up in supporting documents this way:

> *Effective execution of Agenda 21 will require a profound
> reorientation of all human society; unlike anything the world has
> ever experienced. It requires a major shift in the priorities of both
> governments and individuals, and an unprecedented redeployment
> of human and financial resources. This shift will demand that a
> concern for the environmental consequences of every human action
> be integrated into individual and collective decision-making at every
> level.[308]*

307 https://www.discoverthenetworks.org/individuals/maurice-strong/
308 https://americanpolicy.org/2019/02/25/green-new-deal-reveals-the-naked-truth-of-agenda-21/

As reported in 2019 by The Times of India, the specific issue of climate alarmism originated as part of the Club of Rome of 1968 and its 1973 "Limits of Growth" report. One of the Club of Rome associates who played a particularly insidious role in drumming up a range of anti-poor hysterias was Maurice Strong. Simply stated, he had a revulsion for humans. In his autobiography from the year 2000, he dreamed of the day when two-thirds of the world's population might be wiped out. Strong was widely supported by thousands of influential, like-minded people, many of whom are extremely powerful today. Among those powerful people was William Nordhaus, who started a life-long focus on CO2 and has long recommended a carbon tax without ever bothering to check whether CO2 is actually a pollutant. In fact, CO2 is good for all life on earth, which is thoroughly detailed in former Wisconsin State Legislator Frank Lasee's book entitled Climate And Energy Lies: Expensive, Dangerous & Destructive.

The Club of Rome and its associate organizations remain active and operate behind the scenes. There is a powerful network of people determined to use climate alarmism as an instrument to curb agricultural productivity and choke energy use by the poor. Al Gore is perhaps the most well-known, but the group includes innumerable "scientists" who are happy to fudge data, a thorough investigation of which is detailed in Lasee's book. The "Climategate" emails, for instance, demonstrate how these "scientists" operate in the shadows to distort facts and mislead the public.[309]

Also in the 1990s, Strong continued to promote the possibility of a new global order founded upon the tenets of radical environmentalism. From 1991–1993, he served as Secretary-General of the "UN Conference on Environment and Development." Upon taking that post, Strong called for a radical change in the free-market economic system that had created so much wealth in the U.S. and elsewhere. Said Strong: "A shift is necessary, which will require a vast strengthening of the multilateral system, including the United Nations."[310]

Additional examples of Strong's commitment to global governance include the following: Strong served for some time on the Commission

---

309 https://timesofindia.indiatimes.com/blogs/toi-edit-page/looking-behind-the-scenes-of-the-well-orchestrated-climate-hysteria/
310 https://www.mtdemocrat.com/news/agenda-21-regional-planning-and-sustainable-development/article_ec328323-c4f3-5957-8871-09f3cc231973.html

on Global Governance, whose manifesto, titled "Our Global Neighborhood," called for a dramatic redistribution of the world's wealth and political power. It advocated a phasing out of America's veto in the UN Security Council while increasing UN authority over member nations, declaring:

> *All member-states of the UN that have not already done so should accept the compulsory jurisdiction of the World Court." To further advance the cause of wealth redistribution, the report advocated on behalf of: (a) the international taxation of multinational corporations; (b) the imposition of a worldwide carbon tax; and (c) the creation of a new international "Economic Security Council" to ensure that the world's economic growth remains subjugated to "sustainable development" principles.[311]*

Strong also believed that global governance could be achieved by manipulating and exploiting international concern about the alleged degradation of the environment. This, he said, might require an all-powerful, authoritarian government to terminate the voting process by which people have traditionally elected their political leaders. "Our concept of ballot box democracy may need to be modified to produce STRONG governments capable of making difficult decisions," Strong asserted, "particularly in terms of safeguarding the global environment."

Additionally in the 1990s, Strong was a founding member of the Foundation Board of the World Economic Forum, eventually becoming the board's co-chair. In 1995, he was named senior advisor to the President of the World Bank. In 1997, he became Under-Secretary-General of the United Nations and served as a special advisor to Kofi Annan, the Head of the UN at that time. Strong was a leading architect of the 1997 Kyoto Protocol, an international agreement that set binding greenhouse-gas-reduction targets for 37 industrialized countries.

In 2000 and 2001, the Joyce Foundation, on whose board Barack Obama sat at that time, made a grant of $1.1 million to fund the establishment of the Chicago Climate Exchange (CCX), which described itself as "North America's only cap and trade system for all

---

311 https://press.un.org/en/2023/sc15171.doc.htm

six greenhouse gasses, with global affiliates and projects worldwide." Maurice Strong became one of CCX's nine directors. Al Gore's General Investment Management, a carbon offset company, also exerted considerable influence over CCX and other carbon credit trading firms. Strong was a longtime friend of Gore and was a silent partner in Gore's company.[312]

We have been told that all we have to do to restart the economy is rewire everything about our behavior, value, finance, and ethics to decarbonize civilization under a new world regime of central bankers and new green digital currencies, as outlined by the Green Horizon Summit held on 9–10 November 2020. The Summit was hosted by the City of London Corporation, in collaboration with the Green Finance Institute, and supported by the World Economic Forum ("WEF"). The aims of this summit stated: "It's time to reset the relationship between finance and the real economy. It's time for public and private finance to get behind the transition to a sustainable and resilient future for all."[313]

On his death in 2015, The *Telegraph* hailed Maurice Strong as the man who invented climate change, stating: "to this day, global climate policy is still shaped by the agenda of Maurice Strong, a Canadian multimillionaire." But to those who have looked behind the veil of corporate media propaganda, he's known as the Godfather of climate change—Godfather, as in crime boss. He was also one of Klaus Schwab's mentors. Schwab's other mentor was Henry Kissinger. Kissinger recruited Schwab through the "International Seminar," a CIA-funded program at Harvard University, and introduced him to Ken Galbraith. Galbraith was a Canadian-American economist, diplomat, public policy maker, and Harvard intellectual. Kissinger and Galbraith were the real driving force and helped Schwab create the WEF.[314]

Also upon Strong's death, Schwab delivered the following remarks: "[Strong] was my mentor since the creation of the Forum: a great friend; an indispensable advisor; and, for many years, a member of our Foundation Board. Without him, the Forum would not have achieved its present significance."[315]

---

312 https://www.discoverthenetworks.org/individuals/maurice-strong/

313 https://expose-news.com/2022/08/28/maurice-strong-invented-climate-change/

314 https://www.telegraph.co.uk/news/earth/paris-climate-change-conference/12035401/Farewell-to-the-man-who-invented-climate-change.html

315 https://www.weforum.org/agenda/2015/11/maurice-strong-an-appreciation/

So, how does any of this directly relate to relief efforts on Maui and their alleged "grassroots" organizations? As mentioned above, Strong's legacy at the UN was to capitalize on climate impacts, both before and after events, by creating various NGOs, activist groups, and relief funds, etc. This was born out of his late 1980s preparation for the run up to the 1992 Earth Summit. In the years prior to 1992, Strong was behind the creation of various different types of activist groups, NGOs, and relief organizations that were designed to amplify their niche voice into a virtual grassroots "movement" of thousands. This also allowed them to get their foot in the door of local political processes by exerting their influence upon key locals who were some of the most trusted members of their communities, just like what has been seen on Maui. After devising this strategy prior to 1992, it was then adopted by the UN as a standard operating procedure moving forward, and despite the efforts of think tanks like the Tavistock Institute to hide their shell game of shell companies, it will soon be overturned to reveal what's underneath.[316]

The Maui Strong Fund is directly managed by the Hawaii Community Foundation (HCF), which is governed by a CEO and Board of Governors. HCF claims to work "in close collaboration with state and county leaders, non-profit organizations, and community members," as evidenced by the Hawai'i Community Foundation Board of Governors:

- Peter Ho, Chairman (President & CEO Bank of Hawai'i)
- Michael Broderick, Vice Chair (Principal, Broderick Dispute Resolution)
- Tamar Chotzen Goodfellow, Vice Chair (Philanthropist & Community Volunteer)
- Mary G. F. Bitterman, Secretary (President The Bernard Osher Foundation)
- Alan H. Arizumi, Treasurer (Vice Chairman First Hawai'ian Bank)
- Jeff Arce (Senior Advisor, The MacNaughton Group)
- Jason Benn (Senior Vice President & Chief Information Officer Hawai'ian Electric Company

---

316 https://www.bitchute.com/video/PuYYULs1jaUP/

- Kaleialoha K. Cadinha-Pua'a (President & CEO Cadinha & Co., LLC)oahu
- Robert S. Harrison (Chairman & CEO First Hawai'ian Bank)
- Paul Kosasa (CEO & President ABC Stores)
- Jon B. Kutler (Chairman & CEO Admiralty Partners, Inc.)
- Elliot K. Mills (VP Hotel Operations Disneyland Resort & Aulani, a Disney Resort & Spa)
- Catherine Ngo (Chair Central Pacific Bank)
- Judy B. Pietsch (Owner Judy B. Pietsch Consulting)
- Juliette K. Sheehan (Board Member, Atherton Family Foundation James & Abigail Campbell Family Foundation)

As we can see, the Board of Governors for HCF includes the Presidents, Chairs, and CEOs of the Bank of Hawaii, First Hawai'ian Bank, and Central Pacific Bank, as well as the VP and CIO of HECO (the CEO of Hawaii Community Foundation, Micah Kāne, is on the Board of Directors for HECO as well).

The Disneyland Resort, as well as the new owner of the Lotus Honolulu at Diamond Head Hotel, the MacNaughton Group, are also represented among the Board, in addition to the President and CEO of the largest Financial Asset Manager in Hawaii, Cadinha & Co. However, Admiralty Partners tends to invest exclusively within the global aerospace, defense, and federal information technology industries, so it's rather odd to see them involved here as well.[317]

The Maui Strong Fund was actually created in 2019, four years *before* the Maui fire, and the Hawaii Community Foundation had already established four different disaster funds; one for each of Kaua'i, Oahu, the Big Island, and Maui—and had even done "pre-disaster fundraising" for all of them. The Maui Strong Fund (created in 2019) was activated the day of the Lahaina fire, with $1 million already available. The sum comprised of $170,000 from pre-disaster fundraising and $830,000 in overnight donations that included:

> *$500,000 from the Omidyar Ohana Fund*
> *$100,000 from the Goodfellow Bros.*
> *$50,000 from Hawai'i Life*

---

317 https://www.hawaiicommunityfoundation.org/about_us/hcf-board-of-governors

$25,000 from the Cooke Foundation
$25,000 from Shangri La Museum of Islamic Art, Culture and
Design
$130,000 in anonymous donations[318]

Keep in mind, once again, that this first million came in overnight and was already activated and available on the morning of August 9th, before Mayor Richard Bissen or MEMA administrator Herman Andaya could even know the extent of the impact. The fund quickly ballooned to over $61 million just two weeks later. This enabled the Maui Strong Fund to gain traction and exposure ahead of the actual grassroots organizations, allowing it to quickly appear as the leading relief fund, inevitably drawing attention and resources away from other efforts and funneling them into theirs. The *Civil Beat* stated:

> *The public was admonished against donating directly to [the victims'] GoFundMe and to donate instead to established non-profit org funds, with the Maui Strong Fund being the leading fund. Every news outlet and non-profit org, including NPR, that helped to promote the Maui Strong Fund now has a moral obligation to ensure the funds are distributed to the victims.*[319]

According to "Hawaii Community Foundation's" own Facebook posting, at the time of this writing nearly at the one-year anniversary of the fire, the Maui Strong Fund has given only $5 million to the Maui United Way's Emergency Financial Assistance Program, which has been giving the victims $1,000 each in cash assistance.

The *Hawaii Tribune-Herald* pointed out that: "Maui Strong is the largest fund raised, $140 million in the name of directly assisting the victims (currently $190 million, as of April 20th).[320]

It's nothing short of a scandal how little money has actually gone directly to the victims. No one is arguing the need to support the non-profit organizations that provide the services to support the victims. However, **five million out of $140 million?** That's 3.6%, or four

318 https://www.civilbeat.org/2023/10/how-will-the-maui-strong-fund-be-spent/
319 https://www.civilbeat.org/2023/10/how-will-the-maui-strong-fund-be-spent/
320 https://www.hawaiitribune-herald.com/2024/04/20/hawaii-news/maui-strong-fund-tops-190-million/

cents out of every dollar donated. I think most people who have given money to the Maui Strong Fund believed a large portion of their donations would go to cash assistance to the victims, not just four cents out of every dollar they donated.

We can't tell you how disappointing it is to find out that the "Hawaii Community Foundation" is planning to use the funds for long-term development, not short-term cash assistance to the victims.[321]

According to the foundation, "HCF is not collecting a fee for donating to the Maui Strong Fund and is reinvesting any investment earnings derived from Maui Strong Fund assets back into the fund to carry out its purpose." That purpose, as we have seen, may actually be a multifaceted one that includes influencing local political opinion, especially for redevelopment on Maui.[322]

Another interesting connection is found with Micah Kāne, the President and CEO of Hawai'i Community Foundation. His previous work experience includes serving as Chief Operating Officer of Pacific Links International, responsible for operations and acquisitions of all residential and resort development in Hawai'i. He was also the Chairman of the Hawai'ian Homes Commission and the Department of Hawai'ian Home Lands, a 200,000-acre native Hawai'ian land trust. Kāne also served as the Government Affairs Liaison for the Building Industry Association of Hawai'i. Over the years, Kāne has been recognized with various awards, including the "Housing Advocate of the Year Award" from the Building Industry Association of Hawai'i. He currently serves as a Trustee for the Kamehameha Schools, with oversight of an $11.3 billion asset portfolio, and is a corporate Board of Director with the Hawai'ian Electric Company.[323]

With a resume like that, Micah Kāne seems to be the perfect tool for the job of funneling money and influence toward the direction of those who would most benefit from redeveloping Maui, especially his associates at Pacific Links International, the Hawai'ian Homes Commission, the Building Industry Association of Hawai'i, Kamehameha Schools, and Hawai'ian Electric Company (HECO).

Since its activation during the Maui fires, Maui Strong has not only withheld the majority of its funds for the purpose of redevelopment

321 https://www.civilbeat.org/2023/10/how-will-the-maui-strong-fund-be-spent/
322 https://www.hawaiicommunityfoundation.org/maui-strong-fund-faqs
323 https://conference.hec.org/micah-kane/

(instead of the immediate assistance it was in a unique position to offer) but has also been a loud voice in the centralized redevelopment of Lahaina and the rest of West Maui through its outspoken support of the Lele District bill SB3381, the eminent domain bill HB2693, and the associated redevelopment bills SB3068 and SB582. In many of the press briefings, Ways And Means hearings, and other staged public appearances, state senators such as Angus McKelvey are often seen appearing side by side with Mayor Richard Bissen, Governor Josh Green, and members of Maui Strong, who all take their turns at the mic pushing the new *land grab* that they should be opposing. To be fair, some of these groups (like Lahaina Strong, for example) have been misled and have taken the politicians' words at face value without bothering to read what's in the bills and who really stands to benefit from them, while others have simply been bought off through lavish dinners and resort hotel rooms, all while the community they were supposed to represent was displaced and is in need of basic necessities.

This chapter would not be complete without a celebration of a fundraising and information sharing hero and resident of Maui, Eric West. Eric West (YouTube: https://www.youtube.com/@ hawaiirealestateorg) raised money by investing his personal time and money into educating the public about the fires and getting images and drone footage as well as interviews that were not conducted by the mainstream news outlets. Not only did Eric post links to individual GoFundMe campaigns, but he raised $872,000 in just two weeks for victims. Not being a fundraiser, but a real estate agent who lost his job for the work he did as an intrepid citizen journalist, West originally had thirty days to distribute the money he raised through GoFundMe, but didn't realize that he needed more time than that to get a 501c3 approved or else he'd surrender a lot of money in taxes instead of to victims. He donated money to churches that cared for victims.

Importantly, bypassing bloated organizations, existing non-profits and celebrity funds by raising money directly to victims cost Eric his reputation, his safety, his job, and endless hours of time in video recording, editing, and posting. He was even audited by the Attorney General, which must be unnerving, to put it lightly.[324]

---

324 https://www.civilbeat.org/2023/11/maui-realtors-fire-relief-fundraiser-under-audit-from-ags-office/

With Eric posting from the ground thanks to his Starlink internet connection, he was one of the first and only citizen journalists who helped the world see Lahaina and, consequently, donate to the victims. From a pure ratio of funds donated to funds distributed, we know of no other person who donated as much as Eric West, and we applaud him for helping the world see and care about Lahaina. Regardless of what one might think of his theories or Christianity, the man did the job that should have been performed by free speech-empowered journalists or a government that was simultaneously sending billions to Ukraine. They didn't. Perhaps our next book will be a biography about Mr. West and his heroism. The island of Maui owes Eric gratitude not just for what he raised, but for providing a platform that actually got the world to care about Lahaina.

CHAPTER FIFTEEN:
The Psychology of Cognitive Dissonance and Stockholm Syndrome

In the aftermath of the August 8th fires, there was a huge outpouring of support for the victims of this tragedy, albeit brief and sadly funneled into the hands of seemingly corrupt, irresponsible and questionable organizations such as Maui Strong. Previously in this book, we discussed the infiltration of seemingly grassroots organizations that were allegedly intent on raising money to help the victims.

As far as we can tell, Lahaina Strong was assembled in 2018 after the first Lahaina fire that was associated with Hurricane Lane.[325] They were seemingly the most visible group standing up for the interests of the residents of Maui; they made statements in front of the State Capitol and made appearances on local news channels. Initially they did not go along with Governor Green's plans and did not show support for him in any way. They were very outspoken about the lack of disaster relief from the state and county. In a matter of days, there was a huge shift in opinion from the members of Lahaina Strong who seem to be the most influential of the non-profit groups. In this news report, you can see a performance of dancing and chanting in front of Governor Green, his wife, and Mayor Bissen.[326]

Why the change of heart?

325 https://alohailhawaii.org/lahaina-strong/
326 https://www.youtube.com/watch?v=Ch72OjBdUWw&list=PPSV

*How can those that lost loved ones and saw their town burn down
at the hands of the government be celebrating these very same people?*

There are two psychologies that explain why, which illustrate two
very powerful tools used to influence a community in crisis: cognitive
dissonance and Stockholm Syndrome.

"Cognitive dissonance" is the mental discomfort that results from
holding two conflicting beliefs, values, or attitudes. People tend to
seek consistency in their beliefs and actions, and this conflict causes
unpleasant feelings of unease or discomfort, ultimately encouraging
some change in their beliefs or actions to better align and reduce
this dissonance.[327] The inconsistency between what people believe
and how they behave motivates them to take actions that will help
minimize feelings of discomfort. People often try to relieve this tension
in various ways, such as by rejecting, explaining away, or avoiding new
information altogether, instead of adopting a new perspective that
takes the new information into account, and adjusting the actions and
behaviors to align with that new information.

Author of "Safe and Effective, For Profit," Harry Fisher writes:

> *No matter how many tweets or videos I shared on X.com, there were
> and still are trolls who experience distress at the very thought of
> accepting the fact that their actions don't measure up with the truth:
> that they were tricked, scammed, and manipulated. Three booster
> shots, a lifelong diagnosis of myocarditis and a bout of turbo cancer
> don't hurt as much as admitting to one under the spell of cognitive
> dissonance that they were plain wrong.[328]*

Your authors' hope is that by understanding this, the reader will choose
the latter over the former and try to overcome any dissonance that
any new information presented in this book may have caused. Each
of us has a responsibility to do so if we want to maintain objectivity
and have consistency between our beliefs and actions in light of new
information.

Another situation that can create cognitive dissonance is through
forced compliance. You might find yourself engaging in behaviors that

---

327 https://www.verywellmind.com/what-is-cognitive-dissonance-2795012
328 www.fishersbook.com

are opposed to your own beliefs, due to external expectations from work, school, government, or in social situations. This might involve going along with something due to peer pressure, doing something at work to avoid getting fired, or to avoid breaking a law, even if it conflicts with your sense of ethics or morality.

"Stockholm Syndrome" is a descriptive term for a pattern of behaviors that are used to cope with a traumatic situation.[329] This may explain why hostages sometimes develop a psychological bond with their captors, a phenomenon that is generally studied in Psychology 101 across America, ironically. Stockholm Syndrome is supposed to result from a rather specific set of circumstances, namely the power imbalances contained in hostage-taking, kidnapping, and abusive relationships, including the abusive relationship with the government; when victims live in enforced dependence and interpret rare or small acts of kindness in the midst of horrible conditions as good treatment.[330]

Stockholm Syndrome may seem paradoxical at first, because the sympathetic sentiments that captives feel toward their captors are the opposite of the contempt and disdain which an objective observer might feel toward the captors.

The effects of cognitive dissonance and Stockholm Syndrome are often used as tactics that work on the vast majority of people, as shown in the infamous "Milgram Experiment," and to a lesser degree in the "Stanford Prison Experiment."

On August 7, 1961, Yale psychologist Stanley Milgram began an ethically and morally questionable experiment to measure the willingness of participants to obey an alleged authority figure who told them to do things that go against what they believed to be ethical and moral.

Three individuals took part in each session of the experiment:

1. The "experimenter", who was in charge of the session;
2. The "teacher", a volunteer for a single session. The "teachers" were led to believe that they were merely assisting, whereas they were actually the subjects of the experiment;

---

329 https://www.verywellmind.com/stockholm-syndrome-5074944
330 https://en.wikipedia.org/wiki/Stockholm_syndrome

3. The "learner", an actor and confederate of the experimenter, who pretended to be a volunteer.[331]

The subject and the actor arrived at the session together, and the experimenter told them that they were taking part in "a scientific study of memory and learning" to see what the effect of punishment would be on a subject's ability to memorize content. The subject and actor drew slips of paper to determine their roles. Unknown to the subject, both slips said "teacher", and the actor would always claim to have drawn the slip that read "learner", thus guaranteeing that the subject would always be the "teacher". The experimenter was also dressed in a lab coat in order to appear to have more authority. Both were then taken into another room where the learner was strapped into what looked like an electric chair. The teacher was then given a list of word pairs to teach the learner, and would read the first word of each pair and read four possible answers. If the answer was incorrect, the teacher would administer a shock to the learner, with the voltage allegedly increasing in 15-volt increments for each wrong answer, ranging from 15 to 450. The shock generator also allegedly had markings that varied from "Slight Shock" to "Danger: Severe Shock." The "teacher" subjects believed that for each wrong answer the learner was receiving shocks, but in reality there were no actual shocks. Almost every "teacher" subject followed the orders all the way up to the highest setting, with the learner allegedly falling silent.

Milgram devised his psychological study to explain the psychology of genocide and answer whether or not the Nazis during the holocaust were responsible for their actions, despite the defense that they were "just following orders". Milgram elaborated two theories.

The first is the theory of conformism, based on Solomon Asch conformity experiments describing the fundamental relationship between the group of reference and the individual person. A subject who has neither ability nor expertise to make decisions, especially in a crisis, will leave decision making to the group and its hierarchy.[332] (Just like those who obeyed alleged authorities in Lahaina.)

---

331 https://en.wikipedia.org/wiki/Milgram_experiment#
332 https://archive.org/details/obediencetoautho0000milg/page/n7/mode/2up

The second is the agentic state theory, wherein, "the essence of obedience consists in the fact that a person comes to view themselves as the instrument for carrying out another person's wishes, and they therefore no longer see themselves as responsible for their actions. Once this critical shift of viewpoint has occurred in the person, all of the essential features of obedience follow".[333] (Also like in Lahaina, where alleged MPD officers were "just following orders" during the roadblocked evacuation.)

About 10 years later, the Stanford Prison Experiment was conducted in August of 1971. It was intended to be a two week simulation of a prison environment that examined the effects of situational variables on participants' reactions and behaviors.[334] Stanford University psychology professor Philip Zimbardo led the research team who did the study. Volunteers were chosen and then randomly assigned to being either "prisoners" or "prison guards." Those selected to be "guards" were given uniforms specifically to "de-individuate" them, and they were instructed to prevent prisoners from escaping. Over the following five days, psychological abuse of the prisoners by the "guards" became increasingly brutal, and after a psychologist visited to evaluate the conditions, she was upset to see how study participants were behaving and she confronted Zimbardo. He ended the experiment on the sixth day.[335] Zimbardo's primary reason for conducting the experiment was to focus on the power of roles, rules, group identity, and situational validation of behavior that generally would repulse ordinary individuals. He stated:

> I had been conducting research for some years on deindividuation, vandalism, and dehumanization that illustrated the ease with which ordinary people could be led to engage in anti-social acts by putting them in situations where they felt anonymous, or they could perceive of others in ways that made them less than human, as enemies or objects."[336]

---

333 https://web.archive.org/web/20130205025321/http://www.is.wayne.edu/mnissani/
PAGEPUB/milgram.htm
334 https://en.wikipedia.org/wiki/Stanford_prison_experiment
335 https://www.prisonexp.org/conclusion
336 https://web.archive.org/web/20111118040323/http://news.stanford.edu/
pr/97/970108prisonexp.html

The study was funded by the U.S. Office of Naval Research.[337]

Since the 1971 study, ethics concerns allegedly ended these types of studies; however, the presence of projects like "Project Monarch"[338], "MK Ultra"[339], and the "Delphi Method" developed by the RAND Corporation,[340] show that they merely continued studying social engineering behind closed doors. All of these experiments were devised to influence individuals and groups to behave and act in ways that benefit the perpetrators of such crimes at the expense of the victims, just like has been seen in Lahaina.

There has been a public awareness surging about the presence of experimentation such as MK Ultra and others as of late, particularly when the testimony of Cathy O'Brien came out in the 1995 book *Trance Formation of America*. Naturally, if you search the internet, you'll see claims that O'Brien is a "conspiracy theorist."[341] There are a myriad of testimonials from celebrities who've "escaped" Hollywood that MK Ultra is used to control parties, most notably Beyonce, Kanye West, Amanda Byrnes, and Britney Spears. Roseanne Barr has bravely come out publicly to claim that Hollywood is involved in mind control operations.

337 https://www.prisonexp.org/faq
338 https://archive.org/details/CIAandProjectMonarchFullHistoryRonPatton
339 https://en.wikipedia.org/wiki/MKUltra
340 https://www.rand.org/topics/delphi-method.html
341 https://en.wikipedia.org/wiki/Cathy_O'Brien_(conspiracy_theorist)

PART THREE:

Action NOW

CHAPTER SIXTEEN:
An Urgent Message to the People (And Tourists) of Maui

There are several stories about the Lahaina fires that we've heard over and over again, sometimes with a new detail here or there, but otherwise without much new information. However, there's one single story we've never heard. And we believe it's the most important one to the people of Maui right now and in the immediate future... one that affects the island for generations. It has to do directly with the fires, too. This is the story of the high toxin load that people on West Maui are vulnerable to following the August 8th fires in Lahaina.

But first, a little back story.

Co-founders Mike McKeehan and Luis Martinez of a business called "Deconpac" met while working at a fire department. Mike had been involved with his department's anti-cancer group for over seven years at that time. They mourned a recently loss of a young firefighter to liver cancer and began masterminding what they could do to help firefighters, including using supplements that aid in liver detoxification and "binders." The firefighters dedicated themselves to securing ingredients, a manufacturer, packaging, and production for a product that firefighters could use easily and carry everywhere. The product is now recommended for all those who've been exposed to toxicity from both wild and man made fires. In fact, Stephanie has been using Deconpac since January since her visit to Lahaina due to the severe exposure she had staying in the burn, although she was careful not to drink tap water, not to wear shoes in the house, and not to eat fish that were caught anywhere near Maui.

Mike Mckeehan, Captain
Co-Founder Deconpac, LLC

Luis Martinez, Captain
Co-Founder Deconpac, LLC

Just a few weeks after the Lahaina fire on August 8, 2023, two more firefighters died from illnesses attributed to exposure at the World Trade Center in 2001 during the 9/11 attacks. With those two souls, the death toll among just Fire Department of the City of New York (FDNY) is at 343, with cause of death being cited as "a result of time they spent working in the rescue and recovery at the World Trade Center site," according to FDNY. Over 3,500 first responders from the site have cancer and over 11,000 others suffer illness attributed to their work at the World Trade Center disaster response.[342]

According to Deconpac, challenges people exposed to a fire experience include:

> *Exposure to Toxic Smoke:* Firefighters are exposed to toxic smoke containing a wide range of hazardous substances, including volatile organic compounds (VOCs), heavy metals, polycyclic aromatic hydrocarbons (PAHs), and dioxins. Inhalation of these toxic chemicals can lead to respiratory issues, lung damage, and long-term health complications. This exposure can occur while removing bunker gear, working next to the structure in the warm zone, or during overhaul/clean up stage.

> *Chemical Absorption Through the Skin:* Firefighters' skin can also absorb toxic chemicals present in the fire environment. These chemicals can penetrate the skin barrier and enter the bloodstream, leading to systemic toxicity and potential organ damage. Firefighters are being exposed while they are in the structure.

> *Accumulation of Heavy Metals:* Fires often involve burning materials that contain heavy metals such as lead, mercury, and cadmium. Firefighters may be exposed to these toxic metals, which can accumulate in the body and cause various health issues over time.

> *Systemic Inflammation:* Exposure to toxic chemicals during fires can trigger inflammation in the body. Chronic inflammation

---

342 https://www.cbsnews.com/news/fdny-death-911-illnesses-equal-fdny-death-toll-day-of-the-attacks/

is linked to various health conditions, including cardiovascular disease, respiratory disorders, and autoimmune disorders.[343]

It is the strong conviction of firefighters and co-founder Mike McKeehan of Deconpac that the simple once-quarterly Deconpac regimen includes all the essential ingredients for the binders which can reduce toxin load or detoxify the body should be required by Maui Public Health for everybody on the island of Maui. Due to the winds on the island, it's likely the entire island has had toxic exposure.

If you're reading this message, please urge your friends and family on Maui to immediately begin a Deconpac regimen. It's as easy as taking a multivitamin, gentle on the system, and as inexpensive as most supplements you'd purchase in a grocery store or pharmacy. No prescription is required for Deconpac, which you can find at www. deconpac.com.

Deconpac provides a full-body cleanse for more than just firefighters; everybody in our modern world can be exposed to home, work, and environmental toxins and chemicals. Your Whole Foods "Detox Smoothie" probably isn't doing the trick, which is why your authors urge all readers, not just those on Maui, to consider Deconpac to cleanse your body quarterly of toxin and chemical exposure.

Other concerns from experts include the impact on the environment around Maui, including toxins in sea life as well as the water in which people swim and fish. Due to the constant movement of winds, the entire island may be exposed to new molecules and different types of dioxins due to the prevalence of synthetics used to build homes or furniture which were even more prevalent in 2023 than during 9/11 in 2001. There are thousands of dioxins now identified; but even a couple would be dangerous to humans and animal life when exposed.

Another concern is that the air quality was deemed safe in 2023 after the fires so that Maui would open up fully for tourism again, but unfortunately the air was allegedly tested *upwind*, providing an inaccurate reading of air that was in the opposite direction of where toxins may have been blowing, which was, coincidentally, toward the remaining habitable population of Maui on the East side.

---

343 www.deconpac.com

According to experts we interviewed, toxic ash travels a 55 kilometer radius. It is within this radius that residents and tourists are exposed to toxic dust and, consequently, cancers tend to skyrocket in these exposed areas.

The toxic particulates to which people are exposed are undetectable, which is one way that people are even more vulnerable. After all, if it's undetectable, we can't prosecute anybody for leaving the residents vulnerable. The ability to hide the toxicity of the air and water post-fire is convenient for the Hawai'ian government, particularly following an event that's already been shrouded in secrecy and rampant violation of the First Amendment Freedom of Press.

Another convenient way to hide the effects of severe exposure for residents of Maui or visitors to the island is the fact that most of the cancers like leukemias, birth defects, and other problematic health issues don't show up for years, if not decades. Some experts in disaster response have identified that because of the island being small and winds carrying toxic dust all over the island, the fear is that the August 8th fires will have a level of destruction on Maui residents similar to Hiroshima. Unfortunately, fire captains such as Captain Sam Eaton have written about such dangers, but after a 2003 press release regarding the Tubbs fires was scrubbed, we have seen a proliferation of censorship among the firefighters, similar to healthcare workers and political whistleblowers. We suppose this is due to the fact that there's a lot of money in fires; it's referred to as "Disaster Capitalism." After a disaster, thousands of people get richer; and it generally isn't the victims. We'll detail this in a later chapter.

Detoxification Post-Fire

> *"It'll be 5–10 years before we really know anything."*
> Sam Eaton

Following an event like the August 8th fires in Lahaina, the primary concerns are exposure through air, food, and water. The good news is that the "forever chemicals" don't have to be forever chemicals provided the people who've been exposed are responsible with detoxification. Naturally, we the authors feel strongly about supplements such as Deconpac and the binders that flush toxins from the body. One thing that can be done is to have a test performed at a lab (e.g., blood draw) to provide early detection of toxins which could lead to further complications.

In addition, a few things those who've been exposed can do are the following:

1. Never bring shoes in the house. Doctors who wore shoes in their hotels experienced acute systems of toxic exposure on Maui after only a week on the island, according to Captain Sam Eaton. Allegedly one notable doctor, Dr. Pang, reported that physicians were coming down with skin rashes from being in hotels similar to those found on people who worked in the burn zone piles.

2. Keep vehicles clean. Use an industrial cleaner in things like your car, such as Hygenol (https://hygenol.co/uk/aqua-heavy-duty-industrial-cleaner-5-litre/)

3. Don't swim near Lahaina, especially downwind. Never swim in murky water near the burn zone.

4. Sweat. Use of a dry sauna is the best way to sweat out toxins. If you're doing a steam sauna, make sure it's 130 degrees and be sure to dry and clean it out thoroughly when finished. When using an infrared sauna, be cautious of the EMF radiation it may be putting off. There is also a risk of bumping into the heater and lights. This form of sauna is early technology and there isn't perhaps enough evidence to promote it just yet. Dry saunas, however, are the sure thing. Be careful that the wood is not treated with chemicals and you know where it's coming from. You're generally safe with wood coming from Canada. If it comes across on a boat, don't heat it up and breathe it in. A traditional dry sauna with good clean wood at 180 degrees is best. It sterilizes itself in those temperatures.

5. Keep your lungs clean with a hydrogen peroxide nebulizer.

6. Binders such as Deconpac are critical. Also common is the use of activated charcoal, bentonite clay, and zeolite.

7. Keep your liver clean—it's your filter. Many people exposed to toxins from a fire make the wise choice to avoid alcohol indefinitely.

8. Drink purified water and organic foods. Don't eat fish from near Lahaina.

9. Avoid being down wind of Lahaina.

10. Avoid any groundwater.

If you read nothing else, we hope you will take care of your body and the bodies of those you love in and around Lahaina.

CHAPTER SEVENTEEN:
Real Help. Not a Band-Aid.

"It's a way that we can ban together against the elites,
against the perpetrators of this crime."
Eric West

Calcification of the pineal gland... from toothpaste?

Cancer-promoting ingredients... in cleaning products?

In 2023 Stephanie Pierucci encountered a storm in her business. She was publishing the most important medical and legal minds in the world for many years, but less people were purchasing books about "COVID-19," which slowed down the niche Pierucci Publishing served. Then LinkedIn changed their algorithms which almost eliminated her ability to generate new author leads almost overnight. The SBA money that had artificially boosted the economy through money printing ran dry, which meant that less folks were investing in book writing and marketing than in 2019–2022. Finally, in 2022, Stephanie finalized a 2-year legal battle to protect her son from the COVID-19 experimental gene therapy injection that cost her $140,000.

Stephanie and her son were broke, and for a few months, they were homeless.

During that time Stephanie worked to get back on her feet as a single mother running a small business in America and noticed that Amazon was assertively advertising to authors who would previously work with Pierucci Publishing, and away from small businesses like hers. Like the communities around a newly opened Wal-Mart, Whole

Foods, or Target, her business was slowly getting swallowed up by the mega-corporation. It was a perfect storm.

Also during this time, Stephanie had a young child about whose health she cared immensely. She had heard about the dangers of artificially created fluoride components in toothpastes or mouthwashes, but didn't want to succumb to giving her child these products. She invested in "Hello" mouthwash, "Boka" toothpaste, and continued to make cleaning products at home with white vinegar and essential oils. However, one tube of toothpaste or mouthwash could exceed $10 or even $18.00. They were at a crossroads: could Stephanie continue protecting her son from toxic ingredients and still stick within her newly restrictive budget?

This is a question we finally answered during the research of this book, and the answer is **yes**. You can protect yourself and your family from toxic ingredients without breaking the bank. What's more, it seems purely hypocritical that "anti-vaxxers" still use toxic products in their homes, especially in places like Maui where the community is being exposed to toxic dust from the Burn Zone, even today. If you don't want a toxic shot, why do you pick up any other toxic ingredient every morning, noon, and night and rub it on your skin, counters, and kids?

Did you know that the European Union (EU) and the United States (U.S.) have different regulations regarding ingredients in consumer goods and beauty products? The EU generally has much stricter regulations and bans more ingredients compared to the U.S. The EU's Cosmetics Regulation (EC) No 1223/2009 includes a list of substances banned from cosmetic products. As of the latest update, the EU bans over 1,600 substances from being used in cosmetics.

In contrast, the U.S. Food and Drug Administration (FDA) has banned or restricted only about 30 ingredients for use in cosmetics. The regulation in the U.S. is less stringent. **The EU bans over 1,570 more ingredients in cosmetics and consumer goods than the USA.**

These numbers illustrate the significant difference in regulatory approaches between the two regions. More toxic ingredients are legally permitted in the USA consumer goods and beauty industries than in Europe by a scale of *53:1.*

In this book, we have presented a case that globalists are intent on incinerating land in order to erect their projects; interested in their own profits and not in the freedom and sovereignty of the communities they plow over. In the same way, the American economy has been hijacked. Americans have been blindsided by retailers and manufacturers who have refused to create clean consumer goods and beauty products, and who have even begun to affect our food supply.

America is being poisoned; cancer rates are skyrocketing and our dollars are being funneled to mega-conglomerates who continue to sell toxic, disease-promoting products to our families while siphoning our funds into the hands of shareholders, not back into the communities they decimate with big box stores.

What's a concerned anti-globalist consumer to do?

In your community, Walmart, Target, Amazon, and Whole Foods have forced many small American businesses to shut down already and almost all of us regular people will shop with them every few days for the rest of our lives, buying more products from overseas and funding foreign economies.

The Illusion of Choice

The image below illustrates how few companies own nearly everything we buy. What's more, shareholder megacorporations like Blackrock, Vanguard, and State Street control 97% of these companies. Just eleven manufacturing companies produce nearly every (toxic) thing we buy, and they jack up prices at will to please their shareholders.

In the beauty industry there are even fewer manufacturing companies that control the industry. Thanks to Business Insider, the graphic below shows you where your beauty products come from.

182 BEAUTY COMPANIES ARE OWNED BY 7 MAJOR LEADERS

INSIDER

Here's where the rabbit hole begins. Not only do these corporations funnel your dollars into the hands of shareholders to the detriment of your community, and are politically assertive about things such as the destruction of family values in our schools, marriage, the sacredness of life, but they also remove the rights of citizens and farmers to live, lease, and conduct life and business sovereignly. We even believe they incinerate land they want to use for their nefarious purposes. This was illustrated in the first sixteen chapters of this book on various continents worldwide.

Although the book hasn't named one individual criminal, it's been made clear that the globalist entities are making puppets of American citizens, perhaps such as the board of the Maui Strong organization or even members of the police force or legislative bodies who've made bad decisions in the wake of the Lahaina fires. To the credit of these people who are labeled criminals by some, we choose to believe that they have been coerced under duress or even co opted by nothing more than sheer ignorance.

The truth is, although you, too, have no intention of supporting evildoing globalists, **you do.** Every time you purchase a Proctor & Gamble or Johnson & Johnson product, you vote with your dollars to give money to the very criminals who want to incinerate your life and freedoms. And you do it while poisoning your family with toxic products and harming the environment with absurd household items such as a monster laundry detergent container that's mostly water, after all.

If you're like us authors, you have spent years stocking your pantry with items from Costco or Kroger, giving very little thought to the fact that the mega conglomerates that control most of our world's food supply are using your money to gain more power over you and your community.

For instance, are you or somebody you love a victim of food allergies? The lack of transparent labeling and injection of synthetic and toxic ingredients are probably why. This increases medical bills and wrecks your happiness and peace of mind.

Do you or somebody you love struggle with weight but can't seem to stop consuming foods that are processed or unhealthy? That's because there are so many ingredients making those foods addictive.

Do you get a headache merely by walking down the "laundry detergent aisle" in your grocery store? That's your body telling you to get out. But nonetheless, we bathe our homes and children with these products.

But what if you're one of the awakened, conscious consumers who makes the "organic" choice? You might be, unfortunately, under the illusion that your money is going to help "Burt" tend to his bees or "Tom" create his toothpastes in Maine.

Again, you'd be wrong. Companies such as Seventh Generation, Meyers, Tom's of Maine, Burt's Bees, used to be family-owned "healthier" options. However, they have all sold out to mega-conglomerates, as well. Burt's Bees was acquired by Clorox, for instance. Seventh Generation sold out to Unilever. Meyer's sold out to SCJohnson, and Tom's sold out to Colgate Palmolive.

Here are a few examples of brands many of us buy, thinking we are supporting family owned and healthy alternatives.

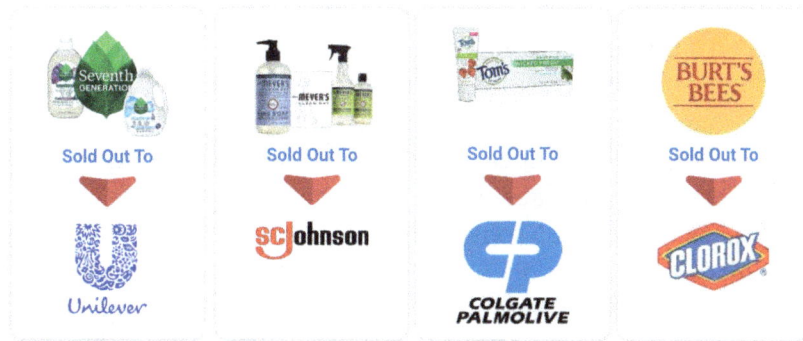

During her late teenage years and early 20s, Stephanie was plagued with painful cysts in her abdomen and developed some in her chest. She was terrified, often tormented before sleep with thoughts of breast or ovarian cancers.

Thankfully, she recovered. However, it wasn't until she made the "switch" from grocery store tampons to cleaner varieties. She learned at this time that arsenic, lead, and fourteen other toxic metals were found in top-selling tampon products, and women who menstruate use more than 7,400 tampons in their lifetime.

"Environmental International" published a study performed by a team of scientists from U.C. Berkeley, Columbia University, and Michigan State University which evaluated thirty tampons from fourteen brands and eighteen product lines. They sought to measure the presence of sixteen heavy metals like lead, arsenic, and cadmium, all sixteen of which were found in the samples. These were detected in both organic and non-organic tampons, with concentrations clearly being higher in non-organic products. However, arsenic was even higher in organic tampons, which might be due, according to the researchers, to the natural fertilizers used to grow cotton for organic tampons. [344] [345] [346]

---

344 https://www.publichealth.columbia.edu/news/first-study-measure-toxic-metals-tampons-shows-arsenic-lead-among-other-contaminants

345 https://publichealth.berkeley.edu/news-media/research-highlights/first-study-to-measure-toxic-metals-in-tampons-shows-arsenic-and-lead

346 https://www.ewg.org/news-insights/news/2024/07/multiple-metals-detected-tampons-new-study-finds

The researchers highlighted the potential health risks associated with exposure to these metals, such as damage to the cardiovascular, nervous, and endocrine systems, as well as increased risks of cancer and reproductive health issues. The study calls for more stringent regulations and better labeling of menstrual products to ensure consumer safety. But that's a pipe dream. We don't foresee accountability by the mega conglomerates or a cleanup of toxic ingredients in the near future. Not a chance.

So what's a conscious consumer to do?

Later in this chapter, we'll tell you how we believe you can protect your body from such products and their inaccurate labeling.[347] [348]

Don't rely on the 11 consumer good conglomerates or the 7 beauty product manufacturers to change. The change must begin with you.

Mega Conglomerate Lawsuits and Inaccurate Labels

It is said that at this time, Procter & Gamble (P&G) and Johnson & Johnson (J&J) are currently facing approximately 600,000 lawsuits for contamination, false or misleading information, cancer promoting ingredients, and harm to children and pets, among other claims. What we believe is that it's cheaper for these companies to pay settlements than it is to clean up their ingredients.

While specific numbers can vary as new lawsuits are filed and others are resolved, both P&G and J&J are frequently subject to litigation due to the vast range of products they offer and their ubiquitous market presence, which is essentially everything you buy, everywhere you go.

Significant P&G lawsuits include:

1. ***Benzene Contamination:*** *P&G settled over 20 proposed class action lawsuits regarding benzene contamination in aerosol products, such as Secret, Old Spice, Pantene, Herbal*

347 https://health.wusf.usf.edu/npr-health/2024-07-11/a-study-found-toxic-metals-in-popular-tampon-brands-heres-what-experts-advise

348 https://newatlas.com/health-wellbeing/tampons-toxic-metals/

Essences, and others. The company agreed to an $8 million settlement to address these claims.

2. **Metamucil Misleading Claims:** *A class action lawsuit claims that Metamucil products contain misleading and false claims regarding their health benefits. This lawsuit, filed in the Northern District of California, alleges that P&G failed to disclose dangerous levels of lead in the product.* [349]

J&J has faced extensive litigation over its talcum powder products, which have been linked to ovarian cancer and mesothelioma. The company has been ordered to pay billions of dollars in settlements and verdicts. Some of these claims include:

1. *Talcum Powder Litigation: J&J has faced thousands of lawsuits alleging that its talcum powder products, such as baby powder, cause cancer. The company has been ordered to pay billions in settlements and verdicts in these cases;*
2. *In May 2024, J&J proposed a $6.48 billion settlement to resolve nearly 54,000 claims related to ovarian cancer allegedly caused by its talcum powder products;*
3. *There have been significant verdicts against J&J, such as a $260 million award to an Oregon woman diagnosed with mesothelioma, attributed to her lifelong use of J&J's baby powder;*
4. *J&J has also faced legal challenges regarding its attempts to use bankruptcy filings to manage the settlement of these lawsuits, which have been met with substantial opposition and legal scrutiny.* [350] [351] [352]

J&J is also involved in litigation related to its role in the opioid crisis. The company has faced multiple lawsuits and settlements related to the aggressive marketing and distribution of opioid medications. For

---

349 https://topclassactions.com/lawsuit-settlements/closed-settlements/procter-gamble-benzene-aerosol-products-8m-class-action-settlement/
350 https://www.drugwatch.com/talcum-powder/lawsuits/
351 https://www.lawfirm.com/product-liability/talcum-powder/settlements/
352 https://www.lawfirm.com/product-liability/talcum-powder/lawsuit-updates/

instance, in 2019, the company was ordered to pay $572 million by an Oklahoma judge for its part in fueling the opioid epidemic. J&J, along with other pharmaceutical companies, has been involved in broader national settlements to address the impacts of the opioid crisis, agreeing to multi-billion dollar payouts to states and local governments to fund addiction treatment and prevention programs.

To add insult to injury, the products you purchase often have labels that are inaccurate. So not only have the mega conglomerates stolen your job, but they're lying through their teeth. Manufacturers like P&G and J&J have faced numerous allegations and legal actions over misleading consumers with false labeling and marketing claims. Here are just a few examples:

1. Tide Laundry Detergent Misleading Claims: P&G was sued over claims that its Tide laundry detergents were advertised as "safe" and "gentle" but contained 1,4-dioxane, a potentially harmful chemical. Plaintiffs argued that the labeling was deceptive and did not disclose the presence of this substance.

2. Herbal Essences Natural Claims: P&G faced a lawsuit over its Herbal Essences Bio line, which was marketed as containing "real botanicals" and being "100% natural." The lawsuit alleged that the products contained synthetic and artificial ingredients, misleading consumers who believed they were purchasing a more natural product;

3. Baby Shampoo "No More Tears" Claims: J&J faced scrutiny over its "No More Tears" baby shampoo, which was found to contain formaldehyde-releasing preservatives and other potentially harmful chemicals. Despite the product's branding suggesting it was gentle and safe for infants, the presence of these chemicals contradicted those claims, leading to consumer mistrust and legal challenges;

4. Neutrogena (a J&J brand) False Sunscreen Claims: Neutrogena faced lawsuits over its sunscreens, which were marketed as providing broad-spectrum UVA/UVB protection. Tests revealed that some products did not meet these claims, leading

to accusations of false advertising and misleading consumers about the level of sun protection provided.[353]

These examples illustrate how even well-established companies get away with misleading consumers, resulting in legal actions and significant reputational damage. But they don't care. They sell enough products to handle the lawsuits and they care more about their bottom line and reputation with shareholders than with their consumers and their lives.

It's clear that it's more profitable to pay out families whose kids get hurt than it is for these manufacturers to clean up their products to reduce things like cancer causing chemicals. We'd like to imagine in this world that we are smart enough to figure out how to clean floors without killing children... but here we are.

In countries outside of the United States where our consumer packaged goods market is not as heavily regulated as other places, these toxic ingredients aren't included in things like laundry detergents, toothpastes, or baby powders.

But here in the USA, sadly, we put profit over people.

Do You Have A Choice?

Your authors have learned that you do have a choice to invest in:

- Great Products
- Family-Owned
- Great Pricing
- American Made
- Great Customer Service

We've searched North America and only found *one* manufacturer that we trust, and which met our criteria. The products are made in Idaho, Tennessee, and Kansas City. In a forty-year history they've never been

---

353 https://www.lawfirm.com/product-liability/talcum-powder/settlements/

sued, settled out of court, and they've never hurt anybody. That's right: in forty years, *they have never been sued.*

They formulate, manufacture, and distribute all under one roof. They have hundreds of patents and they cut out middlemen in order to keep prices low. We understand that making ends meet in a challenging economy can be a struggle. That's why we believe that you shouldn't foot the bill for advertising, middlemen, marketing, and retail store leases when you purchase items you use every day. What's more, in the current grocery store scenario, you pay for a long and expensive distribution system that includes a factory, shipping, warehousing, trucking, costs of store shelving, and staffing those stores, to boot. This isn't just hard on the pocketbook, but devastating to the environment.

What's more, your authors believe that consumer packaged goods is a money laundering scheme for organizations like Planned Parenthood. In fact, J&J was, for a long time, the biggest funder of Planned Parenthood.

If you are a small business owner like Stephanie, it will or already has crushed your family to have your business siphoned by mega conglomerates with war chests full of money. If you work in manufacturing, a lot of those jobs have been switched overseas. The old fashioned Dick Van Dyke or Andy Griffith world, where we go to work and sweat for American companies, is gone.

The Rebellion Against Mega Conglomerates

We need American companies to thrive. Fundamentally, the Maui fire was about disempowering the small guy so that the big guy can roll in and take over. As we've illustrated in Part Two, it's coming to a community near you.

Early in 2020, a plumber named Kristian Hoenicke watched small businesses close and business owners who'd give you the shirts off their backs get pummeled. They often had no savings and when their businesses closed, and many declared bankruptcy. Not all of these businesses qualified for SBA loans to help them through this hard time. Many entrepreneurs didn't meet qualifications for government assistance, such as Stephanie with her small publishing business that began to fail in 2022.

Globalists play by different rules. It's not just the people in Lahaina only received $700 per household for their loss. Entrepreneurs and small business owners have been getting choked and squelched in America for decades. Hoenicke thought, *Well, sometimes, life isn't fair.*

But then he discovered a manufacturing company that produces 500 household items that are clean, non-synthetic, and organic. The toothpastes are free of sugars, full of essential oils, and pure, unlike other "clean" toothpastes, you can obtain these items at grocery store prices. Best of all, they employ thousands of people in the United States.

Reader, please stop giving P&G, J&J, Unilever, Clorox, or other mega conglomerates your money. The pending litigation against these companies includes harm to people, animals, the environment, and even false advertising, as has been clearly illustrated in this chapter.

Your authors were recently introduced to Hoenicke from Eric West and saw him work alongside Eric to bring families from Lahaina into the "switch" away from harmful corporations into American-made, clean, family-owned manufacturers. We are proud to promote an organization that's already helping 1,100 families who've been displaced find meaningful work and income since Covid, with a significant portion of those families in Lahaina.

When you join this local grassroots movement with us and shift your spending for everyday household goods (things you already buy from Target, Walmart and Costco), you redirect lifeblood dollars to an individual or family affected by the Lahaina Fire as well as other families around the nation who've been devastated by globalization.

Every day in America, there's a river of money aimed at the wrong people. Wal-mart makes about $1,000,000 a minute! If 150 or 200 million of us complain about how the world is but continue handing our money over to these mega-conglomerates, we're voting with our dollars. And frankly, we're part of the problem.

The average American can't afford $12.00 toothpaste or $18.00 mouthwash, which was the choice Stephanie faced in the beginning of this chapter. In her first book, Stephanie struggled to lay out steps for political and social action.

But today, we now have a way for the every-man and woman to get involved. If we can act together, we don't have to give them our money. So let's stop.

Your mission, should you choose to accept it, is to join "Switch For Lahana" with your authors. You can become a consumer like the vast majority (82%) of people who make the switch. Or, you can use Switch For Lahaina to bring additional income into your household. The first eight people in Hawaii who made the Switch earned between $1,000-$5,000 extra cash their *first month*.

Let's defund the criminals.

Schedule time with Stephanie (just 20 minutes) to discuss how you can easily make the switch to vote against these criminals with your dollars, and start protecting your family from the silent (but stinky) threat they're lathering up faces, countertops, and floors with all day in your home. Visit www.BuyCleanUSA.com to chat with Stephanie about this mission and, together, let's create a cleaner, brighter and healthier America for ourselves and our children.

CHAPTER EIGHTEEN:
SMART City Defeated: A Sovereign Love Story

On March 11, 2024, the municipality of Pérez Zeledón near San Isidro in Costa Rica quietly enabled public access to the proposal of the "PLAN de ORDENAMIENTO TERRITORIAL" (POT), or land use plan for the Canton of Pérez Zeledón, which was to be submitted to a public hearing before a vote that was to occur on 4/4 regarding an "Eco-Barrio," or "15-minute city."

Dustin Bryce, from "Interest of Justice" (IOJ), reported from the historic and successful protest against the UN "SDG Agenda 2030" in Pérez Zeledón Costa Rica. Interest of Justice was at the front of the line to serve papers to protest and to demand a hearing on science disputes, and other critical legal issues.[354]

The fact that this legislation moved so quickly, especially in Costa Rica, showed how this was against families and for corporations that will follow the WEF guidelines. It pushes small farmers out of their homes and businesses, with land use restrictions that force people from the agricultural areas by banning buildings for homes or business, and prohibiting planting, permaculture, and raising animals, which is how they've lived off the land for generations. The plan would force them into the new "Eco-barrio", or 15-minute city. Ironically, while churches and family homes can't be built under this new plan, casinos, nightclubs, resorts, and hotels would be permitted, all in the name of "protecting the growth and development of land."[355]

---

354 https://interestofjustice.substack.com/p/costa-rica-perez-zeledon-defeats?publication_id=825071&post_id=143284752&isFreemail=true&r=q7mkz&triedRedirect=true
355 https://www.youtube.com/watch?v=PvGPLrWIIww

This may have looked "green" at first glance, but what does it look like in the long run? Small, local farming families that have passed down land and farming practices for generations would no longer be able to afford to do what they have always done to provide for their families and communities as sovereign individuals. They would be forced to move to cities and may have had to depend upon government subsidizing to meet their needs. Farm lands, which are the sources of their food and water, would be regulated and controlled. As farm lands would become abandoned, they would consequently be up for grabs.

Under the PLAN de ORDENAMIENTO TERRITORIAL de PEREZ ZELDON, the municipality of PZ is planning to:

- Implement regulations that may force farmers to relocate to cities;
- Require large, yearly investments of money for permits controlling the crops farmers grow and the animals farmers raise;
- Restrict land owners from passing property rights to their children and families by making it illegal for them to legally divide land parcels.[356]

The WEF is actively encouraging companies to get rid of farmers at the time of this book's writing, with many of their activities detailed in Stephanie's book *Burn Back Better*. The same thing is happening in Canada, where the present government is doing everything that they can to make the lives of farmers difficult to the point that they give up or go bankrupt. This is happening worldwide, to countries that are involved in the WEF. Small farmers are being taken over by the larger companies that will switch over to factory created food.

On the bright side, Costa Rica is a prideful country with roots in family, neighbors, and the "pura vida" lifestyle. And now, they officially sue presidents and champion human rights.

The whole town took to the streets and the defiant people spoke to protest the re-zoning scheme, which was not adopted by the Municipality of Pérez Zeledón. Police guarded the doors, which were

---

356 https://www.pzahora.com/post/ya-est%C3%A1-habilitada-la-propuesta-del-plan-regulador

shut so that none of the citizens could even enter. Those citizens miraculously got the police to shove the papers in the door just before the 6 p.m. scheduled vote. "Thank God for the one nice police officer who helped us make it happen and got the documents inside the building", Bryce said.

This move allows us standing to sue as an interested party if they do not respond in the legal Costa Rican Administrative timeline of 10 business days (they already responded nicely to say they will answer us on time). Pérez Zeledón was heard by our Municipality and thankfully they did not adopt the scheme. The town folk and city officials are getting red pilled and educated in reality and forced to never try to overhaul society to interfere with property rights again! No one will agree to be micromanaged with our own land that is often passed down generationally here. It's our rights and the land use of our own property we are talking about.

We love Costa Rica! This is why we chose here for our headquarters— Justice! It's where humanity will WIN freedom against Globalism. Mark our words. Costa Rica was the only country that kicked the Spanish Conquistadors butts out of the country and won against them, because we are fierce about our dignity and property rights." There you have it. The initial reaction to Costa Rica's first "eco barrio" and "land rezoning" scheme was not a very warm welcome by the people who live here. The Municipality has shown they actually care about their inhabitants and stood down!

The Mayor will still need to provide a hearing and due process if they ever want to resume this crazy idea and try to pitch to the 82% of rural farm people that live here precisely why we want to live in "land use" zones and be forced to get a yearly permit to continue activities of our choice that they "let us" do? We think the UN "eco barrio" (15 minute city) is a doomed plan here and everywhere. Watch it play out and fail midstream. We will sue for as hard and as long as it takes to prove it's either unconstitutional or illegal (or both). We are not accepting these insane, disproportionate and unnecessary plans to restrict our land use and change our lifestyle by the Mayor of the Municipality and his cohort handlers at UN, WEF and WHO.[357]

---

357 https://interestofjustice.substack.com/p/costa-rica-perez-zeledon-defeats?publication_id=825071&post_id=143284752&isFreemail=true&r=q7mkz&triedRedirect=true

CONCLUSION:
Who's Waving Their Hand Over Your Lamp?

Every four years in America there seems to be a new surge of threats from people on every side of the political spectrum who claim "if so-and-so becomes president, I'm leaving the country!" However, what used to be idle talk seems to have legs, so to speak, in the past four years. Your authors have witnessed many acquaintances, friends, and even some family members leave the country or head out of big cities toward smaller towns. Reasons cited include fear of civil war, uneasiness about open borders, disrespect for the wastefulness of the American government and the Federal Reserve's money manipulation, fear of inflation, inability to afford housing, fear of God's wrath for immoral laws, and general disdain for the size of our "big government" in the United States.

President John F. Kennedy once said, "We do not have a democracy now because the little guy in this country has absolutely no say in what's happening with his government... the rise in this violence and the polarization, et cetera.... It [the system] is rigged to shift money upward. It's like a vacuum cleaner. The Fed and all of these—all of our laws and institutions are designed to strip-mine wealth from the American middle class and send it north."

Ironically, these words come from a president who was allegedly murdered by the very government he criticizes in this quote. By and large, the feeling that the little guy has no say in what's happening in a "rigged system" isn't new. When the authors have interviewed acquaintances and friends who've expatriated, become American Nationals, or otherwise left the USA, the exit interview usually includes the same sentiments as President Kennedy expressed so many decades ago. "I'm tired of playing in a rigged game. I'm tired of having no voice, no power, and losing freedoms left and right. I'm tired of my dollar having less purchasing power. I'm tired of toxic media, toxins in food, toxins in the air and water."

As we finalize this book, we ask you to take a few deep breaths with some more positive concluding thoughts. This manuscript contains evidence of the truly depressing reality that we have a government not only capable of death and destruction against its own people, but likely doing it in plain sight. However, we ask in these final sentiments that you will join us in soberly focusing on your potential role in the cleanup. If there is any hope of salvaging the great USA our fathers or grandfathers fought nobly for, you are part of the new war. The war might be less plainly bloody, but it will, no doubt, claim as many lives, if not many, many more.

What happened in Lahaina on August 8th was an act of war. It was and is a wakeup call that without a vigilant and less tolerant populace, a government unchecked is capable of tremendous crimes. The people of Lahaina owned their community and their homes and businesses, but our fear is that they were forcibly stolen in a violent way.

As the evidence in this book suggests, our fear is that your town, too, is vulnerable to such thievery and even destruction. However, because you are reading this book, you may have the opportunity to save not only your home and life, but those of others.

Among the many actions you can take as have been outlined in Part Three include but are not limited to:

1. Switching for Lahaina to USA-made consumer packaged goods;
2. Encouraging your friends on the island to detoxify the toxic dust to which they've been exposed;
3. Refusing to play the climate change or carbon credits game;
4. Getting involved in rejecting sustainable central planning in your community or any other WEF-sponsored initiative;
5. Follow Traci Derwin and Shane Buell on "Brush Junkie" on YouTube to learn about more movements we support in addition to the four listed above;
6. Become an engaged member of your sober-minded or awakened local community;

7. Finally, ask yourself this final question: Who's waving their other hand over your lamp? If you'll recall in Chapter Two, Shane experienced a moment in 2023 when a Hawai'ian girl and old man appeared to him in a vision. He knew at that moment that he was called to investigate the truth and speak out in support of Maui for the benefit of the whole world. All us "little guys," as President Kennedy identified in the quote from the beginning of this conclusion chapter.

If you have the ability to make the switch, collaborate with investigators and researchers such as Shane and Traci, yet involved locally, submit public testimony such as we saw during SB3381, or even begin a local Telegram Group with other concerned citizens, you're taking small but significant steps toward being part of the solution.

Above all, don't make things so complex that you take your eyes off the community you're devoted to. That said, the final and most important request is that you engage with your community actively, intentionally, and swiftly. Church, Rotary and Chamber of Commerce Groups, or business clubs are great places to start. Don't find yourself stuck in small talk with people who aren't of sober mind and heart. Seek out the like minded warriors who, like you, are taking heed of your respective callings; those who recognize and acknowledge the flickering light over the lamp, and who are committed to joining hands with you to make your small local difference which could reverberate to global impact.

PHOTOS: "IN THE BURN"

January, 2024

INDEX